THE
MEN
that TIME *has*
FORGOTTEN

THE
MEN
that TIME *has*
FORGOTTEN

MICHAEL JOHNSON

The Men that Time has Forgotten by Michael Johnson

This book is written to provide information and motivation to readers. Its purpose is not to render any type of psychological, legal, or professional advice of any kind. The content is the sole opinion and expression of the author, and not necessarily that of the publisher.

Copyright © 2021 by Michael Johnson

All rights reserved. No part of this book may be reproduced, transmitted, or distributed in any form by any means, including, but not limited to, recording, photocopying, or taking screenshots of parts of the book, without prior written permission from the author or the publisher. Brief quotations for noncommercial purposes, such as book reviews, permitted by Fair Use of the U.S. Copyright Law, are allowed without written permissions, as long as such quotations do not cause damage to the book's commercial value. For permissions, write to the publisher, whose address is stated below.

Printed in the United States of America.

ISBN 978-1-953150-68-4 (Paperback)
ISBN 978-1-953150-69-1 (Digital)

Lettra Press books may be ordered through booksellers or by contacting:

Lettra Press LLC
30 N Gould St. Suite 4753
Sheridan, WY 828011
1 307-200-3414 | info@lettrapress.com
www.lettrapress.com

CHAPTER ONE

IT WAS DECEMBER OF 1944 driving trucks in Europe in the worse winter in history was not my idea of fighting a war. I was cold as hell and hungry, but here I was fighting for my country who didn't even consider me an equal. I didn't mind though this war was suppose to change everything for Negro's in America. A lot of the men joined thinking they would get a chance to fight, but we were wrong they assigned us to this truck company. I joined in March of 1942 hoping the same thing, but they shipped me off to this dusty base in the middle of Iowa. Since I have been in Europe all we have been doing is driving troops around and supply them. The ways things were going I didn't think we would ever get a chance to fight. We had heard rumors that they didn't need us and we were here to do is serve the white soldiers. The white soldiers were saying we were cowards and would run when we came face to face with the enemy. That get some nerve saying those things about us. I have heard stories about them going AWOL, shooting themselves and even committing suicide to get out of fighting. I thought about going AWOL myself, but I didn't want to get shot and I have a family I have to take care of. They don't believe a black soldier was as good as a white soldier. We all bleed red blood, but to tell those white soldiers that they wouldn't believe it. They think we are some type of sub human who that can't do anything without them. I can't complain I know what I can do, so we better do our jobs and do it well or they will laugh us right out of the Army.

The word had came down from Brass to ship out in August of 1944 a couple of months after the D-Day invasion. I was real exited and also scared I knew once I got over to Europe there was a real chance that I might get killed. The thought of not seeing my family again made things even more frightening. When I was at the base in Iowa I met my good friend Staff Sgt. Willie Earnest Banks III. He was a big man 6'4 250lbs brown eye, dark skin, muscular and black wooly hair. He also was a very handsome man. When he walked in a room everyone stopped and looked at him. He had this walk about him that showed how confident he was in himself. That scared a lot of those white boys they didn't like that. All the ladies wanted to come out of their panties when they seen him. Even the white girls would be checking him out, but he knew and they knew that wasn't possible. Especially back in those days a black knew better not to even look at a white woman he knew he would get lynched. Sgt (that's what I called him) was not a very educated man, but he knew how to take charge. He had joined they Army when the war first broke out. He was driving trucks for the troops in San Diego, Ca. He was so good at it the promoted him to Corporal in 1942. Then he started training Negro soldiers that's when he got promoted to Staff Sgt. The other Negro soldiers feared Sgt especially the white soldiers. I don't think it was fear at all it was more like jealously wishing they were like him. He had a way when he talked people respected him. A lot of people didn't know all he had was a 7th grade education, but he talked like a college graduate. I actually met Sgt by accident. We were doing rifle drills one afternoon out in the burning hot sun. They had us standing out in that hot ass sun in full gear sweat was pouring down my face. My hands were sweating I was tired and they had us running though some damn obstacle course. I was tired of drilling that's all we did and drive those raggedy ass trucks. They told us to load our rifles I loaded my rifle when I went to put it at the ready it accidentally slipped out of my hands a round went off and killed a bird sitting in a tree.

Who the FUCK did that Sgt asked? Everyone pointed at me. He came running over to me mad as hell.

What the FUCK are you doing Pvt. Ross? He got in my face. I ain't doin nutin Sgt. So you telling me your rifle didn't go off killing that bird in that tree over there? Yes Sgt it was my rifle that went off, but it was an accident. He looked at me what this look like he wanted to kill me. An accident? Then he snatched me up by my collar with one hand my feet were dangling in the air. Look Pvt. Ross we ain't got no time for accidents that bird in that tree could have been one of our guys and you just killed him. I'm sorry Sgt. Sorry ain't going to bring that man man back Ross. Don't let that shit happen again you understand Ross? Yes Sgt I understand.

Then he let me go. I was real happy he did that he had some real bad breath. It stink so bad it was burning the hairs in my nose. Got on your feet Pvt. Ross. I picked up my rifle and got back in ranks. I was real mad at Sgt for embarrassing me in front of the whole division. I wanted to shoot him, but I knew he was only doing his job. I had only been with the division a few months and that was the first time he ever got mad at me and it wouldn't be the last time.

We finished our drills and they dismissed us I was on my way back to the barracks when Pvt. Anderson came up to me. Don't worry about what Sgt did he has done that to all of us.Oh yeah. Yeah. I just looked at him and shook my head I was still mad about what he did. When I got back to the barracks I put my gear down on my bunk and sat down I was really tired standing in that hot ass sun had drained me. Hey Ross? Yeah Anderson. Are you coming with us to Sally's tonight or are you going to stay in the barracks like you always do? I might come over there later. Come on Ross that's all you been doing since got here. I'll think about it.

Sally's was a local club the black soldiers hung out at. The white soldiers had the club on base and we couldn't go there. The black soldiers had know where to go, so they all got together and built their own club out in town. They took this old barn and turned it into a night club. It sounded like one of those juke joints back in Houston. Man do I really miss home. I decided to go I was taking my time getting dressed, because I really didn't want to go. I put on my uniform, my shined shoes and grabbed my cover. I was about to walk out the door when I heard a voice call my name. I turned to see who it was. It was Red. Hey are you going to Sally's? Yeah. Okay I'll walk with you. Red was a short man (5'5') with real light skin, green eyes and red hair. They call him Red because his hair was red. His real name was Patrick Simmons. He was a quite man that kept to himself. This was the first time he had said anything to me. We didn't talk much on our way to the club. All he asked me was where I was from. He seemed like a real nice guy, but they would find Red dead two weeks before we were to ship out to Europe. They wouldn't tell us what happen to him, because they were afraid that it would cause a riot on base. We would find out later that he was killed by some white men who caught him with a white woman. He had been seeing this white woman ever since he came to Iowa. When they found him they had cut off his dick and shoved it in his mouth.

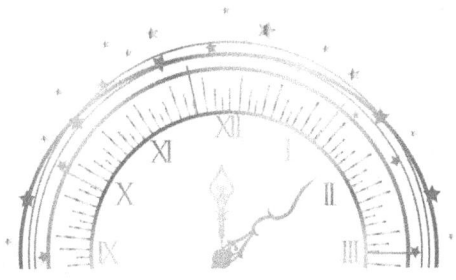

CHAPTER TWO

WHEN WE GOT TO the club from the outside it looked like a run down barn, but when I walked in it was a different story I was shocked to see how well they had fixed it up. I was expecting one of those raggedy juke joints like the ones back in Houston. There was a bar made out what looked like oak. There were bottles of alcohol the shelves behind it, finely stained wooden tables and chairs and a nice size dance floor. It even had a stage where a band (which were guys from the base) playing jazz music. What shocked me the most was all the black women and men there. I didn't think Iowa hand any black people living there. The place was packed for a Wednesday night. I really didn't know anyone so I sat at the bar. The bartender asked me what was I drinking? I told him to bring me a beer. He brought me back my beer I was about to take a sip when I felt a tap on my shoulder. I turned around to see who it was. It was Sgt. Hey Ross what's going on?

Nothing much what's going on with you? Nothing I'm just here hanging out. I'm sorry about this afternoon I didn't mean to treat you that way in front of the whole company, but I take my job very serious. You (sitting down) know Ross they look for mistakes like that to keep us out of this war. You are very lucky Lt. Douglass wasn't out there to see that he would have went and told Capt. Goodwin. Who's Lt.

Douglass? Oh that's right you just got here. Lt. Douglass is the biggest uncle Tom on base.

That Nigga will tell on anyone, so I try my best not to tell his sorry ass anything. So Ross what is your first name? It's Jeffery, but back at home they call me Popeye. Popeye! Why they call you that? Well when I was young I had these big eyes that looked like they were about to pop out of my head. He gave me this funny look and started laughing. He was laughing so loud everyone started looking at us. To get him to stop laughing I asked him his name? My name is Willie Earnest Banks III. I was named after my father. Did you know they made him fight on the side of the French because the U.S. didn't want any black soldiers fighting for them. No I didn't know that. He told me they had to wear these funny looking helmets and they were given rifles from the 1870's to fight with. He told me about Henry Johnson. Who's Henry Johnson. You don't know who Henry Johnson was? No. He was about to tell me who Henry Johnson was when the bartender asked us did we want another drink. I told him no I barely was finished with my first one, but Sgt told him to bring him two more beers. As he was telling me about Henry Johnson he sucked the beer he had. The bartender brought Sgt his two beers. He sucked down one beer as he was telling me this story about Henry Johnson. Henry and my father served in the same company. Another soldier by the name of Needham Roberts came and relieved my father. Around 0200 hours the Germans surprised Henry and Needham . They shoot Henry and left him for dead. They took Needham as their prisoner. When Henry saw them taking Needham away he jumped up and pulled out his 9" bolo knife jumps in the middle of those Germans and started cutting and slashing like a wild man. When he had finished he had killed 29 Germans and saved Needham. He was wounded severely. The papers wrote ll about it. They gave Henry the Distinguish Service Cross and a Purple Heart. He even receive a hero's welcome when he got home. As for my father he was lynched when I was 13 years old. When the soldiers got home the white people started to attack them thinking they wanted the same treatment as whites. Riots broke out all over the south. As he was telling me about that riots. I remember my daddy telling me about them and how his brother and wife were killed during those riots. While Sgt was telling this story he had drink six beers and he was good and drunk. He started to slur his words. I drink the rest of my beers and told him let's get you back to the barracks. I took him by the arm and put it on my shoulder. It felt like a tree trunk was on me. He was so drunk he couldn't even stand up. I was trying to stand him up, but it just wasn't working he was falling all over the place. Now here I am 5'8" 140lbs trying to carry this 250lb man out the door.

Everybody is looking and laughing at me. Damn y'all instead of laughing at me give me a hand. This Nigga is heavy. One of the guys got up and I thought he was going to help, but instead he opened the door for me. I looked at him. You Bastard! You be careful on the way back. I will. Than he closed the door behind me laughing. When I got outside and seen how far I had to go I almost cried. I stood him the best way Icould and started the long walk back to the base. I could barely hold him up all his weightwas on me. Just holding him up was wearing me out. Come on please stand up. I was about to drop him when I felt his weight get light. Let me help you with him Ross. A tall skinny man grabbed Sgt's other arm. Thanks I really needed the help. We struggled to get Sgt to his feet. You got him he said? Yeah I got him. Once we had Sgt on his feet we started walking towards the base. Damn Sgt your ass is heavy the skinny man said.

CHAPTER THREE

IT TOOK US 30 minutes to get Sgt back to the base. The guard on watch opened the door for us. I see Sgt than gone and got drunk again. Yeah he did this time he is good and drunk help us put him in his bunk. By this time Sgt was passed out he was nothing but dead weight. We tossed him in his bunk. Man That Nigga was heavy. That felt like a work out I'm tired as hell. Thank you man. No problem. What's your name? My name is Thomas Walters.

Glad to meet you Thomas my name is Jeffery Ross, but my friends call me Popeye. Popeye!

Why they call you that? When I was a kid I had these big eyes that look like they were about to pop out of my head. He looked at me and ok. We walked out to smoke a cigarette. I took one out and lit one up I took a drag and put my head back. That's when I heard someone calling me name. Pvt. Ross, Pvt. Ross. It broke me out of my daydream I looked up to see who it was. It was Lt. Douglass he was standing over my foxhole. Yes sir. Make sure you and Webb stay awake. Yes sir I will sir. Than he walked away.

2nd Lt. Arthur Douglass was a light skin man with curly brown hair, medium build, 5'8" 140lbs with brown eyes. He was a soft spoken man. The glasses he wore made him look like he was really smart. I thought he was smart. The guys in the company didn't like him. The one thing I didn't like about him was he was really scared of white people. He would do anything to please them even if it was something stupid. He made things hard on us when it didn't have to be. I woke Webb up and told him Lt. Douglass was checking foxholes to see who was sleeping. Damn that motherfucker is always fucking with us. Why don't you just get up Webb, so his silly ass won't come back. Ernest Webb was a short stocky man about 5'6" 245LBS. I don't see how he got in the Army being as heavy as he is. He probably got in because he was a great baseball player. He played catcher in the Negro leagues for the New York Black Yankees. I could see his round face when he sat up. He had this big gap between his two front teeth. He was mad that I had woke him up his stubby little hands grabbed is M-1 rifle stood up and pointed it out our foxhole. When are we going to see some action? This shit is boring sitting here in this foxhole freezing our balls off. Ever since we got here all we been doing is driving those raggedy trucks and burying the fucking dead. I came here to kill me some Germans. I was thinking the same thing I came to to prove that we could fight not drive trucks all over Europe. While we were talking Sgt jumped into our foxhole. Hey Sgt what's up Lt. Douglass told me to go around to see if anyone is sleeping. We know he just came by and told us. Capt. Lewis has been getting on him about guys falling a sleep, so make y'all stay awake. We will Sgt. Hey Sgt. Yeah Webb. My hands are freezing. What the hell you want me to do Webb? You can find me some gloves. I ain't got know gloves Webb nobody does.

Put your hands down your pants. I laughed a little at Webb. I'll be back to check on you two. I got to go check on Neal and Parks Douglass caught them sleeping. Alright Sgt. He jumped out of our foxhole and headed for Neal's and Park's foxhole. You know Popeye I think that Nigga's crazy. Yeah I know, but he is a good friend. What was that? What was what Webb?

That right there. What? SHHHH listen. That sounded like gun fire. Yeah it does, but it's far away. Yeah it is. You know Popeye I was taking a shit this morning when I over heard Capt.

Lewis talking to some of the other white officers about us. What was he saying Webb? He was telling them that we were a bunch of cowards and we were crying about going back home. What! Yeah he told them that he hated Niggers and where he was from they knew how to put Niggers in their place. Where is his ass from? That motherfucker is from Mississippi. That don't surprise me that is a bad place for a Negro. That place I heard is worse than Texas. We knew what type of person Capt. Lewis was. We have dealt with white people like him everyday I hated white people like him. They think they can talk to you like you were a dog in the street. I was about to say something else to Webb when we heard a loud broom. You hear that Popeye? Yeah. The next one was closer. I got my M-1 rifle and stuck it out of my foxhole. Than bombs started dropping everywhere. I could see people running around pieces of dirt hit in my face and helmet. I heard someone yelling stay in your foxholes. It was Sgt running around to each foxholes. Than one hit right next to our foxhole Webb and I crouched down in our foxhole covering our ears from the loud booming sound from the bombs dropping. One hit a tree above our foxhole blowing it's branches to pieces most of the debris fell in our foxhole. I hear people yelling and screaming than just as it started it stopped. I had debris all over me I stuck my head out to see was it ok. I asked Webb was he ok. He didn't answer me, so I called him again. He didn't move, so I grabbed his shoulder to turn him over to see if his was alright. That's when I seen a piece of a branch sticking out his eye. It horrified me when I seen that. There was blood all over his clothes and in the foxhole. I started to get sick. I haven't seen that much blood since I was 12 years old.

 My father found his brother with his head blow off. I yelled for a medic, bout one came. I jumped out of my foxhole to the nearest one. When I got to the foxhole I could see Reuben Scott and Tony Davis still crouching down in their foxhole. I yelled I need a medic Webb been hit. They told me to go to the next foxhole that where Doc Phillips was. I ran to Doc Phillips foxhole other men were yelling for a medic to. When I got to him he was helping another soldier who's legs had been blow off. He was delivering a message to Capt. Lewis when the bombing started. He laying in a big pool of his blood looking at him started making me sick again. I started to get dizzy to. I had to catch myself I almost fell on Doc. He grabbed me and asked me was I alright. Yeah I'm fine Doc, but Webb has been hit. He looked at me like he knew Webb was already dead. We run over to my foxhole. When we got to my foxhole they were already pulling Webb body out of my foxhole. Lt. Douglass and Sgt were there. Where were you Pvt. Ross? I went to look for a medic sir. We told everyone to stay in there foxholes If you would have stay in yours this man probably would be alive. I just looked at him he must haven't seen that branch sticking out of Webb eye that went out the back of his head. If I had stayed or not he still is dead. Staff Sgt. Banks! Yes sir. Get some men to bury Pvt. Webb. Yes sir. Sarge picked me and 4 other guys to bury Webb. We carried his body into the woods. His 245lb body made it seem like he weighed a ton. We find a hole where one of the bombs had left a big hole. We layed him in it, but it wasn't deep enough so Scott and I had to dig a hole deeper hole for his body. We tired to dig a deeper hole, but it was useless the ground was frozen solid it was like trying to dig though cement. After about 30 minutes we just give and layed Webb body in the hole. We started covering Webb body when Scott asked should we pull the stick out of his eye? No Scott let's just bury him and get back to camp. We started burying Webb as we were burying him I started thinking that could have been me. I started to think about my wife and baby girl. That really shook me up seeing Webb die like that. It ain't right for a man to die like that being bury in the ground like a dog so far away from home. I really started to get scared, because I knew this was real now. Scott was scared to he had escaped death several times himself. When we were burying Webb Scott started telling me what happen to him back at home and why he joined the Army.

CHAPTER FOUR

RUBEN SCOTT WAS FROM Washington D.C. A city boy. He was 5'10" medium built man with black hair and brown eyes. He also played for the Negro leagues he played second base for the Newark Eagles. He joined the Army to get away from some trouble he had gotten himself into. He was messing around with this white girl and her father found out. One night he was suppose to meet her in at this park, but instead of the girl showing up her father sent two of his Goons to beat Scott up.

Scott said he was sitting on one of the benches waiting for the girl to show up. One of the two men came up behind him hit him in the back of the head knocking him down. The other man came and started kicking him. While they were beating on him Scott said he pulled out his .22 pistol and shot one of they men in the leg. As the man was falling Scott said he shot again hitting the man in the head. Stunned that this had happen the other man screamed I'M GOING TO KILL YOU YOU FUCKING NIGGER. Scott get up and started to back away when the man came running at him. Scott said he was backing away so fast he fell over a rock and the gun went off hitting the man in the chest killing him. When he fell the man fell on top of him. He pushed the man off knowing he just killed two white men.

He knew right than and there he had to leave town before he got lynched. He said he got on the next bus leaving town and a few days later he joined the Army. By this time Webb body was frozen solid. We place him back in the hole and tried to bend his legs so he could fit, but but they were stiff like boards it didn't matter he was dead we put him in the hole the best way we can. Scott asked me again if we should pull that branch out of his eye? I looked at him and told him to go ahead if it makes him feel better. He went to pull it out, but the stick was frozen in Webb head, so he put his foot on Webb head and pulled it out. When he did that he pulled out some of Webb's brains came out with it. It made me sick, but this time Scott got sick and and throw up. He throw up all over poor Webb I wanted to laugh, but I didn't because I wanted to throw up. We finished burying Webb said a prayer over him and we headed back to camp.

On our way back I started thinking about what Webb said about getting a chance to fight. He got his wish and now he is dead. When we got back to camp everyone was cleaning up all the broken tree branches and debris. Hey Popeye what took y'all so long to bury Webb?

Sgt asked us. Before we could say anything he told us that Russell Parks was killed also. I didn't know Russell well. All I knew about him was that he told a bunch of lies. He claims he was a lady's man, but we never saw him with any women. I heard rumors that he was a Homosexual. I don't know how true that was, but I felt bad that he is dead. I was on my way back to my foxhole when Sgt told me to come up to the CP. Now what does he want with me at the CP? I was already messed up over Webb dying. I walked passed several dead bodies lying on the ground cover up. I wandered which one of those bodies was Russell Parks body.

As I was walking towards the CP I started thinking about my wife Lillian. She didn't want me to join the Army, but I had to make a better life for and my baby girl. We had only been married a a year before I shipped out to Europe. She had this smile that could light up a room when she walked in it. As I got closer to the CP I could see several people standing around. Sgt, Capt.

Lewis, Douglass and other guys from my company. Capt. Lewis told us to gather around.

Capt. John Parker Lewis was a tall man 6'3" 220lb with sandy blonde hair, blue eyes and very pale skin. He had a long face that made him look older than he was. His lips were turning black for all the smoking he did and he was nerves all the time every 5 minutes he was lighting up a cigarette. He drink heavy too. He graduated from West Point, but he finished last in his class. They assigned him to our company because no else wanted him. The Army shit canned him form all the white companies, because of his bad leadership skills. They always give the black divisions bad leaders and he is one of the worse. He got assigned to our company when we first arrived in Europe. We can tell right from the start we were not going to like him. He's been giving us a hard time since he got assigned to us. He doesn't have any respect for us. He doesn't care if we look good or bad and he's never around. So Lt. Douglass and Sgt runs the division. He told us that the bombing tonight was the beginning of something big the Germans are about to do. That the Germans are about to mount a counter attack soon. On this map here there are some machine guns nest and 2 88's in the woods. They need someone to take those out so our troops can get though there. I volunteered our division to take up this task. Lt. Douglass and I will lead two teams into woods.

Everyone looked at each other. My heart almost stopped when he said that. These two are going to lead us we are all going to die. I got really scared. Lt. Douglass your team will be Staff Sgt. Benson, Cpl. Wilkes, Pvt. Davis, Scott and Kelly. My team will be Staff Sgt. Banks. Cpl. Walters, Pvt. Neal ,Ross and Jackson. Doc Phillips you will come along, but you will hang in the back just in case anyone gets wounded. Does anyone have any questions. No said a word. Ok than we will meet back at the CP at 0100 hours and we will be moving out at 0130 hours so get some rest and be back here. Your dismissed. When we were leaving Sgt. Benson stopped me. Hey Popeye I don't know about this we ain't trained for no shit like this. I know, but they don't care Benson it's just some Niggas going in some woods to get killed.

Staff Sgt. Clarence David Benson was a dark skin man with a slim build. He was about 5'11" 175lbs with a slim and a long neck. His adam's apple stuck out his neck like a buzzard. He had graduated from college with a degree in business from Howard University. He came into the Army as an officer a 2nd Lieutenant, but he lost it when he got into a fight with two white officers. One night he was on his way back to base when he ran into two drunk white officers.

They told him that he better give them some money or they were going to beat his black ass.

When Benson refused they attacked him. What they didn't know was Benson was an ex golden gloves boxer. He beat the shit out of them. When the MP'S arrived they didn't arrest the white officers they arrested Benson instead. They thrown Benson in the stockades for a year and took away his commission. Instead of the Army discharging him they wanted to humiliate him, so they demoted him to a Sgteant and made him work for the two white officers he had beaten up. They made his life a living hell. He was transferred to our company before we left for Europe. I could see all all dying Popeye. Lt. Douglass knows we ain't never trained for anything like this. Before he could say another word Sgt interrupted him. Hey y'all Niggas stop complaining you sound like a bunch of little girls crying for your mommies. They was going to give this mission to someone else. Douglass and I begged Capt. Lewis to give it to us. Why you do that Sgt? Those white boys think we are cowards and this is a way to show them what they can do we can do. Now I don't know the way you Niggas are talking maybe they are right. Come on Sgt you have got to admit that Douglass couldn't lead a horse to water never mind lead this mission him or Capt. Lewis. Now you listen Benson you joined the Army to prove what you can do here is your chance to do just that. Now I don't want to here anymore about this. Y'all get some rest and be back at the CP at 0100 hours you got that. Yes Sgt. As Benson and I was walking back to our foxholes Benson said to me that Niggas crazy he knows damn well this is a suicide mission. They always using us to clear the way for those white boys. We do all the hard work and those crackers get all the credit. I could see why Benson was angry he was right we were like lambs being lead to the slaughter. The white divisions couldn't take out those guns, so what gave Sgt and

Douglass the idea that we could do this? I think Douglass is looking to make Captain.

If this mission goes well it will make him look good, but if we fuck this up we will be the laughing stock of the Army and he will get shit canned. So we are going to have to succeed.

Neal stopped me for a light. So what you do you think about this mission Popeye? I don't know Neal. Reggie Edward Neal was what you would call a pretty Nigga. He was light skin 5'10" 165lb black curly hair and green eyes women would flock all over him when came into a room he also was a city boy. He told me he was looking forward to doing this mission it was the only time he could kill a white man without getting lynched for it. Neal had a cool personality about him I guess it come from living in N.Y.C. Doc Phillips told me that Neal told him was a pimp back in N.Y.C. He was forced into the Army, because they found a white girl dead in one of his apartments. When he went to court the judge told him he had a choice go into the Army or he was going to throw his black ass in jail. I don't know how true that is, but he seems out of place to me. He was just doing his time so that he could move on. I gave him a light and I walked back to my foxhole.

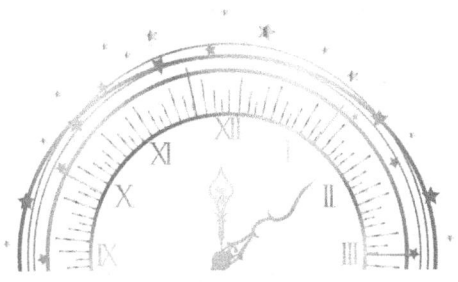

CHAPTER FIVE

I JUMPED BACK DOWN INTO my foxhole I could smell Webb blood all over the foxhole. I sat on the other side in the corner took out a cigarette lit it up. I don't start smoking until I joined the Army. My wife Lillian was shocked to see me smoking when I came home from boot camp.

She told me she wasn't going to kiss me as long as I was smoking. I told her that I would stop, but when I got to Europe I started up again. I tried to think of home, but the smell from Webb broke my concentration. I took my shovel started putting dirt on the bloody mess. I was putting dirt on the blood when I notice something white in the corner. I got down to see what it was. I picked it up it felt mussy, so I held it up to the moon light so I can see what it was.

That's when I realized it was Webb eyeball I throw it down and covered it with dirt. It gave me the chills knowing that eye was in the foxhole with me. I took a long drag of my cigarette and blew it out slowly. I looked at my watch to see what time it was. It looked at it and notice it wasn't working. The time had stopped at 2110 hours it must had stopped during the bombing.

I leaned my head back against the wall to take a quick nap before I had to report back to the CP. I started thinking about my wife Lillian she is the best thing that ever happen to me. I met her at a church dance one night I saw her standing there next to the punch bowl serving drinks. She was wearing a dark blue dress with white buttons going down the middle of it. Her hair was in a ponytail with a blue ribbon around it. She was wearing black 2" heels and she had the most beautiful green eyes I have ever seen. All the men in town were chasing after her, but I was to scared to say anything to her. The reason I was to scared, because she might laugh at me. I didn't consider myself a good looking man. I was 5'7" 130lbs, dark skin.

I had a small round head and big eyes. I also was slightly bowed legged. I was named after one of my uncles and I got my nickname Popeye from my auntie Arlene when I was a child. She saw me one day and said boy your eyes look like they about to pop out your head, so that's how I got my nickname Popeye. I didn't like it at first, but I got use to it. A woman like Lillian wouldn't be interested in a man like me. I would try and talk to women like Lillian before but all I would get is the cold shoulder or laughed at. This one night I decided I was going to go say hello to her what do I have to lose. I took a sip of my punch and started walking towards the table where Lillian was standing. I was about to say hello when all of sudden BIG.

Brenda James grabbed my arm. Where you going Popeye? I'm going to the table to get me some more punch. I seen you looking at Lillian. So you know her? Yeah I know her, but you are not going to get her she got a man. Why don't you (try to put her arms around my neck) come over my house I can show you a go time. Would you move girl I'm trying to get some more punch. She gave me me this crazy look and let me by, but she pinched my butt as she walked away. I've known Brenda ever since we were kids. She was a big girl (300lbs) but she had a very pretty face. She had long beautiful brown hair and light brown eyes. The men were chasing her to, but I think it was more for sex than a relationship with her. About time Brenda moved her big ass out the way another guy had moved in on Lillian. Damn Brenda I got and went mad outside. I don't know if I was mad or relieved she did that maybe she saved me from from getting embarrassed. What would a woman like that want with a man like me? I don't know what I was thinking that she would even look at me. I guess Brenda will be as good as I get. While I was standing there feeling sorry for myself I heard a soft woman's voice say hello.

I turned around to see who it was and I was shocked it was Lillian. I couldn't speak I tried to say hello, but nothing came out. Hello. Ummm Hello. My name is Lillian Crawford. What's Your name? My...my name is Jeffery. Jeffery what? Oh Jeffery Ross. Glad to (putting her hand to shake mine) meet you Jeffery Ross. I shook her hand it was soft like a baby's ass.

Nice to meet you Lillian. I heard that you were checking me out? Who me oh not me. Who told you that? Brenda told me that. Really I'm going to get her for that. So I thought I'd come out here to see who this man was checking me out. She also said that you wanted to ask me out on a date but you were to scared to ask. What! Yeah that's what she told me. All I wanted to do was come over and say hello. When you asked me my name what were you going to do after that? I really don't know I guess stand there and look at you. She started to laugh. I laughed a little myself. So are you going to ask me. Ask you what? Are you going to ask me out on a date or are you just going to stand there looking at me? I would love to take you out on a date. That's if you want to go? I would love to go out with you, but you are going to ask my folks. Ask your folks why? I'm only 17 years old. What! You don't look 17 Lillian. I know I look much older than I am. A lot of boys get in trouble trying to talk to me. I was 19 years old at that time. Ok so who are your folks? Carol and Roscoe Crawford. Roscoe Crawford is your daddy? Yeah. A chill went down my spine Roscoe Crawford is one of the biggest men in town.

He stood about 6'5 and weighed over 300lbs one of his hands was bigger than my head. He was a giant compared to me I started to have second thoughts about talking her out. I didn't want to talk to her father I was scared of him. I finally get the nerve to say ok. So are going to come back into the church? Yeah. I opened the door for her and we went back in the church.

We sat down drink a little more punch and talked, but it wasn't for long she had to leave. I have to leave now my momma and her friends are ready to go. Oh ok when can I see you again? You still want to take me out right? Yeah. Why don't you come by tomorrow you can ask my daddy than. Ok where do you live? I live in the upper 5th ward. Oh you live there?

Yeah something wrong with that? No. The upper 5th ward is where the so called well to do Negros lived. So when shall I be expecting you Jeffery? I'll come over after work. What time will that be? I say around 5pm. Ok I'll see you than. She smiled at me and left. Than I heard someone called my name. Popeye..... Popeye wake your ass up man. Than I felt a sharp pain on my head. I looked up to see who it was it was Sgt. Popeye get your ass up you are late.

Get your ass to the CP NOW! I must have nodded off I grabbed my rifle and ran to the CP.

When I got to the CP everyone was standing around waiting on me. I was still trying to wake up. Capt. Lewis said to me. Glad you could join us Pvt. Ross. Now that everyone is here let's get started. We told by Headquarters that the Germans had several fortified positions beyond these hills (pointing at the map) They have 2 88 guns and 4 machine gun nests. Those 88's have been reckoning hell on our troops they can't advance unless these guns are taken out.

This is where we come in we are going to take out those 88's and machine guns. This will give our troops room to advance. Douglass raised his hand. Yes Lt. Sir do we know how many men are manning these 88's and machine guns? No Lt. I don't know that we will fi out once we get out there. Now I know these fools have lost there minds. They want 12 men who aren't trained to do this time of mission to take out 2 88's, 4 machine gun nests and God knows how many men. They aren't expecting any of us to come back alive even Sgt had a worried look on his face and he ain't scared of nothing. This is a very important mission for you and your country. I've been hearing you boys complaining about not getting a chance to fight. Well here is your chance to prove yourselves. Capt yes Lt. Douglass. Sir we don't have a lot of ammunition sir. Well get some from the boys from your company Lt. We didn't carry a lot of ammunition, because we were truck drivers and they didn't expect to do any fighting. All they gave us was two clips apiece. Lt. Douglass I'll give you boys 5 minutes to gather up more ammunition. Yes sir. You heard him you have 5 minutes to gather ammunition. We all went around gathering ammunition from other guys in our company. I got 10 clips and 6 grenades from other guys. I thought I had enough, but I would find out later it wasn't. Sgt.Staff Benson got real lucky and find a B.A.R. (Browning Automatic Rifle) in one of the trucks. One of the white soldiers left it behind by accident. He also found 600 rounds of ammunition.

Douglass told us to line up. We fell into formation and we checked our weapons. Capt. Lewis told Douglass let's go. Yes sir. Attention! Right face! Forward march! We started walking down this icy road. Walking into the unknown not knowing what's waiting for beyond those hills and woods.

CHAPTER SIX

IT WAS A COLD crisp night the wind was blowing a little, but it cut though my clothes to my bones. There wasn't a moon out that night and it was pitch black. You couldn't see your hand in front of your face. The snow was ankle deep from all the snowing it had done two nights earlier. I had a bad feeling about this. When I get a bad feeling my stomach start to feel funny.

It feels like crabs are rolling around in my stomach. My teeth started to chatter and my toes started to get cold. The longer we walked the colder they got. Now I know how those white soldiers felt landing on the beaches of Normandy facing all that machine gun fire and bombs must have been a terrifying experience for them. Now it was our turn to face the same thing. I wanted turn back, but I couldn't. Capt. Lewis told us to halt at this road that split into two roads. He pulled out his map. This is it. Lt. Douglass you'll take your team up this road I think that's where those 88's are. According to this map there are two machine gun nests up there and two across this field behind us. My team will do a frontal assault distracting them, so you can work your way behind them. It's 0200 hours now when get into position we will start our attack buy shooting a flare in the air. So that means Lt you better have your black ass in position you understand? Yes sir I understand. This will be the rallying point we will meet back here if anything goes wrong. Lt. Douglass you have to destroy those 88's if you don't our troops are dead. I understand sir. Sgt. Benson. Yes sir. Leave that B.A.R with Cpl. Walters.

We are going to need that for more fire power when we attack these machine guns. Benson didn't want to give that B.A.R. Up because he knew what kind of fire power it had. Benson reluctantly give it ti Walters. Can you handle that Cpl? Yes sir I can. Good I'm counting on you to cover our asses just in chance we get into some real bad shit here. Everybody knew Walters was lying he ain't never handled anything like that before and he was the worse shoot in our company. Pvt. Parks was the best shooter in our company and he got killed in that bombing. Doc Phillips I want you to stay behind just in case we have any wounded. Yes sir. Get the moving Lt. Douglass. Douglass and his team started up the icy road, but Benson turned around and gave my an envelope looked at me and walked away. I didn't know what to make of it. I just shoved it in my pocket. Now listen boys we are going to have to crawl across this field on our stomachs stay low and don't make a sound. We want to surprise this Germans. Let's go Sgt told us. We got on our stomachs and started crawling across this field covered with deep snow. The field we had to cross was about 40 yards long. You could see that our troops failed trying to cross this field. There were dead Americans and German soldiers on this field. I crawled pass one dead American soldier with his brains blown out.

Another one died with his eyes open. Looking at their frozen bodies made the hairs on the back of my neck stand up. I knew than we were getting ourselves into some deep shit. I was getting cold crawling there all that snow. My hands were getting cold and trying to hold that rifle wasn't helping me neither. I looked to my right to see how Walters was doing. He was struggling trying to crawl with that B.A.R.

Albert Kevin Walters wanted to be a pilot when he joined the Army, because his brother David was a Tuskegee Airmen, but he fail the exam to be one so he came into the regular Army. He almost killed someone in boot camp while they were on the firing range. They didn't want him in the infantry, so they told him the only job he was going to do was drive trucks. He was assigned to our company a couple days after I got there. He is to much of a laid back guy I think joining the Army for him was a mistake. We were about 10 yards away when an German soldier spotted us crawling across the field. A machine gun opened fired on us. The bullets were flying over our heads like rockets. Capt. Lewis yelled to us to head for the woods. We all got up and started running towards the woods. Walters was still lagging behind everyone. I yelled you better bring your ass on Walters. The bullets were hitting the ground around me. Dirt and snow were flying everywhere. Out the corner of my eye I could see Jackson go down. I was trying to run as fast as I could, but the extra ammunition I had was slowing me down. When I got to the woods another machine gun opened fire on us. The bullets were ripping branches off tree I couldn't see with all the debris flying around. I took cover behind a tree. I seen Sgt and Capt. Lewis talking about something. Sgt ran over to me. Popeye I want you and Neal to work your way around that machine gun and take it out.

Where the fuck is Walters with that B.A.R. I don't know Sgt. Just than Walters came running up. Walters where the fuck you been we need that B.A.R? You need to kept up boy. Popeye you and Walters take out that machine gun Neal you come with me. They started running back towards Capt. Lewis when a bullet ripped though Neal's shoulder. Sgt stopped o help him, but he waved him off. He crawled behind a tree to nurse his wound. Walters I want you to cover me so I get work my way around that machine gun. Ok Popeye. He was shaking real bad he couldn't hardly hold the B.A.R. He went to fire the gun and it jammed on him. What the fuck is going on? I don't know Popeye it just jammed. Will unjam it Walters. Oh no. What! I didn't put in a clip. Well than what the fuck are you waiting for put one in. I'm ready now. Ok I started working my way around that machine gun. Walters was giving me good covering fire.

I was saying to myself I hope he doesn't freeze up on me. As I got closer the covering fire stopped. I was exposed to the Germans hellish machine gun fire. I took cover behind a broken wall. I could hear gun fire off in the distant I said that must be Douglass and his team. I looked over the wall to see where that machine gun was. When I did that they opened fire on me again. Where is Walters and the covering fire? I was yelling like he could ready hear me with all this gun fire going on. I returned fire on them. The two machine gunners and I got into a gun fight. I killed two of them two more came running at me and I killed them. I was shocked that I could kill a man like that. My hands were shaking so bad I couldn't load my gun. My heart was beating so fast I thought it was about to come out of my chest. I was loading my gun when one of the Germans I thought I killed started shooting at me. By this time Walters had joined me and killed him. Thanks Walter. No problem. Hey let's move up to see if all those Germans are dead. We moved slowly towards the machine gun nest to see if all those Germans were dead. As we went by we kicked them to see if any of them were still alive. I think they are all dead Popeye. Yeah I think so to. We were standing there looking at them when a hail of bullets came out of know where. Walters and I drove into that machine gun nest. Where the fuck are those bullets coming from Walters? He didn't answer me. I asked him again. When I looked to see why he wasn't answering me that's when I seen he had been shot in the head. Looking at Walter lying there in a pool of blood almost made me sick, but I knew this was the wrong time for that. When went to reload my rifle I realized I had no ammunition. The fighting had been so intense I had used it all. There were two German soldiers pouring heavy machine gun fire down on me. I didn't know what to do I had no ammunition. All I had were two hand grenades I lost four of them crossing that field. I pick up the B.A.R and started firing back at those Germans. When I stopped to reload out the corner of my eye I could see two German soldiers trying to come up behind me. I whipped that B.A.R around and shot the first one the bullets ripped though his body like paper. The other soldier at a shot off at me missing my head by inches. When he went to cock his gun I got off a couple rounds and one hit him in his shoulder. He dropped his gun and grabbed his shoulder in pain. I let off a couple more rounds one hit him in the eye blowing the back of his head out. I slowing moved over to see if there were anymore Germans in that machine gun nest. When I got there all the German soldiers were dead. I stood over the one I had shot in the eye and said that was for Walters. The machine gun that was firing at us had stopped. I looked out the nest to see what was going on. I saw dead German soldiers everywhere.

Then I seen Sgt walking towards me. I yelled Sgt over here. He ran over to me and jumped in the nest. He had this dazed look in his eyes. Hey Sgt where's Capt. Lewis? He's dead. Dead how? He got shot. We need to get the fuck out of here and meet up with Douglass at the rallying point. Yeah your right let's get the hell out of here. Sgt do you know if Neal is ok? I don't know Popeye we will see when we get to this woods. We started running towards the woods. When we get to the woods we saw Neal lying there dead. He had bled to death. There wasn't a medic to treat his wound Doc Phillips was left behind. I picked up his rifle and took his ammunition. Come on Popeye let's go. On our way to the rallying point Sgt told me that something bad had happen back there. I can't tell you now, but I will tell you later. I didn't say anything I just kept running.

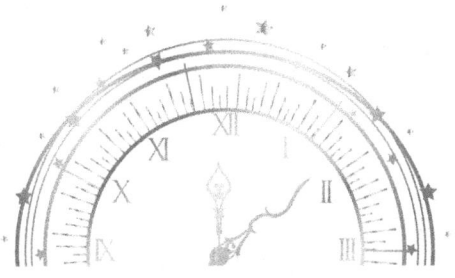

CHAPTER SEVEN

WHEN WE GOT TO the rallying point there was no one there. There was no sign of Lt. Douglass or his team. Where the fuck are they? I don't know Sgt. We ain't got time to wait on them Popeye let's get our asses back to base camp. We were about to leave when we saw two figures coming down the icy road. We the fuck is that Sgt? I don't know Popeye. We aimed our guns at them. When they got closer we could see it was Lt. Douglass and Pvt. Scott.

Scott was badly wounded he had been shot in the leg and shoulder. Give me a hand with this man Staff. Sgt. Banks. Where are the other men at Lt? Their all dead. What! Yes their all dead. Sgt and I looked at each other. Sgt picked up Scott put him over him shoulder and we started back to base camp. We started making our way back to base camp when I notice Lt. Douglass didn't have his rifle. Sir where is your rifle? I lost it Pvt. Sgt stopped and looked at Lt. Douglass. How did you lose your rifle sir? A soldier never loses his rifle. Don't worry about it Staff. Sgt. Let's get this men back to base camp before he dies. On our way to base camp I kept on thinking about what Sgt said something bad happen.

It was 0330 hours when we finally reached base camp. Everybody was out there waiting on us to come back. They were shocked when they only saw the four of us. A tall fat white Lt. Col approached us when we got back to camp. Lt. Douglass where is Capt. Lewis? He was killed sir.

Sgt looked at me when the Lt. Col asked Lt. Douglass that question. How? He was shot sir. He got killed when we were attacking a machine gun nest sir. So you saw this Staff Sgt?

Yes sir I was with him. He looked at Sgt for a second. Ok than get that man to medical. Yes sir. A couple of guys grabbed Scott and took him to medical. Lt. Douglass I need you to come to the CP tent and debrief me on what happen out there. Get cleaned up first and I will see you in 10 minutes. Yes sir. I didn't seem to concerned about they other men who got killed all he was worried about was that redneck Capt. Lewis. That white Lt. Col was Conley Lt. Col Jack Conley was tall about 6'5" 270lbs with brown hair and eyes. He had a big round face, thin mustache and thick eye brows his belly hung over his pants, but he was a real solid man. His uniform always looked sloppy on him no matter what he did. He graduated from West Point first in his class. He wasn't dumb like Capt. Lewis who finished last in his class.

Col. Conley was a very smart man. I would learn years later that he helped plan the D-day invasion. He was the Commanding Officer of all the Negro truck divisions in Europe. He was assigned to us a couple of months before we left for Europe, because something bad had happen at his last command. He didn't care to much for us Negros he never talked to us.

This was the first time I saw him. He would tell Capt. Lewis what he wanted us to do. Now that Capt. Lewis is dead who will carry out in orders now? I was on my way to my foxhole when Lt. Douglass passed me he had this worried look on his face. Something bad must have happen out there and he ain't saying what it was. I was about to jump in my foxhole when Sgt called me to come to medical. I was tired and I wanted to get some sleep. I really didn't want to go over there, but I did anyway. When I got there the medics were treating Scott wounds he was in real bad shape. He had lost a lot of blood and one of his legs had a hole in it. I could see the muscles and nerves hanging out of it. All that started to make me sick, so I stepped back outside. Sgt was standing outside the tent smoking a cigarette. He was smoking his cigarette with this dazed looked on his face. What's wrong Sgt? He looked at me and said. Popeye that whole mission was fucked up. They didn't tell us the truth about those guns. I was taking to Scott and he told me what really happen to them on that hill up there. Those white motherfuckers lied to us Popeye. Why you say that Sgt? Come I don't want to talk here let's go to your foxhole. We walked to my foxhole he didn't say anything to me on our way there. When we got to my foxhole there were two guys in there. Sgt told them in an angry voice to get the fuck out and find themselves another foxhole. The two guys jumped out and left and we jumped down in it. I pulled out a cigarette. Give me one of those Popeye. I give him one and lit it for him. He took a long drag from it. So what's going on Sgt?

    I fucked up Popeye it's all my fault. What are you talking about Sgt? I should have never volunteered us for that fuck up mission. Why is that Sgt? Scott told me that Douglass got all those men killed. What! Yeah he told me that Douglass didn't attack the guns from behind like he was told by Capt. Lewis. He told them to attack those guns head on. Scott also told me that Douglass didn't even lead the attack he was hiding in the woods. Then who lead the attack? Staff. Sgt. Benson lead the attack. Benson and Davis took down the first machine gun nest. Wilkes and Scott took out they our one. Then they all got together and attacked the 88 artillery guns That's when Benson got killed. Scott said he was shot in the head. Scott, Davis, Kelly and Wilkes continued their attack on that 88 artillery gun. They destroyed the gun and killed all the Germans. Scott said that there was only one 88 artillery gun. I thought Capt. Lewis said there were two. Scott said there was only one. They were on their way back when they ran into a squad of Hitler Youths. Scott said they got into a serious fire fight with them.

    Davis, Kelly and Wilkes were killed and Scott was shot in his shoulder. Where the hell was Douglass when all this was going on. Scott said he was in the woods hiding. He finally came out to give them a hand, but he got so scared he dropped is rifle and ran. What! So that's how he lost his rifle? Yeah Doc Phillips told him to come back and give him a hand with Scott that's when one of those Hitler youth boys throw and mashed potatoe grenade killed Doc and that's how Scott got those leg wounds. Scott said Douglass was going to leave him there to die, but he got some balls and came back to get him. That's when we met them at the rallying point.

So what you telling me that we did all that for nothing? That's what I'm telling you Popeye.

They didn't need us to do that. So why did they send us out there like that Sgt? I don't know Popeye I guess to see if we could fight. So those guys died for nothing. Sgt didn't say anything. These motherfuckers don't give a fuck about us. These white bastards are always playing with our lives like we are someone dogs. I'm nobody's dog. I'm a man and I'm sick and tired of it. Sgt you said that something bad happen out there? He looked at me. Give me another one of your cigarettes. He lit it up took a long drag and moved closer to me. What I'm about to tell you is just between you and me you understand? Yeah Sgt. Popeye you are the only person in this whole division I can trust. You can't tell anyone this. Okay Sgt I'm not going to say a word I promise. The reason Sgt trusts me is I'm the only one who would listen to his stories when he got drunk. He was about to tell me when Douglass came to my foxhole and told Sgt that Col. Conley wanted to see him at the CP. Yes sir I'm on my way sir. Sgt climbs out of the foxhole and heads to the CP. Douglass stands over my foxhole looking down on my. How are you feeling Pvt. Ross? I'm doing good sir just still a little shaken about what just happen. Yeah I know what you mean. I told the Col that I'm recommending you Staff. Sgt. Banks and Pvt. Scott for promoted for your bravery out there tonight. You guys might receive medals for what you did. I didn't believe him. He told me when we were back in the states that he had recommended me for promotion that was a year ago. Now as for the medals we will never see them they don't give Negros medals. I don't know why he said that I guess to try and make me feel good. Pvt. Ross. Yes sir. Did you see how Capt. Lewis died?

No sir. He looked at me and did say anything for a second. Alright get yourself some chow and go see Col. Conley. Yes sir. I grabbed my rifle climbed out of my foxhole and headed to the chow tent to get something to eat.

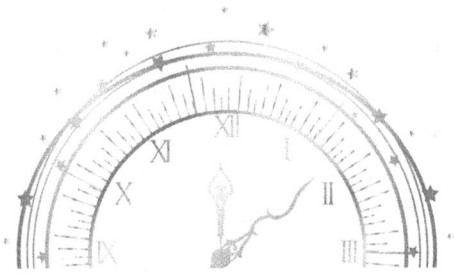

CHAPTER EIGHT

ON MY WAY TO the chow tent I didn't understand why Douglass would ask me that question.

The only person who knew that was Sgt, because he was with him. I also didn't understand why Col. Conley wanted to see me. I figured whatever Sgt told him would be enough. Why would they won't to hear my side of what happen? I had a bad feeling about this. The closer I got to the chow tent I could smell the freshly baked bread. It made me think of home and how my momma made bread like that. My mouth started watery for some of that bread. My stomach started growling I haven't eaten in two days. I went to the washroom to wash my hands if you want to call it that. All it had was a pipe with a bucket under it. I put down my rifle and turned the water on. It was cold as hell there wasn't any hot water. My hands were real dirty from crawling in all the snow and dirt. I dried my hands off of these towels they had hanging up for us. I took out my pack of cigarettes to smoke one that's when the envelope fell on the ground. I pick it and realized it was the letter Benson had given to me. I wanted to read it, but I was hungry and wanted o get something to eat before I went to talk to Col. Conley. I put it back in my pocket and headed to the chow tent. The chow tent is where they prepared all the food for us it looked like one of those circus tents. There were a few holes around the tent from the bombing. All it had were table and chairs. There were a shack of metal trays shacked in the corner. I walked over and grabbed me a tray and some utensils.

There were four big pots over these burners it wasn't a lot of choices to close from. The cooks The cooks gave me two pieces of bread a stoop of powder eggs and what looked like bacon.

I got me a cup of coffee (I had to drink it black) I sat down at an empty table in the back. I I made a sandwich out of the bread, bacon and eggs. I ate that in no time it wasn't to bad, but I was still hungry. I sipped on my coffee which was very nasty I hate black coffee. This gave me time to read the letter Benson had given me. I opened it up and it said.

Popeye, If you are reading this letter that means I'm dead. I'm you you this letter, because you and Staff Sgt. Banks are the only ones I trust in this company. This mission we are going on is a decoy mission. It really has nothing to do with us destroying any guns. It's meant to distract the Germans giving them the impression that our troops are going to attack from the East, but really they are going to attack from the north. They moved those 88's two days ago. All there is are about 20 young boys and old men. You are probably wondering how I know all of this information? A couple of days ago I was going to Capt. Lewis tent to ask him a question when I over heard Capt. Lewis and Col. Conley talking about this mission. Capt. Lewis told Col. Conley we didn't have a snow ball chance in hell making it back alive. He told the Col he would hang back and watch things go bad for us. Than he would report back that we fucked the mission up. It was all planned Popeye to send us to our deaths. Tell Staff Sgt. Banks about this and don't tell Douglass you know how he is.

Your Friend Staff Sgt. Clarence Benson. P.S. There was someone else at that meeting to. Lt. Douglass.

I was shocked I couldn't believe what I was reading. These motherfuckers really set us up to die. They knew all along that this was a suicide mission. That's why the Col is asking all these question about what happen to that racist motherfucker Capt. Lewis. He wasn't suppose to die. I'm glad his ass is dead good men died for nothing.

While I was pissed off about what I just read Douglass came into the chow and told me to go to the CP now. I put the letter back in my pocket grabbed my rifle and headed to the CP. Before I left Douglass asked me what was I reading. I told him it was a letter my wife sent to me. I didn't know you guys got mail. We didn't sir it's an old letter I carry around with me. He give me this suspicious look. I put on my helmet walked out the tent to the CP. I started to turn around and blow his fucking brains out. He knew I was reading something what he didn't know. I walked up the hill to the CP. As I was walking I was trying to figure out what kind of Negro Douglass was. I have heard about Negros like him who would sell out there our people to make it in the white man's world. We had Negros like that back in Houston who would anything to please the white man. I never thought I would meet someone like him. How could he let them do this to us? I got to the CP and stepped in. I saluted them Pvt. Ross reporting as ordered sir. Pvt. Ross come and have a seat. I took my helmet off and sat down in the chair in front of them.

There were three men in the tent. It was Col. Conley another by the name of Col. Moore. I had seen him once back in the states. They other Col I have never seen him before he was a skinny man skinny man that wear glasses. His big ears stuck out from the side of his head. His name tag said Col. White. Col. Conley asked me did I know why I was here? I know why I was there, but I acted like I didn't. No sir. Your here because we want to know what happen on that mission? Okay what do you want to know? Were you with Capt. Lewis when he was killed?

No sir I wasn't Well where were you? Walters and I were pinned down behind a brick wall. So Walters was killed right? Yes sir. During that time did you ever see Capt. Lewis? Yes sir he was with Sgt I mean Staff Sgt. Banks. When the Germans started shooting at us they both ran in the same direction. What happen after that Pvt? After I took out the last few German soldiers Staff Sgt. Banks came running over to me. Was Capt. Lewis with him? No sir he told me Capt. Lewis was dead. They started looking at each other. I'm sitting here thinking I know they don't think Sgt killed that redneck. That would be crazy for Sgt to do that he knows what would happen to him. Killing a white officer is punishable by death. I was getting scared not for me, but for Sgt. They are trying to pin Capt. Lewis death on Sgt? My stomach started feeling funny. I sat there looking at them as they talked among each other. I was trying to hear what they were saying, but they were talking real low. Col. Conley told me I was dismissed.

Yes sir I saluted and I was about to leave when Col. Conley told me that he was promoting me to Cpl. I was shocked. You boys did a hellva job out there keep up the good work. Thank you sir I saluted again and left. That put a little smile on my face knowing I'm going to be a Cpl now Douglass was telling the truth this time. I smoked a cigarette to celebrate my promotion.

Cpl. Ross that sounds good to me. They must really like me they skipped over Pvt first class and promoted me to Cpl. While I was patting myself on the back I saw out the corner of my eye Douglass go back into the CP tent. I was wondering now what more do they want from him? I got to find Sgt. I asked several guys have they seen Sgt? One soldier told me he was in my foxhole. I ran over to my foxhole and found Sgt smoking a cigarette. I jumped down in my foxhole. How long you been sitting here? Oh about an hour waiting on you. They done talking to you? Yeah. What they asked you? They asked me what happen to Capt. Lewis.

What did you tell them? I told them I didn't know. What did they say to that? They didn't say anything they just looked at each other. Sgt why are they asking all these question about Capt. Lewis? What about they other men who were killed? They ain't white Popeye they are less Niggas they got to worry about. On my way back here I saw Douglass go back into the Cp tent. Oh yeah. Yeah. What's going on Sgt? He just looked at me and said. They trying to say I killed Capt. Lewis. What! Why? I was the last person he was with. He was suppose to come back not us. Capt. Lewis was your boy even though he was a fucked up motherfucker.

He was kissing Col. Conley ass for the next promotion and he was going to get it off our deaths. I took out the letter Benson gave me and handed to Sgt. Here read this Benson gave it to me. I know what is says. You do? Yeah when Benson heard thee plan he came to me and told me. I told him to write everything he heard down and give the letter to you. I figured you would get killed so I told him to give it to you. He left a few details out. Like what?

Capt. Lewis lied to us. They knew they had moved at least 6 of those 88 artillery guns a couple of days ago and they left a half of a Panzer division behind. We weren't suppose to come back. We were lucky were got out of there alive. They were shocked when they saw us.

I'm surprised you hung in there Popeye. Why you say that Sgt. I know you were scared and the sight of blood makes you sick. Yeah it does, so did something happen between you and Capt. Lewis Sgt? He looked at me and shook his head like I told you before what I'm about to tell you stays between you and me. I understand Sgt. I took at another cigarette to smoke it, because what ever he's about to tell I know it's going to be something bad. My stomach started feeling funny.

CHAPTER NINE

WHEN WE WERE CROSSING that field all I could think about Popeye was all of us were going to die. When those Germans started shooting at us Capt. Lewis and I ran to an empty machine gun nest. You and Walters were taking a lot of gun fire. Capt. Lewis told me to circle around that machine gun and he would cover me. So I worked my way around that machine gun nest and killed the two Germans soldiers. By this time Capt. Lewis had joined me. We were about to take out the machine gun that were shooting at y'all when out of know where 5 German soldiers came running at us. I cut down three of them while one stopped to reload one kept charging with his bayonet. I knocked him down and hit him with the butt of my gun.

Then I pulled out my knife grabbed him by his hair and cut his throat. The one German who stopped to reload started shooting at me. I grabbed Capt. Lewis .45 from him and killed that German. What was Capt. Lewis doing during all this. His sorry ass was coward down in the corner of that machine gun nest. I told him to get his ass up and give me a hand, because Germans were coming from everywhere. He told me that he didn't need to help me and to get my Nigger ass. You do what I tell you to do. Now get your Nigger ass over there and take out that other machine gun. I looked at him and put my gun in his face. He stood up and said.

You want to shoot me Nigger go right ahead it will be the biggest mistake in your fucking life.

That's while a bullet ripped though his head and split his head in two. His blood and brains fly all over me. I stood there for a minute in shock, but a couple of bullets flew by my head brought me back. So you didn't kill him? Hell no I ain't killed that motherfucker. I thought you were going to tell me you had killed that redneck bastard. Naw I ain't stupid Popeye. I wanted to kill him. So why do they think you killed him? We were not suppose to come back alive only him, so they figured I killed him since I was the last person to see him alive. You see Popeye Capt. Lewis is a good old boy and Col. Conley liked him. Col. Conley thought we were going to mess this mission up, but we didn't instead we made him look bad. So you think that's why they promoted us? Oh yeah to make his ass look good. Now you know he's going to take all the credit for it. Yeah I know. Douglass got promoted to 1st Lt he's been a 2nd Lt for 3 years now. He is way over due for and promotion. Douglass is a weak man that's why they use him. He's to scared to to say anything. Do you remember a Lt. Bates? Lt. Bates yeah I remember him what ever happen to him? They got rid of him, because of Douglass.

Why? Douglass would run back and tell Capt. Lewis everything Lt. Bates would say.

Douglass and Lt. Bates didn't get along, so when Lt. Bates found out that Douglass was running back and telling Capt. Lewis everything he called Douglass and uncle Tom. Capt.

Lewis told command about it the next day Lt. Bates was gone. Where did they send him? The sent him to Georgia where two weeks later he was lynched. How do you know all these things Sgt? I know a lot of people Popeye. Hey Sgt a voice said. Yeah who's that? It's Pvt.

North. What do you need Pvt. North? Lt. Douglass told me to tell you to come to the CP.

Why? He said we will be moving out soon. Yeah the Germans had broken through our defenses in some forest cutting them in half. So pack all your gear, because we won't be coming back. That doesn't sound good Sgt. I know Popeye, but it's our job let me go and see what the plan is. I'll see at the trucks. Ok Sgt. I grabbed my rifle jumped out of my foxhole and headed to the trucks. While the other guys were running I was taking my time. I wasn't in any hurry to go to where ever this fucking forest was. Hey up Popeye the Col has to brief us on where we're going. When I got to the trucks everyone was gathered around Col. Conley's fat ass. The reason we are moving boys is that the Germans has broken though our defenses in the Ardennes Forest in Belgium. Where the fuck is that at I said to myself. The Allied Forces are retreating they need supplies, it's our job to get then those supplies. This means you probably will be going into the line of fire. This will be the first taste of war for the most of you and boys I'm going to be honest with you it isn't pretty, so don't panic when you see dead bodies lying all over the roads. Capt. Douglass. Yes sir. Capt. Douglass! so they promoted him to Capt? Sgt looked over at me and shook his head. We are in some deep shit now. We'll be moving out in two minutes, so let's load up. Good luck and God bless you.

Now that was a bunch of bullshit he just said he could careless if we die or live. God bless who the hell does he think he's fooling. I got in the truck with Sgt. He put Douglass in charge now he ain't got nothing to worry about. Douglass is really going to do some ass kissing now.

All the supplies were loaded on to the trucks and Douglass told them to move out. We started on our way to the Ardennes Forest it will later be called The Battle of Bulge. The roads were really icy we were sliding all over the place. Sgt to us to listen up. The Germans has broken though and catching our troops off guard. They believe that this is Hitler's last ditch effort to win the war. Our troops weren't ready for this. They thought Hitler was finished, but he fooled everyone. We were not ready for a long winter war neither a lot of our troops don't have any weather gear, so be prepare for a fight for your life. I knew this was going to be bad. We have no weather gear and it's colder as hell in Belgium. Now how did Douglass get promoted to Capt Sgt? I don't know Popeye, but you how that happen. Oh yeah I forgot to tell you Scott died this morning. What! Yeah he lost to much blood and they couldn't save him. Did he have any family? Yeah he had a wife and two kids. That made me think about my wife and little girl who's going to take care of them if I get killed. Sgt. Yeah Popeye. I want you to promise me something. What's that? If I die over here I want you to go tell my wife what happen. Oh Popeye ain't nothing going to happen to you I got your back. The truck started sliding all over again. Who in the hell is driving this damn truck? I don't know Sgt It's Pvt. Bowman Sgt. Sgt banged on the back of his seat and told him to slow this motherfucker down for you kill us before we get there. We had been driving for a while when we started seeing soldiers. Hey Popeye look. We seen soldiers that were wounded, bloody and beaten. Where the hell they going? I don't know, but they are going the wrong way. Why you asking me all these questions Popeye I know just as much as you do. I didn't ask Sgt anymore question he looked like he was getting mad. As we were driving by the soldiers there were bodies lying all over road. Bodies were stacked up along side of the road like firewood. Than the trucks came to a stop some white officer had stopped us. He and Douglass was talking about something I could see Douglass nodding his head to what ever he was saying. Than Douglass told us to get out and to start unloading the trucks. 1st Sgt, Cpl. Ross yes sir. They need some volunteers to move these dead bodies off the road. I volunteered you two, so get a few more men and go ahead and get that done. 1st Banks you are in charge of this task. Yes sir. Take a couple of trucks and you need to hurry before it gets dark. Yes sir. Sgt picked 10 guys we got in the trucks and started down the icy road. Sgt and I were in the lead truck.

Hey Sgt I didn't know they promoted you to 1st Sgt? I know I didn't want you to know. I didn't say a word he had his reason and I wasn't about to ask him. The driver of our truck was a big guy by the name of Ronnie Brown. Everybody called him bad news Brown he got that name because everywhere he went trouble would follow him. He had these very large hands. He was also from Texas just like me, but he was from Dallas. A rumor was going around that he had killed a man with his bare hands. I don't know how true that is, but I didn't want to mess with him. Brown was driving crazy. Damn Brown slow down Nigga before you kill us. Don't worry Sgt I got this. We could hear bombs dropping in the distant. Sgt you hear those bombs?

Yeah Popeye I hear it. We could go any further, because there were trees, dead bodies and debris blocking the road. Then we heard what I thought was a tank. Brown stopped the truck than we saw it come crashing though the trees and it stopped right in front of our truck. You see what I see Sgt. Yeah Popeye I see it.

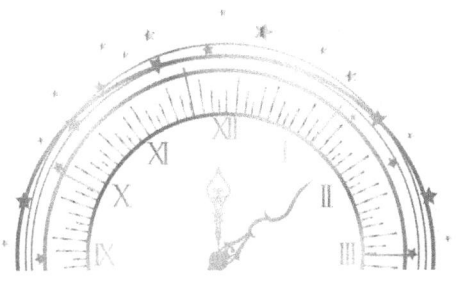

CHAPTER TEN

IT WAS A TIGER tank it is the deadest tank the Germans have. It could rip apart any one of our tanks our tanks didn't have a chance against this tank. What are we going to do Sgt? I don't know Brown, but we better think of something quick. It pointed it's barrel at us. Before it could fire it's gun Sgt, me and Brown jumped out of the truck. The shell went though our truck and hit the truck behind us. It blew that truck to pieces I could see guys jumping out on fire. The trucks behind us turned around and got the hell out of the before it could get another. It fired off another round hitting one of the trucks that was driving away killing everyone. The German gunner on top of the tank let lose a hail of bullets from his machine gun cutting our men down as they tried to run away. Sgt and I jumped into a ditch. We started firing at the tank, but it had no effect. Sgt told me we had to take out that tank if that tank gets by us we all are in trouble.

I looked at him like he was crazy. Now how in the hell are we going to take this tank down?

Than North and two other guys joined us. Where the hell y'all come from? We come from the last truck we jumped out when we seen the truck in front of us blew up. What are we going to do Sgt? We are going to take down that tank. What! Are you crazy Sgt? We are going to get killed doing something like that. You shut your mouth and you do what I tell you North.

You can stay here and die or we can take down that tank. Popeye I'm going to need you, Brown and these two guys to gave me and North cover fire while we try and get on top of that tank to throw a couple of grenades down in it. Are you ready North? Yeah I'm ready. Popeye y'all ready? Yeah we ready Sgt. Okay here we go cover us. We give Sgt and North covering fire as they ran towards the tank. I told one of the guys we had to take out that gunner. I shot and clearly missed him. I shot again my second shot knocked his hat off. I saw him grab his shoulder somebody must have shot him in his shoulder I know it wasn't me. My third shot hit him square in the chest I saw him fall forward on the tank. By this time Sgt and North had worked their way around behind that tank. They climbed on top North opened the hatch and Sgt throw two grenades down in it. The tank stopped moving Sgt and North jumped off the tank, because a small unit of Germans were shooting at them. Sgt ran straight at them shootingthem down. He shot them all down like they were nothing. This was Sgt element you could count on him to kill without showing the enemy any mercy. He belonged in war this is where he could take all his angry out on white men without getting into trouble. After he killed all of them he was looking for more blood to spill. He seen this one German soldier trying to crawl away. Sgt took the butt of his gun and smashed his head in. Then the bombs started dropping again. Sgt told us to take cover we all jumped back into the ditch and covered heads. Sgt had jumped back in the ditch with us he was covered in blood. The smell of the blood started making me sick. Popeye those are our planes dropping those bombs.

How you know that those are our planes? We control the air. As the planes flew over us the bombing stopped. You can stand up now Popeye. When I stood up everything in site was destroyed trees, trucks on fire, the tank we stopped was burning there were holes from the bombing everywhere. Sgt where is North? I don't know Popeye. We slowly started walking towards the tank and that's when we seen him or what was left of him. All that was left of North were his two legs and a part of an arm. When I saw that I throw up. You alright Popeye?

Yeah I'm fine Sgt. Damn! He must have got caught up in that

bombing. You know Sgt a man shouldn't have to die like this. I know Popeye, but this is war and things like this happens. I didn't know North at all I didn't even know his first name. Let's pick up what's left of North off this road and burying him. The two guys with us each grabbed a leg and I grabbed his arm which was still holding his rifle. Sgt find us a place in the woods where we could bury his body parts. How are we going to bury him Sgt we ain't got know shovels? Damn! Well are just going have to put him in that hole over there. We placed his legs and arm in the hole covered it with snow. While we were burying North we heard someone call Sgt name. You hear that Popeye? Yeah I heard it who could it be? Sgt. Banks the voice said again. Who is that? It's me. Me who? Me Brown. Sgt and I looked at each other. Where are you Brown? I'm over here in this ditch. Come on Popeye let's got see where he is. You two stay here and cover us. Sgt and I move slowly towards the ditch a German could have had a gun to Brown's head telling him to call Sg t over to him. As we got closer to the ditch we could see Brown laying there.

Help me Sgt my leg. We jumped down in the ditch and saw that part of his leg had been blow off. Calm down Brown we're going to get you some help. Hurry up Sgt before I bleed to death.

I don't want to die. SgT torn a piece of cloth off a dead German and tied it around Brown's leg to stop the bleeding. Popeye go found something so I can wrap his leg with. Like what Sgt we ain't got know first aid kit. I don't give a fuck go find something now! I got up ran though the woods looking for anything. The first German soldier I came across was frozen solid, but the one lying next to him was carrying a first aid bag. it had the Red Cross symbol on it. I ripped it from his frozen hand and ran back to Sgt. Hey Sgt I found a first aid bag, but the look on his face I knew that Brown had died. He had died from shock and the cold weather. He was sitting there looking at his hands covered in blood. Popeye it's to much dying. I know Sgt, but we need to get the hell out of here before more of those Germans come back. Come Popeye help me cover him with snow. Ok I have never seen Sgt like this before. Brown's dead had a real bad affect on him. We cover

Brown's body and started making our way back to the other guys. I kept that first aid bag just in case we needed it. When was making our way back when we heard trucks coming up the road. Get down Popeye it might be some more Germans. We drove in the snow and waited to see who it was. We were relieved it was our trucks. It's our troops Popeye you can stand up now. We stood on the side of the road thinking they were going to pick us up, but they just kept going. Than the last truck stopped a tall dark skin man with pearly white teeth got out. You boys need a ride? Hell yeah.Okay hop in. Hey where are you guys coming from? We are coming from a supply depot in France. What divison is this? This is the 455th supply division. Sgt and I looked at each other. Now where in the hell is division? I don't know. You boys staying or you riding with us? We are going with y'all. Hey Sgt let's not forget the two other guys back there.

Yeah Hey Pvt. Yes Sgt. We have two guys guys to pick up they just down the road here. Okay no problem we'll pick them up. Sgt and I jumped in the back. There were 10 other soldiers back there too. How y'all doing this one soldier asked us. We are doing fine. What are you guys doing way out here? We were told by our Capt to help remove dead bodies off the road when we were attacked by a tiger tank. Oh really, so those are y'all burned out trucks? Some of them are. Sgt didn't say a word I did all the talking. They all were looking at Sgt strange, because he had all that blood on his jacket. Hey Pvt. Yes Sgt. Did you guys pass a bunch of supply trucks on your way out here? Yes we did, but they took another route. The Capt that was in charge told them not to come this way because this road was crawling with Germans. Sgt and I looked at each other. That damn Douglass Sgt said. What's that? Nothing. We came this way, because we were told that this road was clear and it was safe to come this way. What you think about what he said Sgt? I don't know what to think Popeye, but when we get to this supply depot I'm going to ask Douglass why he sent us out here. The rest of the way we didn't say a word. It took us about 45 minutes to get to the supply depot. On the way we passed dead bodies, burned out equipment that littered the roads. When we got to the supply depot are company was already there. Look Sgt there is our division. Yeah I see. We jumped out the back of the truck and walked towards our division. I see y'all still alive? Yes we are Pvt. James. Why you asking us that? We heard you guys were killed when that Tiger tank blew up y'all truck. Who told you that? Pvt. Thomas told us. Who the hell is Pvt. Thomas? He was driving the last truck when he saw y'all truck get blown up. He turned around and got the hell out of there and got back to the supply depot and told Capt. Douglass that the road was crawling with Germans. Capt.

Douglass told Col. Conley. Than Col. Conley told Capt. Douglass to find another route out of to this supply depot. That motherfucker left us out there to die. Yeah he did Sgt. He knew we were out there. Now I was mad. He didn't even anyone out there to see if we were still alive. still alive. What I don't understand Sgt is why would he send us out there knowing that road was crawling with Germans? I don't know Popeye. Hey Sgt where is Brown, North and the other guys that was with you? They were killed in that bombing. Damn! We are losing a lot of people. Come Popeye let's go get something to eat I'm hungry as hell. We started looking for the chow tent. There were a lot of Negro divisions at the supply depot I didn't know that we had this many Negros in Europe. Hey Sgt look at all these Negro divisions. Yeah I see them you you think we were they only Negro division over here? We found the chow tent and got in line.

CHAPTER ELEVEN

THE LINE WAS REAL long and Sgt was very angry he had to stand in that long line. Fuck this I ain't standing in this long line. Come Popeye we are going to the front. I stood there for a minute. Come on Popeye what are you waiting for? Then I realized that none of these guys had finish fighting like Sgt and I. When we walked to the front of the line no one said a word.

I think the reason they didn't say anything, because Sgt had all that blood on him. I got to the front Sgt handed me a tray. Here you go Popeye. Thanks Sgt. The cooks were looking at Sgt with fear and the blood on him. What are you looking at boy? Give me some of that food I'm hungry as hell. Yes Sgt he said, He gave Sgt four slices of bread an a big stoop of what ever that brown stuff was. I guess he give Sgt so much he didn't want to make him mad by giving him a small portion. It was a different story for me. He give two slices of bread and a small stoop of that brown stuff. He gave me some green beans and I got myself a cup of warm coffee. We sat down at one of the tables and ate our food. I took one bite and wanted to throw it away, but I knew I had to eat it there was nothing else to eat. I just choked it down.

I told Sgt that was the worse meal I have ever had. I know it was, but it hit the spot. He took out a cigarette from his crashed pack. It was flat from all the fighting we had done. His were dirty and covered in Brown's blood it was dry by now. Hey Sgt you need to wash your hands.

The Men that Time has Forgotten

I'll wash them later Popeye. You want a cigarette? Yeah give me one. He lit mined and his cigarettes and he took a long drag. You know Popeye those men didn't have to die like that. I still think about how Brown died. There was nothing we could do for him Sgt. I know but it still bother's me. Hey Sgt a voice said. We looked to see who it was. Yeah Pvt. What do you want? I've been looking all over for you Capt. Douglass wanted me to find you and Cpl. Ross to tell you he needs you two at the CP. Alright Pvt we'll be there when we finish smoking our cigarettes. He didn't go anywhere he just stood there. We are coming Pvt get your ass the fuck out of here. Ok Sgt. What do you think he wants with us this timme sgt? I don't know, but he better explain to us why he sent us out there to die like that. Let's go Popeye and see what the hell he wants. We put out our cigarettes grabbed our gear and headed to the CP.

As we were walking towards the CP we passed several trucks full of the dead and wounded soldiers. The Germans have done a job on us the last couple of days. We came over to Europe with 2,000 men in our division. We have lost over 300 killed and over 600 wounded.

The morrow of the men were real low most of them thought the war would be over be Christmas. I was hoping the same thing, but it looks that ain't going to happen. When we got to the tent that was Douglass CP he was sitting behind his desk he made out of sandbags writing down something. 1st Sgt. Banks and Pvt. Ross come in and have a seat. You wanted to see us sir? Yes I did come in and have a seat you two have seen a lot of action? Yes sir we have sir. We have lost a lot of good men also sir. Yes we have 1st Sgt. Sir I have a question for you? Okay 1st Sgt go right ahead. Sir why did you send us out there to that road when it was crawling with Germans? I didn't send you out there since you asked 1st Sgt do you remember that white officer? Yes sir. He told me that he needed us to to that, because they were pulling out. Sir you know this company was never trained for combat. I know this 1st Sgt, but we have to do what we are told to do weather we like it or not. Sgt didn't say anything. Hey look I'm not even suppose to be here. Why you say that sir? I worked for Lt. Col Conley back in Washington D.C.

I was his orderly. You were his orderly? What is an orderly sir? It's like a secretary. We looked at him funny. I did all his paperwork for him. So how did you end up here sir? He looked at Sgt fixed his glasses took a sip of his coffee and he began to tell us his story. One night Conley went out some some white officer's club and got real drunk. I was his orderly so they called me to come get him. Nobody wanted to take his fat ass home. I was shocked he said that about the Col. Nobody really liked his fat ass, so I had to get out of my bed and go down to this club and get his ass. When I got there he was passed out on the bar. I hurried up and got his ass out of there. When I was I doing this they were calling every name in the book. We were on our way back when he stumbled and fell into this big water fountain. I trying to get his fat ass out when two white officers came and asked me what was I trying to to that white man? I told them I was his orderly and I was trying to get him back to his barracks. One of them said I looked like I was trying to drown him. I told him I wasn't trying to drown him. He told me are you trying to get smart with me Nigger. I said no I'm not.

During all this Conley manage to pull his fat ass out of that water fountain. They recognized who he was he told them to give me a hand getting him back to his barracks. It took the three of us 45 minutes to get his ass back to his barracks. The next day those two white officers reported that incident to a Col. Roger Mason. Col. Mason didn't like Col. Conley he thought he was nothing but a fat slob. The reason Col. Mason didn't like Conley is that Conley grandfather is a General in the top brass. Conley got into West Point because of his grandfather. They were in the same class in West Point. Conley finished first and Mason finished 5th in there class. Everyone knows Conley is to fat for the Army, so when Mason heard about what happen he went right to command with it. A week had passed and I was hearing rumors that they needed a CO for a newly formed truck division out of Iowa. A couple of weeks later Conley had orders to Iowa. So you thought that you were going to stay?

Yes I did 1st Sgt, but The next day I got orders to report to Iowa also. So here I am. Sir can I ask you a personnel question? It depends

The Men that Time has Forgotten

how personnel it is 1st Sgt. He took another sip of his coffee. Go ahead 1st Sgt. I want to know why do you go around here kissing Conley's ass like that? You do whatever they tell you even if it's something that doesn't make any sense.

You act like you are scared of these white folks not to mention you don't help us at all. He just smiled and said. Let me tell you something 1st Sgt I'm an educated man. I came from a well to do Negro family. We told were told by my father not to talk like Niggas. Not like you two I'm playing this game to get ahead in life I don't want the white man to think I'm like you two if you you know what I mean. 1st Sgt you have to step on a few people to get ahead in life even if it's your own kind. That's the way life is. He had this big grin on his face when he was saying all this shit to us. Cpl. Ross or is it Popeye. My friends call me Popeye sir. Well anyway I was the one who got you that promotion. They weren't going to give you shit. I told them that you had done a good job out there. Conley don't like you he knows the only reason your black ass is still alive is because of 1st Sgt. Banks. I wanted to blow his head off for taking to me like that. Now as for you 1st Sgt. Banks they think you are a real animal. You always getting drunk and Popeye here dragging you back to base. You know all that built up angry you have they like that and the way you kill. They can send you out there knowing the job will get done. Your a real killing machine. You are just as dumb as the rest of these Niggas. I saw Sgt grab his 45 I put my hand on his hand and shook my head. What did you want to see us for sir? I seen you talking to Scott in the medical tent before he died. Yes I was sir. What did he say to you?

Nothing sir. Cpl. Ross I seen Staff Sgt. Benson give you a envelope. Yes he did sir, but I lost it I think you two are lying. Is that all you wanted sir? No I want you to report to your new platoon leader a Lt. Glenn Jones. It that it sir? Yeah that's it 1st Sgt. We stood up to salute he just looked at us. Your dismissed. Oh sir one more thing. What is it 1st Sgt. Does Col. Conley know that you didn't lead that attack on those 88's and that you dropped your rifle and ran like a little girl? I bet he doesn't know that. After Sgt said that we left. You see the look on that cowardly motherfucker's face? Yeah I seen it Sgt. Who the fuck do he think he is talking to us like that? That Nigga must think he is white. Those white folks don't give a damn about his black ass. Sgt why was he so worried about what Scott had talked to you about? There was more to what Scott had told me. Oh yeah what was it? Popeye do you trust me? Yeah Sgt I trust you. Than stop asking me all these questions I'll tell you when the time comes. Now let's go find this Lt. Jones. Now I was lost I didn't know why Sgt wouldn't tell me what really happen. I think he doesn't trust me like I'm going to run and tell someone.

CHAPTER TWELVE

WE WALKED ACROSS THE yard looking for this Lt. Jones. We didn't even know what he looked like. Sgt Douglass didn't even tell is what he looked like I wonder if he is black? I don't know Popeye. We stopped this one Pvt and asked him did he know a Lt. Jones? Yeah he's over there in that tent. Thanks Pvt. We walked over to the tent where Lt. Jones was. He was in there talking to our division. He stopped and looked at us. May I help you Sgt? Yes sir we were told by Capt. Douglass to report to you sir. Oh yeah you must be 1st Sgt. Banks. Yes sir I am. You must be Pvt. Ross? Yes sir. I was expecting you come in and grabbed a seat I was briefing the division on our next task.

Lt. Horace Jones was a tall (6'2") dark skin man with black hair and eyes. He was a clean cut officer. His uniform was neat and clean and his boots were shined like mirrors. You can tell he was new. When we sat down everybody was looking at us. I guess because how dirty we looked compared to them. Pvt. Ross. Yes sir. Where did you get that first aid bag from? Sir I got it off a dead German soldier sir. Ok well give it to one of the medics we are going to need it where we are going. When he said that my stomach started feeling funny. That told me we are going into something bad and we are right in the middle of it. Our main task will be to guard the roads coming into Belgium. The Germans are retreating our forces are finally pushing them back. We also been hearing reports that German soldiers have been dressing up as Army officers. They have killed several of our soldiers and gotten pass our road blocks.

So from now on if anyone wants to get though our road blocks they are going to have to show you their ID card. Sir. Yes Pvt. Ross. How would you tell if they had a fake one? Good question Pvt. Ross. The ID card you were issued has an eagle on it. If it doesn't have eagle it's a fake. Does that answer your question Pvt. Ross? It's Cpl. Ross sir. Cpl. Ross? Yes sir Cpl. Ross. Than why are you not wearing your Cpl stripes? I just got promoted a couple of days ago sir and I haven't had a chance to sew them on. Well Cpl. Ross you better get them sewn on immediately. Yes sir I will sir. 1st Sgt. Banks get the men ready we will be moving out in 10 minutes. Yes sir you heard the man let's move. Where do you think we are going now Sgt? I don't know Popeye, but I can tell you this it ain't know where nice. We loaded onto the trucks and started on our way to God knows where. Riding on the back of that truck made me think of when I was small boy we had to ride in the back of my daddy's truck going to the fields to pick potatoes. This old white man by the name of Norman Dixon would pay my daddy and his friends 15 cent an hour to pick his fields. I hated that type of work it made me feel like I was back in slavery. We came to a stop at this dirt road. Alright 1st Banks I want you to take 10 men and guard this road here. Yes sir. 1st Sgt. Yes sir. Guard this road with your lives. Yes sir we will sir. He gets back in his jeep and leaves. What did he think we were going to do let those Germans just walk though here? I guess. The guys we were with were new guys who had just came in. I want you two to set up that machine gun on the other side of this road in those bushes. Okay Sgt. I want you two to stack up this sandbags over here and you two havethe first watch. Every four hours we will rotate. Okay Sgt. Come on Popeye grab a couple of those sandbags and let set up our own CP in these woods over here. I grabbed one sandbag because that's all I could grab one bag was heavier than me. Sgt grabbed two of them like it was nothing. We walked though the deep snow until we found a spot to build our CP. Here's a good spot Popeye. After stacking sandbags for 20 minutes we finished our so called CP. It was late in the afternoon and it was getting real cold. I sat down in the corner of the CP to try and get warm. Damn Sgt my hands are cold. I know it's cold Popeye, but what do you want me to do? We can build a fire. Popeye you know we can't build no damn fire put your hands in your pockets. I put my hands in my pockets, but it didn't help. Sgt do you think we will get out of here alive? He smiled at me yeah I told you I got your back. We could hear bombs dropping in the distant a few came close. That made us real nerves. I was real tired I haven't slept or ate in a couple of days. I didn't know what was keeping me up I guess the fear of dying was. I saw Sgt nodding off. I wondered to myself how long we were going to be out here. Damn! I'm hungry they better bring us some food soon. I'm hungry to Sgt. That meal they feed us back at that depot didn't do nothing for me. Than we heard a jeep pull up.

Let's go see who that is Popeye. I grabbed my rifle to go see who it was. It was Douglass and he had a black Sgt with him. 1st Sgt. Banks, Cpl. Ross this is Staff Sgt. Melvin Hicks he'll be giving you a hand with the division. Glad to have you Hicks we need all the men we can get.

How long have you been in country Hicks? I only been in country for a cuople of days I have been trying to catch up to you guys for a month now. Yeah we have been moving around a lot. the month. We are glad to have you Hicks. Sir. Yes 1st Sgt. When are they going to bring us some food sir? I don't know Cpl. Ross when the Germans broke though our lines they cut off our supplies. It's going to be hard getting supplies to you, so do the best you can. Yes sir. 1st Sgt. Yes sir. We have been getting reports that there have been German soldiers posing as American officers in this area, so keep your eyes open. Yes sir we will sir. Do you have anything for me 1st Sgt? No sir I don't. Well I'm going to head back to the CP if you need anything just call me on these radios. I will sir. He gets in his jeep and leaves. Damn I'm glad he's gone. He almost talked me to death he was really getting on my nerves. Let's walk back to the CP. So where you from Hicks? I'm from Atlanta, Ga. Oh an old Georgia boy. Where you from Sgt? I'm from St. Louis and Popeye is from Houston, Texas. Capt. Douglass was telling me those Germans is beating us pretty good. Yeah that's what we hear, but we ain't seen nothing or heard anything out here. So how long have y'all been out here. We just got out here a couple of hours ago. Have y'all seen any action. Yeah me and Popeye have. Were you scared? Hell yeah we were scared wouldn't you be scared if someone was shooting at you? Y'all killed anyone? Sgt and I looked at each other. We have killed a few. He didn't ask anymore questions after that. Hey Hicks do you have any food in that duffel bag of yours?

Yeah I do Sgt. He reached in his bag and pulled out a box of K-rations and give it to Sgt. thanks Hicks. So Popeye what is your real name? My real name is Jeffery Ross and Sgt what's your real name? His real name is Willie Ernest Banks III. This right here is a real killing machine. He has killed a lot of Germans since we been out here. Yeah I have just hope you ain't got to kill anyone. If it come to that Sgt I'll be ready. Hicks you ain't never going to be ready when it come to killing someone. Hicks looks at Sgt and didn't say anything. Hicks I want you to go check on the other guys. Okay Sgt. He grabbed his rifle and went to check on the other guys He's going to get killed he thinks he knows what to do. A guy like Hicks don't last long out with an attitude like that. Well we will see Popeye. Hey Sgt let me get some of those K-rations. Oh yeah here. I grabbed the box sit in the corner and started eating what was left.

CHAPTER THIRTEEN

K-RATIONS WAS AN INDIVIDUAL daily combat food ration given to soldiers in the field. It provided three separately boxed meals units breakfast, dinner and supper. It came in a unbleached tan colored rectangular card stock box with black letters that between the three meal suppose to to give you 2,830 to 3,000 calories for energy. The Breakfast unit came with canned veal or chopped eggs and ham, biscuits, dried fruit bar, precooked oatmeal, cigarettes, chewing gum instant coffee and sugar. I had the Supper unit which was better than the Dinner unit. It had more things to eat. It had canned meat (sausage, pork and beef), carrots, apples, biscuits chocolate bar, cigarettes and a powder drink which was orange, grape or lemon. It also came with toilet paper. I didn't like K-rations the food was really nasty, but I had no choice there was nothing else to eat. I tasted it and wanted to spit it out, but I just choked it down. I ate what little left Sgt had eaten most of it. The next bite I took I imagined it was my wife's Lillian's cooking. I could smell the pig feet a mile away when she was cooking. The cornbread, collard greens, peach cobbler and ice tea what I wouldn't give to have a meal likethat now. I'm in the middle of now where and I don't know when all this madness is going to end. Hey Popeye hurry up and eat those rations we got the next guard watch. Okay Sgt. I finished up the rations grabbed my rifle and headed back to the road. It was dark now the wind was blowing hard my hands were freezing I could barely hold my rifle. When I got to the road Sgt was telling the two other Pvts to go to the CP and get some rest. In a 4 hours you will relieve us you got that. Yes Sgt. Hicks had joined Sgt at the machine gun. Hicks you go get some rest to.

I'm going to need you out here with these men. Alright Sgt. Sgt it's really cold out here. Yeah I know Popeye go ahead and test the machine gun to make sure that it don't freeze up on us.

Go ahead and fire off a couple of rounds to keep it warm. I fired off a couple of rounds. It looks good to me Sgt. I hope it doesn't start to snow that wouldn't be good we don't have any weather gear I bet those white boys do. Those white boys don't have any weather gear either Popeye they are freezing their asses off just like us. Sgt how come you didn't change your jacket at the depot? I didn't want to Popeye. The blood on his jacket was frozen you could pick it off. Sgt what was it you were going to tell me? He looked at me out the corner of his eye. I took out a cigarette and lit it up. I would like to know you told me you would tell me later. It ain't later yet Popeye. Look Sgt I have a wife and baby at home I would like to get back to them alive. He took a drag of his cigarette paused for a minute. Okay this is what happen. He was about to tell me when we heard a jeep coming towards us. We couldn't see it, because it was so dark Popeye get on that machine gun. I got on the machine and Sgt cocked his Tommy gun. Who could that be Sgt coming from that direction? I don't know Popeye you just have that machine gun ready. The jeep started getting closer. Halt who goes there Sgt asked them. The jeep stopped. It's Lt. Hartman and Lt. Silvermann. Come close so you can be recognized. One of them got out of the jeep and started walking towards Sgt and he was as a tall man about 5'10" or taller. I couldn't see the color of his hair, but he had blue eyes. He wore a long Army officers coat that came down to the top of his boots. He was wearing a scarf around his neck and leather gloves. He was well dressed to be a combat officer. The one thing that caught my attention was his boots were shined. That's when my stomach started feeling funny I knew something was wrong. My I help you sir? Yes Sgt. That's 1st Sgt sir. Okay my mistake 1st Sgt. My name is Lt. Calvin Hartman and that's Lt. Kyle McDonald we are looking for the supply depot. Why do you need to go to the supply depot for sir? I have a message from a Col. Welch 1st Sgt he told me to deliver this message in person.

Why didn't just send it over the wire sir? The lines are down in this area. Really? Yes 1st Sgt.

Okay than well let me see your ID card. My ID card? Why would you want to see my ID card?

It's a new rule that just came down all officers have to show their ID cards. I'm surprise you being an Army officer you didn't know that. Now you listen Nigger I don't have to show you shit. Well sir you won't be getting though here unless you show me your ID card. I started to see the other officer start to get nerves I slowly put my hand on the trigger. One move by him and he was a dead motherfucker. I have never here of this rule before. Well sir that's what they told us. Alright 1st Sgt I'll be back and you can rest ashore someone will be getting court- martial. I'll be right here when you get back sir. He jumped back in his jeep and drove off. We watched them as they disappeared into the darkness. I told Sgt those weren't Army officers those were Germans. Yeah I know if they were real Army officers they would have known about the new ID change. They came out here to see how many of us were out here. Popeye go wake up Hicks and the rest of the guys. Hicks came out of the bushes. I heard everything those were Germans. What we going to do Sgt you know they are coming back. Hicks go get the rest of the guys. Ok Sgt. Hicks runs back to the CP and gets the other guys. Hicks I'm going to need you to go over with a couple of guys and form a firing line. Ok Sgt. What's your name Pvt? Pvt. Martin Sgt. Pvt. Martin I need you to get on that radio and try to contact Lt. Jones and tell we are about to come under attack and to send help. You got that Pvt? Yes Sgt. I need you two to form a line along those bushes. Don't fire until I tell you to.

Popeye you ready with that machine gun? Yeah Sgt I'm ready. Sgt ducked down behind the sandbags. Keep your eyes open Popeye. It was quiet to quiet for me. I started looking around to see if I could see anything. I couldn't see shit it was dark as hell. I tried to focus my eyes to the dark when I thought I saw something moving along the trees. Sgt I think there's something moving in those trees. It probably the trees moving Popeye. I looked and seen it again, but this time it stood up. Sgt trees don't stand up and walk those are Germans. Sgt yelled for us to fire, but when I squeezed the trigger nothing happen. I tried to fire again still nothing happen. Popeye fired that damn gun. Sgt it won't fire it's frozen. What! It's frozen.

Sgt came over to help me, but he couldn't get it to fire. We were taking fire from all directions. You need to get this gun working Popeye or we are done. I had to think of something fast I pulled out my lighter and started heating up the trigger. When I seen the ice start to melt so squeezed the trigger but nothing happen. I heated it up again and tried it again this time it fired. I could see the Germans coming up in front of us I pulled the trigger and let lose a hail of bullets that killed at least 6 Germans with the first burst and with the second 5 more. I was like a mad man out of control I was firing all over the place. Popeye cover me. I cover Sgt as he moved to a better position. He moved like a cat looking for it's prey. He killed two Germans in his first attack and shot another in the back as he tried to run away. I started getting fire from my left I swung my gun around and killed several more Germans who were coming up behind me. I could see them start to run away, so I continued to fire at them as they ran away. Two German soldiers started walking towards Sgt with their hands in the air.

Sgt walks towards them and shot one of them in the head. I knew he was a killer, but damn he didn't have to do that. It didn't bother me they would have done the same if it was one of us. I heard they were to shot us if they captured us they had know respect for Negro soldiers.

I yelled to Sgt to get back. I'm fine he said I think they have all retreated. This was a small attack Popeye to soften us up to see how many men would be defending road. Hicks came running over to me. You alright Popeye? Yeah I'm fine. Where are the other guys at? They are over there they're alright. You think they coming back. Yeah they probably will. I think I killed me a couple of those fucking Germans. Hicks was proud he had killed a man, but it turned my stomach to see all that blood the snow was covered in it. I don't like killing but it was my job and I had to do it. It was better them than me. I saw two German soldiers walking towards me with their hands in the air I pointed my machine gun at them I seen that Sgt had captured them. I captured these two trying to play dead. Keep your hands up I told them. I don't know if they understood what I was saying. Sgt started searching their pockets after he finished he told them to sit down. These soldiers look young Sgt. Yeah they are this one is only 15 years old. What! 15 he's just a boy and this one here is only 17 years old. I could tell they were young the 17 year old had baby blue eyes and he was scared. You could tell they didn't want to fight by the looks on their faces. Sgt said something to the 17 year old in German. Popeye I didn't know Sgt could speak German. I didn't neither he never ceases to amaze me. What is he saying Sgt? He said that they were told to attack this road so they could break thought to the supply depot. He also said their whole division is made out of Hitler Youth between the ages 13-18. You mean to tell me we were fighting boys? Yeah that's why it was so easy to beat them. Hicks started to feel bad that he had killed a young boy. I told him don't feel bad he didn't know. Then we can hear the trucks coming up the road. Pvt.

Martin had done his job.

CHAPTER FOURTEEN

DOUGLASS JEEP PULLED UP along side us, but this time he had LTC. Conley fat ass with him. He gets out and walks over to SgT. 1st Sgt. Banks we got word that you boys were under attack by a division of Germans. Yes sir we were, but they were only a small company of Hitler Youth and I captured these two as prisoners. Good job 1st Sgt your country is proud of you.

You'll get medals for this. We just looked at him we all knew he was lying He was only saying that to try and make us feel good. Sir where is Lt. Jones? Oh we send him to another division that needed him. Sgt. Milford. Yes sir. Take these two prisoners back to the depot for interrogation. Yes sir. You boys are doing a good job 1st Sgt keep up the good work. Yes sir.

Sir I have a question sir. What is it 1st Sgt. We need food and weather gear it get real cold out here and we haven't eaten in a couple of days. I can get you the food, but the weather clothing we just don't have you are going to do the best you can to stay warm. The weather clothing is for the troops who are doing all the heavy fighting. Yes sir I understand that, but we have been in some real heavy fighting ourselves look at our uniforms. The LTC looked at all the blood on Sgt's jacket it almost made him sick. I see what I can do 1st Sgt. Thank you sir. Capt. Douglass make sure you get these boys food and water. Yes sir. LTC sir we are going to need more men out here it's only 10 of us out here.

That was a small attack if we are attacked by a bigger division we will be in trouble. Capt. Douglass you take care of that. Yes sir I will sir. You know I have a better idea Capt. Douglass why don't you stay out here and make sure things run smooth. Douglass looked at the LTC stunned he wasn't to happy with the LTC just said. We weren't to happy neither we didn't need his sorry ass out here with us.

We were doing fine without him. LTC got his fat ass back in his jeep and drove off. Douglass pick 20 men to stay behind. 1st Sgt. Banks. Yes sir. I want these men to start digging some foxholes and to set up a defense premier and send out patrols. Yes sir. Did you guys make a CP. Yes sir we did it's though those trees over there. When you finish with all that 1st Sgt I need to talk with you, Hicks and Ross back at the CP. Yes sir. An hour later they finally brought us some food, water, ammunition and some blankets. We needed the ammunition I I had ran out during that last fight if those Germans had attacked us again all I could do was throw snowballs at them. I'm also glad they brought us some blankets I was about to freeze to death out here. I grabbed some ammunition and loaded the machine gun. Sgt sent a couple of guys on patrols. I grabbed a couple of boxes of K-rations and a canteen of water. I sat down to eat my K-rations when I felt this sharp pain in my arm. I dropped my K-rations and grabbed my arm when I did that I felt something warm. When I looked at my arm again I saw it was blood. When I saw it was blood I started to go into shock and I started to get dizzy. I got on my feet and yelled for Sgt. Yeah Popeye. I've been shot. What! I've been shot. He came running over to me. Let me see where you been shot at? It's my shoulder. Move your hand and let me see. He looked at my wound. Damn! Take your jacket off Popeye. When I took my jacket off I could feel the cold wind cut though my body. Sgt had this real look of concern on his face. That looks real bad Popeye. By this time the medic had joined us. Let me take a look it's not that bad it went in and out. The medic was this guy the called Slim, because he was so skinny his real name name was Robert Brooks. He and Doc Phillips was always together. I had seen him with Doc Phillipps before, but we never speak to each other. He took a dressing out of his medical bag. He tore open the package and sprinkled the white substance on my wound. Damn! Slim that shit stings. He just looked at me and shook his head. Now let put this dressing on your wound. We got to get you back to the depot so a doctor can get a good look at that wound. Somebody call for a truck to come pick up a wounded man. Hey Pvt. Martin get on the radio and call the depot for a truck. Tell them we have a wounded man here. Okay Sgt. Tell them to hurry up before he bleeds to death. I got scared when Sgt said I might bleed to death. Sgt don't let me bleed to death. Don't you worry Popeye if I got to carry you to the depot myself that ain't going to happen. Hey Sgt they are on their way. It took the truck minutes to get to us. Sgt picked me up and put my on the truck. Your going to alright Popeye. You ain't going to die. Come on let's go Slim told the driver. He jumped in the back with me and the truck pulled off Sgt was waving at me. I would have waved back, but my shoulder was killing me. I guess from all that excitement I didn't feel the bullet hit my shoulder.

On my way to the depot I couldn't help but think what if that bullet would have killed me. I would never see my wife or baby girl again. It me think about all the other guys who have died and they will never see their families again. My eyes started to water up and tears started running down my face. Slim put his hand on my shoulder and told me everything was going to be fine. I still thought about the other guys and what happen to them. All they were going to get is a letter saying how they died for their country. That's a bunch of bullshit they died over some stupid shit. The truck came to a stop we were back at the supply depot. Slim and the driver helped me out the truck. Come on Popeye let's get you over to the medical tent so the Doc can take a good look at that wound. The medical tent was nothing but a big green tent with tables, chairs, cots and operating tables. There were wounded soldiers lying every where moaning and groaning in pain. The smell from all that blood was making my sick. They had rig lights to light the tent up. Slim took me to a room in the back this room was for all the wounded Negro soldiers. I couldn't believe it. Here we were thousands of miles away from home fighting a war we didn't start and we still get treated differently. I was they only one there, because it only had a couple of cots. At least it was warm in there I needed that after being out there in that cold weather. Come on Popeye sit down on this cot and let's get your shirt off so I can look at that wound again. He helped me take off shirt it was covered in blood.

I could see the hole in my shoulder. How bad is it Slim? It ain't as bad as I thought. It went in and out like I said. Is that good? Yeah if it had stuck in your shoulder I would have to dig it out and that would have hurt real bad. The Doc will be in here to look at it in a few minutes. So just sit there and relax you are going to be fine. Than a short white man walks in the room.

He looked like to be in his late 40's his hair and mustache were gray. Slims stands up to salute him before he can get a word out he asked him. What is wrong with this soldier? He was shot in the shoulder sir. He looks at me Cpl get that light and bring it over here, so I can look at this wound. Slim grabbed the light and it fall apart in his hand. He put it back together and brought it to the Doc. The light looked like it was going to fall on the Doc. Hold the fucking light still Cpl, so I can look at his wound. Yes sir. Slim looked at him like he wanted to bust him in the head with it. He grabbed my arm with no regard to the pain I was in. Oh it's not that bad it's just a puncture wound. He stuck his finger in the hole. I wanted to punch him in his face for doing that. He made it hurt worse and it started to bleed again. Cpl. Yes sir. I want you to clean that wound out bandage it up let him rest for a day and send him back to his company Send him back to his company sir. Sir he's going to need more than a day to heal what if he goes back out there and it gets infected? The Doc looked at me. Okay Cpl give him a couple of days. Thank sir. He seemed mad about it, but I didn't care I was wounded and I needed the rest. Thanks Slim. No problem. You know why I did that? No why? They are always sending us back out there quicker than those white boys. These white boys would be in this medical tent for weeks and half of them ain't nothing wrong with them. There was this one Negro soldier who had a bad cold all they give him were a couple of pills and they sent him back out there. The man could barely walk do

Michael Johnson

you know he died. What! Yeah if they would have treated him right he would be alive today. There you go Popeye you are good as new. He left the room and came back with a new T-shirt. Put this on to keep yourself warm lay down on this cot and rest up. I took off my boots and layed down on the cot. He got a blanket and layed it over me. I'll be back to check on you later. Okay Slim. He left to go back to the division. It felt good to take those boots off and to lay down on something besides the cold ground. Now I know why those white boys don't want to leave. It feels got to lay down. I don't blame them for not wanting to leave. Shit I might not want to leave myself. This wasn't a bed, but it will do. When I put my head on that pillow I was out.

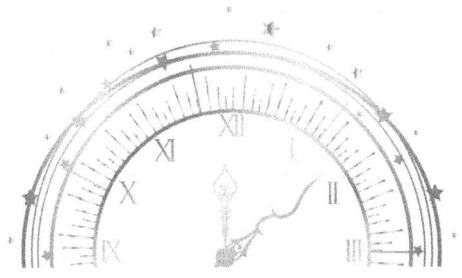

CHAPTER FIFTEEN

I STARTED DREAMING ABOUT THE day I had to go ask Lillian's daddy could I take her out. I decided to go over there when I got of work, but before I went over there I cleaned myself up first I didn't want to go over there in my dirty work clothes. Lillian live in a two story brick home her daddy Roscoe built by himself. It took him over 3 years to complete it. The closer I got to her house my stomach started acting funny. It always gets that way when I get nervous. I heard he ran some boy away with a shot gun, because he wanted to take one of his daughters out.

I walked up slowly to the door. My hand was shaking so bad I couldn't knock on the door. I stopped for a minute gained my composer and than I knocked on the door. It was so light I don't know if anyone heard it. I knocked again this time I knocked a little harder. A loud voice said who is it. It scared the hell out of me. It's Jeffery Ross. I said it so low he didn't hear me.

Who is it? It's Jeffery Ross sir. Than the door swung open a giant man stood in front of me.

My eyes almost popped out my head when I saw him. He looked own on me. What do you want boy? How you doing sir my name is Jeffery Ross. I stuck my hand out to shake his hand he just looked at me. So what do you want boy? Well sir I met your daughter Lillian at the church dance last night and I was wondering would it by possible for me to take her out on a date with your permission sir? He looked at me and stepped down off the pouch in my face. How old are you boy? I'm 19 years old sir. You know Lillian's only 17 years old. What do you want with her? She is younger than you. She a nice girl and I want to get to know her sir.

Oh really you want to get to know her in what way? What do you mean sir? You said you wanted to get to know her right? Yes sir I do, but not the way you are thinking. He gets real close to my face. What way am I thinking son? Now I was sacred. I want to know what she likes to do and what are her hopes and dreams. I was saying anything to get him out of my face. He looked my up and down than he started to laugh. Come on in here boy Lillian told me you were coming. She did? Yeah I'm just messing with you. Oh alright. We walked in the house and Lillian was standing there looking beautiful with a smile on her face. Hey I said.

Hey Jeffery. She was wearing a red and white dress with flowers on it. Her hair was down on her shoulders and she was wearing white socks with black shoes. Her daddy give me this mean look. You can come in here boy and sit with me. I smiled at Lillian as I walked into the living room. The living room was painted all white with pictures hanging on the walls. There was a long brown sofa against the wall under the small window. A small wooden coffee table sat in front of it. There was a small glass color swan sitting on top of it. There were two small chairs sitting next to the fireplace. A radio sat on a table in the corner. Mr. Crawford told me to sit down in one of the chairs. So Jeffery who are your people? Do I know any of them? I don't know sir. My mama name was Hattie Mae and my daddy name was James Ross. Oh yeah I know him ain't he the one who died in some accident at his job. Yes sir that was him. I got a little lump in my throat I miss my daddy we were really close. They never told me what happen to him. Where do you live at Jeffery? I live outside the 5th ward on Collins St sir. You taking about that boarding house Mrs. Hutchinson runs? Yes sir that's the one. He looked at me funny. You know Jeffery Lillian is my second oldest. No sir I didn't know that. So you have others daughters? Yeah

I have two more daughters and a son. So Jeffery you came over here to ask me can you take Lillian out on a date? Yes sir I did. Why you want to take Lillian out? I like her sir. Oh you do. Yes sir I do. So where are you going to take her? I want to take out to a movie. To a movie? Yes sir. Which movie house you are going to take her to? The one over on 9th street. The on 9th street you ain't taking my daughter over there a lot of bad things happen at that place. I can promise you sir ain't nothing going to happen to her. He gave this hard look. Alright than Jeffery you seem like a nice boy and you got a lot of guts to come over here and ask me can you take Lillian out. A lot of boys wouldn't dare do what you just done. You know I ain't going to let you take her out on this date by herself. She can't? No she can't her older sister Pam will be coming with y'all. I didn't like the idea of her sister coming with us, but what can I do. You can come back around 7:00pm and pick Lillian up she will be ready. Alright sir I'll be back than. We shake hands when I got up to leave, but when I went to let his hand go he gripped my hand hard. Let me tell you something Jeffery if anything happens to my daughter Nigga I'm going to kill you. The look in his eyes I know he meant it.

Than he let my hand go and he smiled at me. You better not be late boy you understand me.

Yes sir I understand. I left the living room and Lillian was peeping around the corner. I smiled at her and got the out of there. I was scared to death, but I was glad it was over. I was so happy I ran all the way home. When I was running home I thought about I better not be late. I knew he was testing me to see if I would show up on time. If I didn't he wouldn't let me take Lillian out. I got to the boarding house where I lived. When I got there Mrs. Hutchinson was sitting out on the porch How you doing Jeffery? I'm doing fine how you doing? I kissed her on her cheek. I'm making it. Hey Jeffery there is some food on the stove if you are hungry.

Thank you I'll eat later I want upstairs to my room.

Mrs. Arlene Marie Hutchinson was a short (5'2") light brown skin woman with long silver gray hair that came down to the middle of her back. She had the most beautiful hazel eyes I have ever seen. Her skin was smooth like butter she didn't have a mark on her face. My momma told me that she thinks Mrs.

Hutchinson is half Indian. She had a very nice shape for a woman her age. You can tell she was a very good looking when she was younger. I don't even know how old she is, but she looks good. Mrs. Hutchinson took me in when my momma died. They had been friends since they were little girls. When my momma got sick it was Mrs. Hutchinson who take care of her. My momma got sick right after my daddy died. She died a year later I was 10 years old. Some people say she died of a broken heart. I didn't know what that meant, but I was mad at everybody. If it wasn't for Mrs. Hutchinson I don't know where I would be. I thank God for her everyday. I wanted to get something to eat, but I was to excited to eat even though I was starving. I didn't want to blow this date with Lillian. I know if I did I would never get another chance. I needed to find something nice to wear. I didn't have a lot of clothes. I looked in my closet most of the clothes I have were my daddy's and they were old. I knew I had to put something together to wear. I looked in this old chest that belonged to my daddy I seen a pair of brown pants and a brown shirt they were old but they would have to do. I looked at my shoes and realized that they needed to be shined. They were old and this was the only pair I had. It was 5:00pm and I had two hours before I went to pick up Lillian. I needed to iron my clothes to. I went downstairs to get the iron from the kitchen. The food Mrs. Hutchinson cooked started to make me hungry. I put my clothes down grabbed me a plate off the shelf and a spoon. She had cooked lima beans, rice, cornbread and my favorite pig feet. I fixed a plate fit for a king. I got me some ice tea out of the icebox sat down and started stuffing my face. When I was eating I thought about how Mrs. Hutchinson cooking reminded me of how my momma would cook meals like this for my daddy. I miss her so much. When I was daydreaming about my momma's cooking I heard a voice that I didn't want to hear. How you doing Mrs. H? I'm doing fine how you doing baby? I'm doing good my momma told me to tell you hello. Well you tell her I said hello. I will. Is Jeffery home? Yeah he's upstairs in his room. Damn! it was Brenda now what the hell she want?

CHAPTER SIXTEEN

I WAS TRYING TO EAT my food fast when I heard her coming down the hallway. It was to much to eat that fast. She passed the kitchen and didn't see me sitting at the table. Than Mr. Sutton came into the kitchen. Hey boy how you doing? I'm doing good. I see your girlfriend went upstairs looking for you. She ain't my girlfriend. That ain't what I heard coming form your room two weeks ago. I looked at him.

Mr. Sunny (Samuel) Timothy Sutton was an old man (I think he was over 50) who had been living in Mrs. Hutchinson boarding house for years. I remember seeing him when I was a little boy when my momma would come over to see Mrs. Hutchinson. He was a tall skinny (6'2") man with black hair and a gray beard. He had these blood shot eyes from all the moonshine he drink. I over heard my daddy telling his friends how him and Mr. Sutton ran moonshine back during the depression when they were young. It look like Mr. Sutton drank more than he ran. So what do you mean she's not your woman? Like I said she ain't my girlfriend. Oh Nigga you lying the way you was laying that dick on her a couple of weeks ago she back for some more. He was taking about when Brenda and I had got together one night when we were drinking some moonshine we stole from Mr. Sutton. I was never attracted to Brenda like that. It was a big mistake that we got togethernow I can't get rid of her. This ain't the time to be coming over for seconds. Let me tell you something boy whenthat loving is good to a woman she will always going to come back for some more trust me I know. Mr. Sutton with his big mouth told her where I was at. Hey Brenda he's down here in the kitchen. He smiled at me and left. I could hear her coming down the stairs. Oh there you are. What you doing trying to hide from me? I ain't trying to hide from you Brenda I was down here eating. I went to your room are those your clothes on the chair? Yeah. So where are you going? Why? I just want to know. I going on a date. You going on a date with who? I'm going on a date with Lillian Crawford. Lillian Crawford! Her daddy going to let you take her out? Yes he is I went over there today and asked him. Really and he didn't chase you away? No. So what we did two weeks ago didn't mean anything to you? Look Brenda that was a mistake we were both drunk and we did something that we shouldn't have done. Now I like you, but not like that. I could see the hurt in her face. So that's how you feel? Yeah and I'm sorry. Well I guess I came over at the wrong time I thought we could spend a little time together, but I see I was wrong. So what time are you coming back. I don't know. Well I'll just get out of your way. You have fun with Ms. Lillian. You know if it wasn't for me you wouldn't be going out with her. She got up slammed the chair against the table and stormed out. I could hear her tell Mrs. Hutchinson bye. I felt a little bad, but just because we spent one night together doesn't make us a couple.

 I don't care if she is mad all I'm thinking about is getting over there on time to pick up Lillian. I didn't tell her what time I was going to pick up Lillian, because I didn't want her to ruin my date I finished my food grabbed the iron went upstairs to iron my clothes. I ironed my clothes, shined my shoes. When I had finished it was 6:30pm. When I went downstairs Mrs. Hutchinson was still sitting on the porch. Where you going looking so nice? I got a date. You got a date with who? With Lillian Crawford. Lillian Crawford! Ain't that Russell Crawford's daughter? Yes ma'am. He going to let you take her out? Yeah I went over there today and asked him. What! He didn't chase you away? No. Boy you are crazy. You must really like this girl to go over there and

The Men that Time has Forgotten

ask him. You got more heart than must of these boys out around here. They wouldn't dare go over there and ask him something like that. You better watch yourself Jeffery that Nigga is crazy about his girls. I know one thing she's better than that damn Brenda. She's a pain in the ass. You ain't the only one fucking her. What! Yeah you didn't know she damn near fucking everybody in the 5th ward. She been fucking since she was fourteen. I heard she was messing around with a lot of men. You heard right, because she is. I don't blame you for not wanting her. So where y'all going? I'm going to take her to a movie. Alright you got any money? I got a few dollars. She reached in her bra and pulled out a big roll of money. Damn I didn't know Mrs. Hutchinson had money like that. She peeled me off five dollar bill. Here you go Jeffery. Thank you. Now you go have you some fun and don't worry about Brenda. I kissed her on her cheek and left. You be careful Jeffery. I will. I felt like a millionaire. I had nine dollars that's including the four dollars I already had. Now I can buy her some popcorn, candy and maybe I can take her out for a milkshake after the movie.

    I looked at my watch it was 6:45pm. It was an old watch it belong to my daddy my momma gave it to me when he died. I had a little time. I wanted to get her some flowers, but there ain't no flower shops where I live. I walked to 7th street and crossed over to 9th street where the movie theater was. I got to the railroad tracks which spit the upper 5th ward from the lower 5th ward. There really any difference between the two. The upper 5th ward had better homes at was it. I walked pass this one house that had some nice looking flowers in their front yard.

    I stopped and looked around to see if anyone was looking. Than I grabbed a hand full of those flowers and walked away. I got to Lillian's house at 7:00pm I knocked on the door. Who is it a woman's voice said. It's Jeffery Ross ma'am. The door opened a medium tall (5'7") woman light skin woman stood in the doorway. This must be Lillian's momma. How you doing ma'am? I'm doing fine. I here for Lillian. She stood there and looked at me for a second. Yes I know my husband told me you were coming. Come in and have a seat in the living room Lillian will be down in a few minutes. I sat down in one of the chairs. How you doing Jeffery a deep voice said. I looked up it was Roscoe. I'm doing fine sir. He came in and sat down. Now where did you stay you were taking my daughter? To the movie theater on 9th street. I don't want you to take my daughter there we have one up here y'all are going to. Aright sir. Pam Lillian's older sister will be going with y'all. Ok. Y'all going out for milkshakes after the movie?

Yes sir. You know you are going to have to buy Pam one to. Yes sir I will. He yelled for Pam come into the living room. Yes daddy. Pam was a very good looking girl. She was tall (5'10") with light brown skin, black hair, brown eyes with long beautiful legs. She had this soft voice that would make any man melt when she spoke. I see why Roscoe is so protective of them.

This here is Jeffery. Hi Jeffery. How you doing? You will be going with him and Lillian to the movies tonight. After the movie y'all can go out for a milkshakes and y'all bring y'all ass back here. You understand me. Yes daddy. Now go get Lillian and tell her to bring her butt on. Now Mr. Ross if you try anything with any on my daughters I'm going to kill you. You got that? Yes sir I got it. Good. He said that with a smile. I was so focus on what he was saying I didn't notice Lillian standing there. Hello Jeffery. Hello Lillian. I looked at her and my eyes almost popped out of my head. You look beautiful. Thank you. Are those flowers for me? Yes they are. Where did you get those flowers from boy? I got them out of Mrs. Hutchinson garden. He didn't say anything he just looked at me. You ready to go Lillian? Yes I am. Ya'll have a nice time and be careful out there. We will daddy don't worry. You remember what I told you Jeffery. Yes sir I remember. We walked out the door headed to the movies. Roscoe watched is as we walked up the road and out of sight. When got up the road a little Pam asked us. Hey y'all let's go to Little Joe's. What! Pam you know we can't go to Little Joe's daddy will kill us.

What do you know about Little Joe's Pam? I know more about that place than you think. I was shocked Pam knew about Little Joe's. I have never been in there, but I know what goes on in there. My momma told me never to go in there that was a place for grown folks. Does Little Joe's have food in there Pam? Yeah they have everything over there.

Let's go get something to eat first and than go to the movies. What you say Jeffery? I don't know Pam. Come on y'all stop being so scared all we going to do is eat and leave. Where is this Little Joe's at? It's in the lower 5th ward. I don't know Pam I heard that was a bad part of town. It ain't that bad I live over there. You do? Yeah I do. She smiled at me. Come on Lillian stop being so scared daddy ain't never going to find out. Okay let's go get something to eat. I don't want to stay to long I want to still go to the movies. Okay we won't come on let's go. Pam wanted to go to Little Joe's for a reason, but I had a feeling the reason she wanted to go she wanted to go see someone there.

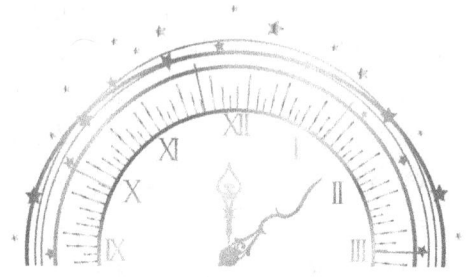

CHAPTER SEVENTEEN

LITTLE JOE'S WAS THIS shack that was turned into a juke joint. It sat on the corner of 8th Ave. It had only one street light that lit the way to the front door. Who ever built it was in a rush with all the different types of wood that held it together. This was the first time I ever seen it up close and I wasn't impressed by it. I'm glad my momma told me to stay out of here. Is this it Pam? Yeah this is it. Pam this look like a shack I don't want to go in there. I know it looks like a shack, but folks be having fun in there right Jeffery. I guess I don't know. What do you mean you don't know? I ain't never been in there Pam. So you telling me you don't knows what goes on in there. Yeah that's what I'm telling you. I had lied to Pam I know what goes on in there. I just didn't want Lillian to do that. My momma were go in there and pull my daddy out of there. He would go in there and get drunk after running moonshine. So what are we going to do. Well let"s go in since we are here. I'll go first Pam. I knocked on the door a slot in the door slide back. What you want boy? I came to get some moonshine and get something to eat. He looked at me close the slot and opened the door. The door looked like it about to fall off he had to hold it up. Y'all come on in you ain't got to be scared. Hey Pam how you doing?

Lillian and I looked at each other in shock. Pam you know him? Yeah this is Tiny how you doing Tiny? I'm doing fine. Who is this beautiful lady? This here is my little sister Lillian.

Damn! She your little sister? Yeah. Well how you doing Ms. Lillian? I'm doing fine. This here is her date Jeffery. Who cares I'm surprised you with a woman like that. Why you say that Tiny? You don't think I can get a date like her? When the last time you had a woman Tiny?

He didn't say anything he just looked at me.

Tiny (his real name is Larry Pepper) was this fat slob who lived behind Little Joe's. He weighted about 300 pounds. He was short and stocky (5'7). His stomach was so big he couldn't even bend over. His hair was nappy like he hadn't combed it in days. He had worked for Mrs. Hutchinson running moonshine at one time. She got rid of his fat ass when she found out he had been stealing bottles of moonshine from her. Mrs. Hutchinson said he ain't never had a woman, because nobody wanted his lying fat ass. The only job he could get was this doorman for Little Joe's. I grabbed Lillian's hand her hand was soft like cotton. We walked across the small dance floor to a table in the corner. Let's sit here y'all. When we sat down a short dark skin woman wearing an apron came over to our table. What y'all having?

Pam told the woman she would like some ribs, collard greens, cornbread and some tea. Ok what y'all two having? Let me get some pig feet, collard greens, cornbread and some lemonade. I'll have what he is having. I looked at her and smiled. You know what instead of bringing me some tea bring me some of that moonshine y'all got. Okay y'all want some moonshine to? No we're good. Okay I'll be right back with y'all food. Pam you know you can't be drinking that moonshine. Stop worrying some much Lillian I'm just going to have a little taste that's all. Alright daddy's going to kill you if he smells that moonshine on your breath.

Jeffery I thought you were going to have some moonshine with me. Naw I don't want any. I know you then had you a taste living over there with Mrs. Hutchinson. I have tasted it a couple of times. Oh by the way call me Popeye. Popeye why they call you that? Well when I was young I had big eyes that look like they were going to pop out of my head. Really I think you have beautiful eyes Jeffery. My heart melted when Lillian said that to me. Thank you no one has ever told me that before.

She smiled at me and grabbed my hand under the table. I thought to myself I can't believe I'm with a woman like this. The woman brought our drinks and than our food. We sat there and talked for a while when this tall dark skin man came over to our table. He had some flowers in his hand. When Pam saw him she got this big smile on her face. Hey Pam he said. How you doing Benny? Everybody this here is my friend

Benny Rice. Hey how y'all doing. We doing good. How you doing? I'm doing good. Benny Rice was a real lady's man. He was 5'11" dark skin, 175lbs, black hair that was wavy.

He had these gray color eyes that all the women loved and a very sharp dresser. He was a real smooth talker. Mrs. Hutchinson use to talk about him all the time. She said he was the sorriest motherfucking man she has ever seen. I think the reason she talked about him like that, because he had dogged her niece out real bad. Benny this is my younger sister Lillain.

Glad to meet you Lillian. This here is her date Jeffery, but they call him Popeye. Your name sounds familiar. Don't live over there in Mrs. Hutchinson boarding house? Yeah I do. Yeah I use to live there a few years back. Yeah I remember you. Mrs. Hutchinson had throw him out because he was always late with his rent. How Mrs. Hutchinson doing? She's doing good.

Tell her Benny said hello. I will. The band started playing some music. Come on Pam let's dance. Benny grabbed Pam by her hand and they go out to the dance floor. Would you like to dance Lillian? No. Oh okay I was shocked she said that. I'm not saying no, because I don't want to dance with you. I'm saying no, because I don't know how to dance. Now that was shocking to me by looking at her you wouldn't think she didn't know how to dance. I loved to dance I might not be the best looking man in Houston, but I can cut the rug. We sat there and looked at Benny and Pam dance. Pam was really enjoying herself What time is it Jeffery? I looked at my watch. It's 8:45pm. Lillian don't have to call me Jeffery you can call me Popeye.

No I'm not going to call you that. I'm going to call you Jeffery I don't like Popeye. I didn't say anything. Let me go get Pam, so we can go catch the last movie. She got up and walked to the dance floor. Man she she beautiful and she got a nice fat ass just the way I like them. I can't she she was saying something to Pam and she was shaking her head no. They got into a little argument. Then I could see Lillian was mad when she came back to the table. Hey what happen Lillian? She said to go ahead when the movie finishes come back and get her.

You sure you want to leave her by herself? Your daddy might come up here and catch her.

My daddy Jeffery would never come in a place like this. Lillian must don't know her daddy.

He's a regular in this place on Friday nights. Alright let's go. We were about to leave when Pam came running over to us. Hey y'all don't forget to come back and get me. We won't Pam. Alright I'll see y'all later. We left. It had gotten a little chilly outside I help Lillian put on her coat. So Jeffery what are we going to see? I don't know. She looked at me you don't know. I don't know what's playing I figured once we got there we can pick out a movie we both like. I got and better idea. What's that? Let's go over to your place. What! My place? Yes your place is there something wrong with that? Oh no are you sure? Yes I'm sure come on let's go.

Okay let's go. We started walking to my place. So you live with Mrs. Hutchinson in her boarding house? Yeah I do. I've heard a lot about that place. You have like what? My momma and daddy talked about that place all the time. They did? I had an uncle who lived over there a while back. Oh yeah what was his name? His name was Teddy Payne. Oh yeah ain't he the one who got chased out of town for messing around with some white woman? Yep that was him. What ever happen to him? He lives in Kansas City now. We talked all the way to the boarding house. She asked me about my family and what happen to them. All I could think about how nice this was being with this beautiful woman. It made me feel good about myself for once. When we got close to the house I could hear Mr. Sutton big ass mouth on the porch talking to one of his friends. He seen us coming up the street. Hey boy where are you coming from? Who is this pretty girl you got with you. This here is

Ms. Lillian Crawford. Lillian this is Mr. Sutton. How you doing pretty lady? I'm doing fine. Ain't you Roscoe Crawford's daughter?

Yes I am. How is he doing? He's fine. That's one crazy Nigga. I seen him one night beat the shit out of three Niggas at one time. Roscoe and I use to run moonshine back in the day.

Lillian looked at Mr. Sutton funny. My daddy use to run moonshine? Hell yeah that's how we made our living running moonshine. Lillian looked at me in shock. I knew he ran moonshine Mr. Sutton would talk about how they would chase women together. I didn't think it was my place to tell her. Well Mr. Sutton we are going to go in the house talk with you later. Alright now. Nice meeting pretty lady. Nice meeting you to sir. We went into the house.

CHAPTER EIGHTEEN

WE WALKED INTO THE living room and I turned on the light. The living room was the best room in the house and also the cleanest. It was the smallest room in the house. It had a long couch with flower designs on it that sat up against the wall. A small hand made table sat in front of it. There was a table with two chairs around it. The fireplace had several pics of Mrs.

Hutchinson when she was young and picture of a little baby. Mrs. Hutchinson didn't allow anyone to sit in the living room. I'm not suppose to be in there, but Lillian was my guest and I didn't want to take her to my room. Come on in Lillian and have a seat. She sat on the couch I sat in one of the chairs. This is nice Jeffery. Yeah it is nice nobody ever sits in here. So Jeffery how long you been living here? Since I've been 10 years old. You like it here? Yeah it's ok. Why you sitting way over there? I don't know. Come over here and sit next to me I promise I won't bite you. I was scared at first, but what the hell. I sat at the end of the couch.

Lillian looked at me funny. Jeffery come sit next to me. I got up and sat down next to her. You ain't scared of me are you? No I ain't scared Lillian. I was laying I was scared to death. She grabbed my hand. You have some very rough hands. I know it come from working in those fields all day makes your hands rough. My daddy won't let us work in the fields. Why not? He said he didn't want those fields to mess up his girls. I grabbed her hand. You know Lillian I really like from the first time I saw you. I like you to Jeffery I think you are a very nice man and a brave one to. What do you mean by that? No boy and I mean no boy has ever come to my house and asked my daddy could he take any of his girls out on a date. Really? Yeah that's why he let me go, because he knew you were a good boy. Then I heard a voice I didn't want to here. What y'all talking about Popeye? I turned around and it was big ass Brenda.

How y'all doing? We are doing fine Brenda what the hell do you want? I came by to see Mrs. Hutchinson.

Well she ain't down here. Now you know Mrs. Hutchinson don't allow any one to sit in the living room. What you doing in here? Hi Lillian? Hey Brenda. I seen Pam down at Little Joe's your daddy allow y'all to go into places like that? I thought y'all were to good for places like that. Brenda was pissing me off she came in here to be nosey. Well I'm going to leave you two love birds alone I'll see y'all later. Where you know her from Jeffery? We went to school together. She lives here? No she lives up the street thank God. Yeah was boyfriend and girlfriend at one time right? No we were never boyfriend and girlfriend we are just friends.

The way she was talking and looking at you funny gave me that impression y'all were. I wouldn't dare tell her what happen between Brenda and I two weeks ago. She grabbed my hands. This is nice. Yes it is. We looked at each other and gave her peck on the lips. She looked at me funny. Is that how you kiss someone? She grabbed my face and gave me a kissed that almost took my breath away. Now that's how you suppose to kiss me. I was heaven until I heard Mrs. Hutchinson scream from upstairs. What the hell. We ran upstairs to see what was going on. What's wrong Mrs. Hutchinson? I was listening to the radio and I heard the Japanese just bombed Pearl Harbor. What! We stood there in shock. It was December 7, 1941. My evening was ruined by some fucking bombing. I could have killed me a Jap right about now. You better be getting home Lillian before your daddy comes looking for us. We walked back downstairs back out onto the porch. Mr. Sutton was

The Men that Time has Forgotten

still sitting out there. Did you here what those fucking Japs did to Pearl Harbor? Yeah we heard. You know we are going to war now. I didn't say a word I just walked passed him. Jeffery we have got to go back to Little Joe's and get Pam. Yeah I know let's hurry up. You alright Jeffery? You seem a little upset. No I'm fine, but I wasn't it always seems like things happen at the wrong time for me. When we got to Little Joe's Pam was already standing outside talking to Benny. Did y'all here what happen? Yeah we heard. What's wrong with Benny? He's upset, because his uncle is a cook on one of the ships in Pearl Harbor. I'm sorry to hear that Benny. Thank you he joined a couple of years ago. We don't know if he is dead or alive. Pam we need to get home before daddy comes looking for us. Yeah we better get going. I'll see you later Benny.

Alright. Jeffery you going to walk us home. Yeah I'm going to walk y'all home. When we were walking to Lillian's house everybody was outside talking about the bombing. When we got to their house their momma was standing outside waiting on them. Where the hell y'all been it's 10pm? We went to get something to first than we went to the show momma. She looked at us like she knew Pam was lying. So y'all must have the news? Yes ma'am we did. I hear talk going around that a lot of men are going to join. Jeffery are you going to join up? I don't know ma'am. I don't think they are taking boys my age. How old are you? I'm 19 years old ma'am.

She just looked at me. You two get inside. Bye Jeffery. Bye I guess I can come over tomorrow

Yes Jeffery you can come see Lillian tomorrow. Thank you ma'am. I'll see you tomorrow than.

Yes you will. I watched Lillian as she went into the house thinking to myself what might have happen if the Japanese wouldn't have bombed Pearl Harbor. I was so happy I ran all the way home. When I got home Mrs. Hutchinson was sitting in the kitchen. Hey Jeffery. Hey Mrs. Hutchinson. So that's one of those Crawford girls? Yes ma'am it is. She's a pretty girl. Yes she is with a big smile on my face.

I'm going to tell you something Jeffery. What? You better watch yourself with a pretty girl like that. Why you say that? Those type of girls will brake your heart fast, so don't get to wrapped up in her. A pretty girl like that always get men chasing them. I didn't want to hear what she had to say. She was making me real mad, but she had a point Lillian is a beautiful girl guys are always trying to talk to her. If I don't watch myself I could be out standing in the cold. Well Mrs. Hutchinson I'm going to go to bed. Ok Jeffery. I kissed her on her head and headed to my room. Oh Jeffery before I forget I need you to help Sunny with moving some boxes tomorrow. Yeah I'll give him a hand. I got to my room and closed the door. I took my coat off and throw it on the chair. I took my clothes off and got into bed. I thought about the date with Lillian and the bombing of Pearl Harbor. I just fell asleep thinking about Lillian.

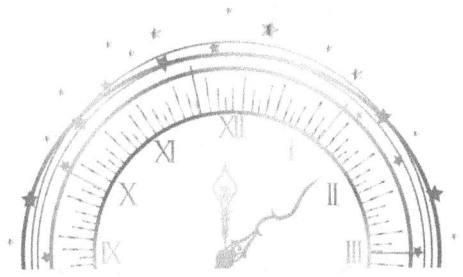

CHAPTER NINETEEN

THE NEXT MORNING I was waken up by the sound of Mr. Sutton's big mouth. I could hear him coming down the hallway. He banged on my door. You up in there boy? We got a lot of work to do today. Yeah I'm up give me a few minutes. Alright than hurry up. I really didn't want to get up it was cold and I was tired form the night before. I got up and sat on the edge of the bed. Damn! I don't feel like doing this bullshit today. The sun was shining bright in my face. I got dressed and went downstairs. Mrs. Hutchinson was in the kitchen drinking a cup of coffee.

Morning Mrs. Hutchinson. She didn't say anything. I said morning to her again. I heard you the first time. Is there something wrong Mrs. Hutchinson? We at war with the Japanese. The President declared war on them this yesterday. I sat down at the table. She looked at me with tears in her eyes. You know those fucking Japs killed over 2,000 men and sunk 20 ships.

What! Yeah and over 35,000 men joined up today. Oh yeah. Are you going to join? Who me?

No I ain't going to join for what? Why not Jeffery? I'm to young and I don't like guns. I never told you about my husband did I? No you didn't. He was killed in World War 1. Your husband fought in World War 1? Yes he did and he was a good man to. He did what he had to do to take care of his family. The white man didn't want them fighting along side them. They prove themselves and still they were treated like dogs when they came home. They give me this medal for him. She handed it to me. I looked at it I didn't know what kind of medal it was, but I would find out later myself it was the Purple Heart. You know Jeffery if you were to join that pretty girl would look at you differently. Women love men in uniform especially young girls. I looked at like she was crazy. I'm not joining no damn Army just to impress some girl, but than again I really liked Lillian. I'm going to have to think about that one Mrs. Hutchinson. Alright I'm going to tell you what's going to happen between you and that pretty girl of yours. One of these young men is going to come home in his uniform looking good and with lots of money in his pocket. She going to see him and starts liking him. What do you think is going to happen? What going to happen? He's going to take her away from you and you are going to be left out in the cold. I just listened to her I don't care what she thinks I'm not joining the Army. Mr. Sutton came in the kitchen and interrupted our conversion. Are you ready to go boy? Yeah I'm ready. I'm glad he came in I was tired of hearing Mrs. Hutchinson mouth.

Come boy we got a lot of work to do. I grabbed me a couple of biscuits and left. Mrs. Hutchinson was standing at the door when we left. You think about what I said Jeffery. I will. I got into Mr. Sutton old beat up truck and we drove off.

What she talking about? She wants me to join the Army. What! Yeah she wants me to join.

Hey don't let talk you into something you might regard later. She tell you the story about her first husband? Yeah she did. She he was killed in World War1. She's always telling that story.

Did you know her husband? Yeah we served together in the same company. Really? Yeah I was there when he was killed. I didn't know him that well, but we had talked from time to time. So how do you know Mrs. Hutchinson? When he died I was the one who came and told her. I was on my way home to Dallas and I stop to tell her what happen to him. Well I'm not joining know Army. I don't want to get killed. You worried about that pretty little girl of yours? I just looked at him. Yeah you are I could see it in your eyes. All I'm going to tell you this real soon it's going to be a lot of young boys walking around in uniforms with lots of money in their pockets. Women love a man in a uniform especially young girls. I know trust me. Now he had me thinking. We turned down the dirt road where Mrs. Hutchinson hid her stash of moonshine. So we got to deliver moonshine today? Yeah just a couple of boxes. We pulled up in front of the barn got out Mr. Sutton unlocked the barn door and we started loading the boxes on the back of his truck. Where we taking these boxes to? We got several stops to make our first will be Little Joe. Little Joe? I thought he stopped buying moonshine from Mrs. Hutchinson? He did, but he changed his mind when his supplier left town. Why did he leave town? The cops found out that he was selling and he didn't want to go to jail, so he left town.

Come lets finish loading these boxes we got a lot of stops to made. We loaded all the boxes on the truck. Hey do you want to drive? Yeah I'll drive. He throw me his keys I got in cranked it up and we drove off. I started to think about what he said about those guys in uniform. That made me think about Lillian. I started to wonder would she leave me for a guy in a uniform.

This was a question I had to ask her. When I pulled up in front of Little Joe's Pam was standing out in front. Pam what are you doing out here? Hey Jeffery I came to see Benny.

Benny? Yeah didn't you here? Here what? His uncle was killed in the Pearl Harbor bombing. Really I'm sorry to hear that. How did you find this out? His sister came by the house early this morning told me what happen to meet him in front of Little Joe's. Where is Lillian? She's at home waiting for you to come over. Oh here comes Benny now. Hey Pam tell Lillian I'll be when I finish here. Ok I will. Come boy lets get these boxes inside. So what is that y'all got in those boxes? Moonshine. Moonshine! Jeffery you run moonshine? No I'm just helping him out. Well let me go. Hey don't forget to tell Lillian. I won't Jeffery. We took three boxes of moonshine into Little Joe's. Tiny fat ass was sitting at the door when we went in. Hey Sunny how you doing? I'm doing good Joe how you doing? I'm making it, so what you got for me today? Joe looked at the boxes reached in his pocket and gave Mr. Sutton $150.00 for the delivery. Thank you Joe. No problem Sunny. Come on Popeye lets deliver the rest of these boxes. We got back in the truck and left. We delivered the rest of the moonshine to Mrs.

Hutchinson clients and we went home. It was about 10:30am when we got back to the house.

Mr. Sutton gave me $20.00 dollars for helping him out. I still had a little time before I want over to Lillian house, so I decided to cook me something to eat. All I had for breakfast were those biscuits. After I finished eating I went upstairs to take a bath. While I was there soaking in the tube I thought about Benny's uncle. I wonder how his family is feeling that he died for nothing. I don't want that to happen to me they can have that war. Besides that a white man's war and he don't any Negro's in it. A knock on the door broke my out of my thoughts. Jeffery?

Who's that? It's me Lillian. Lillian! What you doing over here so early? Hold on I'll be out in a few. I was shocked she came over so early. I want to grab my towel and realized I didn't bring one in with me. Damn! I can't go out there without no towel. I cracked the door open. She was standing there with this big smile on her face. Hey Lillian. Hey. What you doing. I'm taking a bath. I need you to do me a favor. Ok what's that? Could you go to my room and grab me a towel and bring me my clothes I set out please. Which one is your room? The one on the right. She went in my room and grabbed those things for me. Thank you. Give me a few minutes to dry off get dressed and I'll be out soon. That's the fastest I have ever dried off and got dressed. When I came out she was sitting in my bed in my room. What you doing over here so early? Didn't Pam tell you that I would be over to see you later? Yeah she did, but I wanted to come over to see you. That brought a smile to my face when she said that.

Well don't you have chores to do? Yeah I finished them all early this morning, so I could come over here to see you. Does your daddy know you are over here? No I told my momma I was going over to my auntie house. I didn't like that I was afraid he might come over here looking for her. Don't worry Jeffery my auntie will cover for me. She's not like my momma always checking up on us. Well let finish getting myself together and I'll walk you home. Ok I'll be downstairs. Alright. I hurried up and finished getting myself together I didn't want her daddy to come looking for her. I knew if he caught her over here he would kill me. When I went downstairs I could hear Lillian talking to Mrs. Hutchinson I don't know if that was good or bad. When I came downstairs Mrs. Hutchinson was asking her what brought her over here so early? Morning Mrs. Hutchinson. Morning Jeffery. You are right Jeffery she is a pretty girl.

Yes she I said that with a smile on my face. So where y'all going so early in the morning? We are going for a walk. You going for a walk this early in the morning? No he's going to walk me back home. Ok than Jeffery hurry up back I want you to do something for me. Ok I will. Come on Lillian lets go. Damn! I wasn't planning on coming back. I wonder what the hell she want me to do now. I hope it ain't moving that moon shine I'm tried of that shit. Bye Mrs. Hutchinson. Bye baby. We Left. Lillian didn't seem to me to be like those girls Mrs. Hutchinson was talking about earlier. I still couldn't believe I was with her.

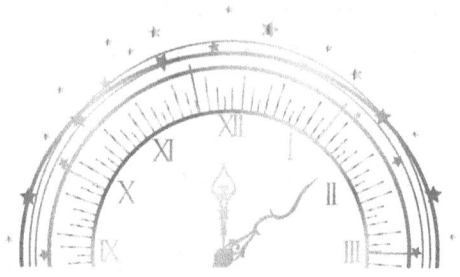

CHAPTER TWENTY

WE TOOK A SHORT cut to her house behind the old Benson Sawmill. The Benson Sawmill use to be a very profitable business for the people who lived in the 5th ward. It went out of business during the depression and never opened back up. All that is left of it is and abandon building, rusted out equipment and rotted wood. The wood that didn't rot away the people used it to build their homes. My daddy worked at that mill. This is where he died or killed from what some people say. We were holding as we walked. Mrs. Hutchinson seems like a real nice lady. Yeah she's alright, but she gets on my nerves sometimes. She was telling me that you were thinking about joining the Army. What! Naw that ain't true Lillian. Then why would she say that? Her husband fought and died in World War1 and she wants me to join. She thinks that if I don't join I'm going to lose you to one Army boys. I hear a lot of men are joining. My daddy said if he was young he would join. I didn't like what Lillian was saying. I stopped and looked at her. Lillian there's something I have to ask you. What is it? If I don't join the Army would you look at me differently? No I wouldn't if you want to join Jeffery that is your choice.

I'm not going to force you do something you don't want to do. You wouldn't leave for some guy in a uniform would you? No I wouldn't. Why you asking me these questions Jeffery? Well Mrs. Hutchinson was telling me that girls like men in uniform. So what does that got to do with me. The only way I would leave you if you didn't want me. I want you Jeffery and no one else. That made me feel good, but I hope it's the truth. I feel for the first time I have finally someone who likes me for me, but I was still a little cautious. I didn't want to get hurt like in the past when I thought that some girl liked me and she didn't. Lillian is a very beautiful girl she could have any man. What makes her what a man like me? We walked hand and hand passed the lake. Even though it was cold she wanted to sit by the lake. We sat on the bench next to the lake. It's cold out here. Come on let me hold you. I held her in my arms. We kissed her lips were soft like a baby's bottom. Jeffery I have to tell you something. What? My momma and daddy didn't want me to go out with you at first. Why not? The didn't think you were smart and you weren't that good looking. My momma said I could do better. My heart dropped when she said that. So why did your daddy let me take you out? He didn't want to hurt your feeling since you came over there to ask him. He thought that was really bold of you to do that. So who was the guy they wanted you to go out with? Ricky Bell. Ricky Bell I know him he use to pick on me all the time in school. So what did you want to do? I told them that I wanted to go out with you, but if I didn't like you than I would go out with Ricky. Now I was feeling really bad knowing now I was not her first choice. I wanted to cry, but I couldn't. I've been though this before, so it wasn't a shock to me. To be honest with you Jeffery I wasn't attracted to you at all. When Brenda came over and told me you wanted to meet me I laughed at first, but when she started to tell me all these nice things about you I told I'll think about it.

So what made you come out to the patio that night? I was curious I wanted to see to what type of person you were, but when I looked in your eyes I could see the kindness in them I knew you were not like the other boys around here. Most of them all they want to do is get in your pants. I didn't see that in you. The things she was saying were hurtful, but a least she was honest. I was happy she was honest with me telling me how she felt. Maybe Mrs. Hutchinson was right and I'm the fool. She grabbed my arm and put it around her and she moved closer to me. We started to kiss. I could feel myself getting hard. I put my arm over it to keep her from see it, but the more we kissed the harder I got. She seen what I was trying to do. I see somebody is happy. You are going to have to control yourself I won't be doing that until I get married. When she said that I went down like a deflated balloon. Come on lets go before your daddy come looking for you. I was still hard a little. You better do something with that sticking out like that. Lets walk slow so it can go down. We both started to laugh. We walked slowly to her house. When we got there Pam and Benny was standing in front of the house talking. Where y'all coming from? We coming from around the lake. The lake in the cold? What was y'all doing at the lake? Sitting on the bench talking. Well anyway Benny's going to join the Army today. Yeah a bunch of us are going down to the Recruiting Office to sign up. He came over to ask daddy could he marry me. What! I was shocked to. Now why would Pam marry Benny? He's a lady's man. Pam how long have you knew Benny? We have been seeing each other about a year or so now. You have? Yeah. Daddy never knew anything about it. Has he asked daddy yet? No he hasn't, but he's going to. I didn't say anything I could see Benny getting his ass kicked by her daddy. Well Lillian I got to go Mrs. Hutchinson has something for me to do. I know she's wondering what happen to me. Ok I'll see you later?

Yeah I'll be over later. We hugged and I left. I left them standing there wondering how Benny was going to ask their daddy could he marry Pam. Good luck with that Benny.

When I was walking home all I could think about is what Lillian said to me. It didn't shock me she felt that way about me. She ain't the only one who has told me that, but it still hurt. Now as for Benny marrying Pam that ain't never going to happen. Lillian mentioned about getting married. She ain't got to worry about that I won't be asking her daddy for her hand in marriage unless I can take care of her. When I got to the house Mrs. Hutchinson was sitting in the living room looking at some old pictures of her husband. I didn't want her to see me, so I turned around to leave when she called my name. Jeffery is that you? Damn! Yes ma'am it's me. Come on in here and let me talk to you. Where you been? I was a Lillian's house talking with her. She seems like a nice girl. Yes she is. Do you hear the news? What news? Tony Bell his brother Ricky and Benny Rice are all joining the Army. Yeah I heard Benny told me when I took Lillian home. So what do you think about what they are doing.

I don't know what to say if that's what they want to do. I'm fine with it. Before she could started talking about that Army bullshit again I changed the subject. Benny told me that he was going to ask Pam's daddy could he marry her. Marry who? Benny wants to marry Pam. What! Ain't she the oldest child? Yeah. Now why would Roscoe let his daughter marry a low down dirty dog like Benny? I don't know Mrs. Hutchinson I've been asking myself the same question. It must be love.

Love my ass he's been fucking that girl ever since she was a teenager. I looked at her. Yeah you didn't know that? No and Roscoe didn't know this? Hell no he can't watch them all at one time. One was bend to get away from him. If he found out he going to kill Benny. Roscoe ain't going to let that sorry Nigga marry is daughter trust me Jeffery. So what was it that you wanted me to do? Oh don't worry about it Sunny took care of it. Well if you need me I'll be in my room. I was about to go upstairs when she asked me. Jeffery what was you and that girl doing at the lake. I hope you weren't having sex. No ma'am we weren't having sex we were just sitting there talking. This would be a bad time for you to start having babies. You are to young to be having babies now. Yes ma'am I know. Ok I'm just telling you. I went upstairs took my coat, shoes off and laid on the bed. I was lying on my bed thinking Mrs. Huthinson must think she knows what's best for me. I'll be 20 years old next month. If I want to have some kids I will, but on the other hand she was right. I don't have a real job and I can't take care of a family on what I'm making. There are a lot of men having babies and can't take care of them. I don't want that to happen to me. The holidays were coming up soon I had to think about what I was going to get Lillian for Christmas.

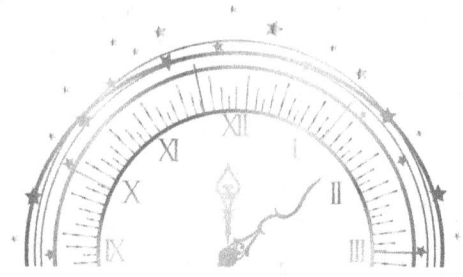

CHAPTER TWENTY-ONE

I SPEND THE HOLIDAYS WITH Lillian's family. Lillian and I were spending as much as we can together with her going to school and me working. She's graduating this year so she been studying hard. I even started eating over her house on a regular basis which made Mrs. Hutchinson mad which I didn't care.

Since I been spending time with Lillian all of a sudden she has all this work for me to do. At one time she didn't ask me where I was going. Now she asked me all the time where I'm going. I think she's jealous of Lillian. This was my life and I didn't want to be around her all the time. She even stop talking to me, because I spend Christmas with Lillian and her family. I had someone I really like and who like me I was really enjoying myself. The war had been going on for about a month now. I hear things ain't going to well for us over there. I really didn't care they can have that war I don't anything to do with it. My birthday came on the 20th of January I turned 20 years old. Lillian and I planned on spending the whole day together. Mrs. Hutchinson was going out of town to see her sister I Dallas Mr. Sutton is going with her. I heard a rumor that they were married. I don't know how true that is, but they'll be gone for a couple of days. Since they'll be gone I can do what I want. There won't be anyone here trying to figure out I'm doing. I don't have to worry about the other boarders they ain't hardly here. I started cleaning up my room which I hadn't cleaned in a month. I picked all my clothes lying around and throw them in my chest. I swept my room which was real dusty it took me about an hour to get all that dust out of my room.

After finished cleaning my room I took me a nice hot bath put on my new clothes I had brought with the money I saved up form doing all the odd jobs and running moonshine with Mr. Sutton. I made the most money running moonshine. During the holidays folks drink more moonshine than anytime of the year. I also brought myself a new pair of shoes. The old ones I had holes in them and were falling off my feet. I really liked them they were brown in color. I know one thing they will last longer than those old ones. I told Lillian I would pick her up at 7:00pm and we would go to dinner and than a movie. I took one last look at myself in the mirror. I looked good you couldn't tell me nothing. I had saved up $75.00 dollars from all the work I had done. I put on a little cologne Lillian had given me put on my new coat Mrs.

Hutchinson brought me for Christmas and headed out the door. On my way to Lillian's house I stopped by the flower shop picked up some flowers for her. These were leftover flowers from the holidays. I also saw a box of chocolates I got that for her to. It cost me $12.00 dollars for the flowers and chocolates. I didn't care I was feeling good about myself. I was on my way to Lillian's house when I ran into her brother Larry. Larry was a big boy for his age. He was about 6'3" 250 lbs with curly brown hair, light brown eyes and dark brown skin. He wasn't a fat boy but he was solid he was built like a grown man and he was only 15 years old. Where are you going Popeye with those flowers and candy? I'm going to pick up Lillian we are going to the movies. Today is also my birthday. Oh yeah that's right she has been talking about you all day. She was really getting on my nerves talking about you. She at home waiting on you.

Where you going? I'm going to see my girlfriend. Alright than I'll see you later. He went on his way. When I got to Lillian's house I could see her sitting in the living room. I knocked on the door and her younger sister

Patrice answered the door. Hey Jeffery how you doing? I'm doing good Patrice. How are you? I'm good showing her pearly white teeth. We hugged. Come on in Lillian's sitting in the livingroom waiting on you. So it's your birthday? Yeah it is. Well Happy Birthday. She gave me another hug, but she pressed herself real hard against me. Thank you. Patrice was the third oldest she was a year younger (16) than Lillian. She was a short slim girl about 5'2" 115lbs with black hair, brown eyes and dark brown skin. She was the out spoken one of all the kids. Lillian was telling me that she has been given her momma and daddy a ard time. When I walked into the living room I was shocked to see Tony Bell sitting there.

The good feeling I had just went away. I looked at Lillian like what the fuck is he doing here?

Hey Jeffery (she gets up and hugs me). Hey Popeye. Hey Tony. I thought you had joined the Army like your brother? I did, but I had a cold at the time so they told me to come back in a month. I'll be leaving for basic training tomorrow. Oh yeah will good for you. I sat down in the chair in the corner. Lillian looked at me funny. Tony Bell was another one of those pretty boys. Him his brother Ricky and Benny ran together they would see would could get the most women between them. Rumor has it that Tony is Ricky's half brother. Mrs. Hutchinson was telling Mr. Sutton one day that Tony daddy was some white man his momma use to work for a while back. They come from a well to do Negro family. Tony and Ricky's daddy is the only black Dentist in Houston. Tony looks more white than black, but his brother Ricky doesn't. So Tony what brings you over here? Well I came to ask Lillian if she wanted to go out on a date with me before I left for basic training tomorrow, but she told me you and her were going out to celebrate your birthday. That's good how old are you now? I turned 20 today. So you are old enough to join the Army? Yes I am, but I won't be joining. Alright you have that choice.

Well I better be going home to get some rest I have to get up early tomorrow. He kissed Lillian on the cheek and left. You take care of yourself Tony. I will Lillian bye. Bye Tony. Lillian came back and looked at me. I was mad, but I didn't show it. I didn't want to ruin our evening together. I know what you are about to say. What? What was he doing over here? Yeah you are right. Jeffery he just came by to say good bye to me before he left. Alright no problem. I think Tony came over for a different reason. I believe he wanted to take Lillian out and try and have sex with her, so he could go brag to his buddies. Lillian would have been nothing, but another notch in his belt. Are those flowers and candy for me? Yeah. Thank you they are some beautiful. She give me a big kiss I started to feel a lot better. So where are we going to have dinner at? I figure we go on over to Mrs. Hattie's place over on 16th street. That's sounds good to me they got some good food over there. Let me get my coat and we can go. I helped her put on her coat. Momma and daddy we are leaving now. Alright now y'all be careful out there. We will. Hey Pam ain't coming with us? No. No! I thought your daddy said y'all couldn't go on any dates unless one of your sisters came with you? Well he trust me with you now Jeffery. A big smile came over my face. We said good bye and left. On our way to Mrs. Hattie's place Lillian asked me was a mad Tony was at the house? Yes I was Lillian. Tony ain't never come over there before not as long as we have been seeing each other. Than out of the blue he comes wants to take you out on a date. I thought it was something fishy about that. You know Jeffery he was the boy that my momma and daddy wanted my to date. I kind of figured that. Why? Your daddy wouldn't let him in his house. I know Jeffery he's just a friend that's all. Alright as long as he is just your friend I'm fine with it. I didn't want to talk about it anymore so I changed the subject. You looked really beautiful tonight Lillian and she did. The black dress she was wearing was hugging her body like a glove. She was wearing the new shoes I brought her for Christmas. I put my arm around as we walked to Mrs. Hattie's.

I took us about 20 minutes to walk to Mrs. Hattie's restaurant. It was a packed a little this wasn't one of those run down jute joints like Little Joe's. This was a well respected family restaurant where well to do Negro's bring their families to eat at on the weekends and to eat a good home cooked meal. It's a brown stone building which use to be a warehouse where Hattie and her husband Jimmy spent two years turning it into a restaurant. It's been around for about ten years and it's the best restaurant for Negro's in Houston. I open the door for Lillian and we went in. We were met at the door by a young girl. How many? Two please. She grabbed to menus and told us to follow her. We followed her to one of the booths in the back.

We sat down and she gave us our menus. My name is Carol I'm going to be your waitress for to night. Can I start y'all off with something to drink? Yes could you bring me and ice tea with lemon in it. Yes and you sir? I'll have the same. Alright you need time to look at the menu?

Yes. Alright I'll be back with your drinks.

CHAPTER TWENTY-TWO

THE INSIDE OF HATTIE'S restaurant looks like one of those white restaurants I use to wish dishes for when I was younger. It had booths that run down both sides of the restaurant. The tables with the chairs were in the middle. All the tables and chairs were made out of fine maple wood. Each booth had it's one little light. On all the tables had salt and pepper shakers, napkin holders, ketchup, hot sauce and toothpicks on them. This was the first time I had ever been in here. It was real nice. So Lillian what are you going to order? I'm going to order this rib tip dinner. What are you going to order? You know what I'm going to get. Pig feet right?

You know it. You know if you eat those pig feet all the time you will start to grow feet like them. We both started laughing. Carol came back with our drinks. Here y'all go y'all ready to order? Yeah I want the rib tip dinner. Alright and you sir. I want the pig feet dinner. Alright give me about 10-15 minutes and I'll be back with your food. I grabbed Lillian's hand. Jeffery do you ever think about marriage? I looked at her she caught me off guard with that one. Yeah I do sometimes. Well if you do why don't you ever talk about it with me? The reason I didn't is that we only been seeing each other a couple of months and I figured it's to early in our relationship to be talking about marriage. Your still in high school and I want you to graduate first before we do something like that. I will graduate for high school I want to know if you are going to feel the same about me? Yeah I will. Why you asking me that? All these questions she's asking me must be from when Tony was at the house. He must have told her something and it got thinking about if something goes wrong between us. I grabbed her hands listen baby when we decide to get married I want to make sure you are will taken care of. I don't want to struggle to make ends meet. That doesn't matter to me Jeffery as long as I'm with you. I'm in love with you. I was stunned I knew she liked me, but I didn't know she was in love with me. I was about to tell her I love her to when Carol brought over our food.

Who had the rib tip dinner? Me. Alright here you go and here is your pig feet dinner sir. Y'all need anything else? No we are fine. Well let me know if you need anything. I will thank you.

This looks good Jeffery. We said our grace and than we started eating. Hey speaking of marriage what ever happen when Benny asked your daddy could he marry Pam. She looked at me. He told him HELL no and throw him out. My daddy knows what type of man Benny is.

What did Pam do? She started to cry. She really love's Benny, but my daddy wasn't having it.

He also told Benny if he ever sees him around Pam again he was going to kill him. I was laughing I knew that was going to happen. You still haven't answered my question Jeffery?

Lillian does all this talk about getting married have anything to do with Tony? Yes it does.

When she said that she had a serious look on her face. He told me if things didn't work out between you and I before he got back from basic training he would marry me. What she said kind of hurt me, but I knew I had to say something to make her happy. Look Lillian I do love you and I do one day want to marry you, but I want to make sure I can do that ok. Yeah I understand. I felt good about myself I never told a woman I loved her, but this was different Lillian was special. You know what Jeffery? What? I don't want to go to the movies. Really?

Yeah let's go over to your house. Ok A big smile came over my face. Now she was saying something I wanted to hear. We finished our food and I paid the bill. I gave Carol a little tip than we left and headed over to my house. On the walk over to my house I was thinking about what Mrs. Hutchinson said about women who like men in uniforms. She was right. Lillian would leave me for Tony. He would have come home in that Army uniform looking good and with money in his pocket he would have taken Lillian away from me. If I hadn't said I loved her I believe she would have left me for Tony. Lillian I have to ask you a question? Alright what is it? How would you feel if I joined the Army? Is that what you want to do I'm fine with it. I thought you said you wanted nothing to do with this war? Now does this has something to do with Tony. Yeah it does I see you like men in uniform. Why you say that Jeffery? Well Tony is going into the Army he is going to be coming back in a uniform with a lot of money in his pocket. If we are not married by the time he gets back he's going to take you away from me.

We stopped walking and she put her hands on my face. Is that what you are worried about Jeffery? Yeah Lillian. You don't have to worry about that I love you not him. I don't care if he came back here with a million dollars. That made me feel a lot better, but I was still a little concerned. I would join the Army to keep Lillian that might sound stupid I would to keep her.

When we got to my house it was empty all the boarders were gone and all the lights were out.

I unlocked the door and we went upstairs to my room. I cut the light on so Lillian could see. I see you cleaned up your room. Yeah I do it took me all day to do it. You must be expecting someone with a smile on her face. Yeah I was you. I helped her take off her coat and I laid it on the chair. I than took mine off. I sat down on the bed and she sat on my lap. So Jeffery what do you want for your birthday. All these wild crazy thoughts ran though my head. Before I could saying something she started kissing me. I could feel myself getting hard. I see someone is awake. The more we kissed the harder I got. I was so hard I felt like I was about to bust out of my pants. I started to feel her breast, but I could feel anything because of her dress and bra. So I started rubbing her thigh. I was surprise she didn't slap my hand away, because of my rough hands. I laid her down on the bed and asked her if she was sure she wanted to do this? Yes I'm sure I love you Jeffery. Are you a virgin Lillian? Yes I am are you?

Yeah I'm one to. I had lied to Lillian if she knew I had sex with Brenda in this same bed three months ago she would get up and leave. We stood up and I started taking off her clothes. I slowly unzipped her dressed. My eyes almost popped out of my head when I seen how beautiful her body was. It was smooth like butter there were no mark on her. When I saw that my dick shot up like a rocket. She smiled at me when she saw that. Could you help me unhook my bra. I unhooked her bra for her. Her beautiful breast looked like to round melons.

Her nipples were the size of half dollars. I couldn't wait to suck on them. The only thing that turned me off about her were her underwear. They looked like grandma panties. They messed up her whole body. I watched her as she got in bed. Are you going to stand there or are you going to get in bed with me? I hurried up and took off my clothes and got into bed with her. It felt funny at first, but than we started to kiss. Than she stopped me. What? Jeffery before we make love I want you to know I love you very much. I wouldn't be doing this if I didn't. Ok I could tell she was scared, because when I held her she was shaking. Relax Lillian it's going to be fine. I went to kiss one of her breast and she stopped me. I'm scared Jeffery. Just relax it's going to be fine. We started kissing I slowly to relax her. I slowly started kissing her breast. I was thinking to myself I better make this a good one, because if I don't I know I won't get another chance no time soon. I slowly tired to put my hands down between her legs, but she had them closed tight. The more I sucked on her breast the more she started to loosen up. She even started stroking my dick. That for some reason relax her more. She was stroking my so hard I get hard again. I slowly tried to put my hand between her legs. This time I was able to do it. I was stroking her pussy gently she was wet and ready to go. I hesitated a little I didn't want to rush it. What's wrong? You sure you want to do this?

Yeah I'm sure Jeffery. I laid her flat on her back and we make love several times that night before we went to sleep. I got up and sat in the chair by the window. I watched Lillian as she slept the light form the moon was shinning on her beautiful face. She looked like an angel from heaven that God had sent to me. I thought about all the disappointments I had in my life with women. I wondered what did this woman see in me the others didn't? I knew now that she was the one for me. I didn't want to disappoint her, so I decided that I was going to join the Army. I'm going down to the Recruiting Office tomorrow and join up. I looked at the clock it's 1:00am. Damn! I better be getting Lillian home. Lillian baby get up it's 1:00am you better be getting home. So what. So what girl you better get up your daddy is going to kill us if I don't get you him now. Stop worrying Jeffery they know where I am and besides it's Friday.

You can take me home tomorrow. Now get back in bed and hold me. I didn't know what to say I got back in bed. Kiss me she told me. I started kissing her and she grabbed my dick. I got hard again. I see someone is awake.

CHAPTER TWENTY-THREE

MORNING CAME QUICKLY IT felt like I had just went to sleep I was tired a little also. I guess it came from all that love making we did last night. I looked at Lillian she was sound asleep.

The sun was shining bright and I could hear the wind blowing. It was 8:00am I was hungry from all that love making. Come on baby wake up. What time is it? It's 8:00am. Come let's go get some breakfast all that love making made me hungry. I'm going to take a bath you coming? Yeah I'm coming with a smile on her face. We took a nice hot bath together and made love while we were doing it. We finished taking a bath got dressed. You sure your folks didn't mind you staying with me all night? Your only 17 years old. No I'm really 18 years old.

What! Your daddy told me you were 17 and so did you. I know I do that to keep these men off me. I started school late, because I had the chicken pox. So how old is Pam? She 20 years old. I'm 18, Patrice is 17 and Larry is 15. So that's why Benny wanted to marry Pam she was old enough to get married. Yep. We finished getting dressed, but before we left I pulled the sheets off the bed. They had blood spots on them I throw them in the closet with the rest of my dirty clothes. The smell of sex was still in the air, but I didn't care I was a grown man I could do what I wanted. I helped Lillian put on her coat. It was real cold outside the wind wa blowing hard to. So where are we going for breakfast? Let's go to Mrs. Hattie Place I hear her breakfast is the best in Houston. We left and started walking towards Mrs. Hattie Place.

We held hands while we walked there. Jeffery I had a nice time last night. So did I Lillian.

Lillian I know you told me if I joined the Army you would back me, but if we get married I got to do something to take care of you. There are no good jobs and the money I'm making I can barely take care of myself. I told you Jeffery what ever you do I'm behind you 100%. Well since you said that I was going to go down to the Recruiting Office today and join up. What!

Why today? I want to spend the rest of the weekend with you. Why don't you do it on Monday. Alright I'll go down there Monday. We got to Hattie Place and Carol we was our waitress last night met us at the door. I see you two are back again. I'm going to sit y'all at the same booth as last night. Is that alright with y'all? Yeah that's fine. She took us back to the booth. Y'all want something to drink? Yeah I want some orange juice. What about you sir? I'll have the same. Y'all need time to look over the menu? No we are going to order now. Ok what you having ma'am? I want the bacon, eggs, grits and toast. So what are you having sir. I'll have the biscuits and gravy with a cup of coffee please. Alright I'll be back with y'all food and drinks. I really enjoyed myself last night Jeffery. So this makes us officially boyfriend and girlfriend? Why you asking me that? You been my girlfriend from the first day I met you. Oh really who told you that? I told myself that. How could you say that when you were to scared to talk to me. Brenda had to come and tell me that you liked me. I was on my way to say something to you, but Brenda got in my way. We both started to laugh. Than Carol brought our food and drinks over to us. Here Y'all go. Thank you we told her. Y'all need anything else just let me know. We will. This looks good and I'm hungry to. It must be from all that love making we did last night. She looked at me with a smile. We ate our food talked and laughed a little. I paid the bill and left Carol a little tip. I walked Lillian home. When we got there her younger Patrice met us at the door. Where you been all night? You know momma and daddy been asking about you.

Why they knew where I was at. You better go see what they want. Let me go see what they want Jeffery. Alright I'll come by later. She gave me a passionate kiss and whispered in my ear. I love you. I whispered back I love you to. Look like somebody's in love. I smile at her I'll see you later Patrice. Bye. I think Patrice had a crush on me. It would be crazy for me to think that we could be together. It an unwritten rule you never mess around with your girlfriends sisters. I decided not to go straight home, but stop by the Recruiting Office. I know I told Lillian I wouldn't go until Monday, but I just wanted to know what I had to do to join up. The Recruiting Office sat on the corner of Maple St it use to be an insurance office before the war started. It had all these posters saying Uncle Sam wants you for the Army and all the things that come with joining the Army. I opened the door and walked in.

There were a lot of desk with Negro soldiers behind them. There were several guys in there taking to them. My I help you a voice said? Yes I walked over to his desk. Yes my name is Jeffery Ross. How are you doing Mr. Ross (shaking my hand) please have a seat. I'm Sgt.

Russsell Lampkin everyone around calls me Rus. Sgt. Russell was a medium built man about 5'9 175lbs with dark brown skin, black hair and eyes. He had a long face with a thin mustache. His was greased back in a wavy style. He spoke like he was white that told me he wasn't from the south especially from Houston. I think he might be from up north some where. So Mr. Ross what can I help you with? I want to know what I have to do to join the Army? Alright first of all how old are you? I'm 20 years old.

Really? You don't look twenty to me. You are going to have to prove it to me. I took out my wallet and pulled out a folded piece of paper and gave it to him. He took it from me and read it. Alright this is your birth certificate and it says here you were born on January 20, 1922, so you are twenty? Yes that's what I told you. Well since you are of age what I'm going to need for you to do is (he reached in his desk and pulled out this folder full of papers) fill out all these papers. He give them to me and looked at them. How long is it going to take me to fill out all these papers? It's going to take you about two hours. Two Hours? Yes two hours unless you want to come back later. I looked at my watch it was 10:00am. I thought to myself I'll be done by 12:00pm and still have to to go home clean my room than go see Lillian.

Alright I'll fill them out. Than Mr. Ross take a seat at one of the desks. If you have any question about the paperwork just ask me. Alright I will. He gave me a pencil I sat at one of the desk and started filling out the paperwork. A lot of the stuff I didn't understand I was a damn good reader, but trying to understand how white people talk was confusing. I was asking Sgt. Lampkin a lot of questions I know I was getting on his nerves. I looked at my watch it was 11:00am and I wasn't even half way finish filling out the paperwork. It was a lot of guys in there sterching their heads. One guy had came in when they showed him all the paperwork he had to fill out he turned around and left. I struggled filling out that paperwork for another two hours. When I finally finished with all that damn paperwork it was 1:00pm. I got up and give my paperwork to Sgt. Lampkin. So you finally finished? Yes I did finally. That was a lot of paperwork to fill out. He looked though all the papers to make sure I had fill out all the papers right. Alright Mr. Ross it looks like everything is good. Now you are going to have to take a test. A test! Yes a test. You have to take a test in order for you to join up. Really? So when do I have to take this test? You will be scheduled to take it Monday morning at 0700 hours. That's 7:00am for you. Oh okay. You will have to be here at 6:00am there are a lot of things they have to go over before you take the test, so make sure you are here at 6:00am.

I'll be here then. Well Mr. Ross you have a good day (shaking my hand) and I'll see you Monday morning. I rushed out of there and ran home to clean my room. When I got there Mrs. Hutchinson and Lillian was in the kitchen talking. I was surprise to see both of them. I wasn't expecting Mrs. Hutchinson to be home so soon. I told Lillian I would be over later.

Good afternoon Jeffery how you doing? I doing fine and you? Well you know me. How was your trip to Dallas? It was good my sister told me to tell you hello. Hey baby (I kissed Lillian) what you doing over here? I came to see you, but you weren't here. Yeah I know I was down at the Recruiting Office. The Recruiting Office! I thought you said you wasn't going to go down there until Monday. I know, but I just went down there to see what I had to do to join up.

It took you all this time to ask that? Well no I was taking to this Sgt. Russell Lampkin he was telling me what I had to do in order to get in the Army. Lillian just got slient.

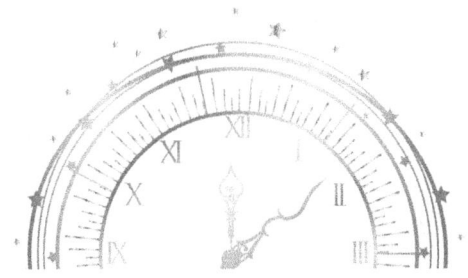

CHAPTER TWENTY-FOUR

I COULD TELL BY THE look on Lillian's face that she didn't want me to going down there talking to those Recruiters, but Mrs. Hutchinson had this big smile on her face. I didn't want to tell her that I had fill out some papers to. So you decided to join up Jeffery? Yeah I did. So what changed your mind about joining? I didn't say I was joining I just went down there to talk with someone. You probably are going to need to join from the look of those sheets I pulled out your closet. Lillian and I just looked at each other. We were both embarrassed by what Mrs.

Hutchinson said. She just sat there and looked at us with this strange look on her face. I'm going to go up to my room. You coming Lillian? Yeah. I kissed Mrs. Hutchinson on her forehead and we went upstairs. Don't y'all be doing nothing up there you hear me. Yes ma'am. We get up to my room and Lillian ask me. How do she know what we were doing?

What is she doing looking around in your closet? She's nosy Lillian I have been spending all my time with you and she's jealous. She washes my clothes and she must have seen the sheets. I don't like that for now on if you want you clothes wash give them to me and I'll wash them for you. I smiled and gave her a kiss. I don't want her in our business Jeffery. Okay.

We spend the rest of the weekend together talking about our future and what if I joined the Army. I took her out to dinner than we went to the movies. The movie was old, but it was new to us. I walked her after the movie. We didn't get a chance to make love again, because Mrs. Hutchinson was at the house. We know we couldn't do anything like that at her house. I went to church with her on Sunday. This was the first time in a long time I had been to church. The last time I went was when my momma was alive. When I moved in with Mrs. Hutchinson she never went to church, but she is always praising God and she never step foot in church.

After church I went over to Lillian's house for dinner. Her momma cooked a big meal. She cooked collard greens, candy yams, fried chicken, butter beans, cornbread and peach cobbler for desert. I ate so much I could hardly walk. I told Lillian lets walk around so I could walk some of this food off. You know I got this that test tomorrow. Yeah I know. You know if I pass it they are going to let me in. Yeah I know. You don't look to happy. I'm not, but I told you I will be behind you on what ever you want to do. But you don't like it? No I don't. I been hearing terrible things happening over there. I don't want you to go over there you might get killed. I don't know what I would do if that happens. She started to cry. I held her and told I know if I would even past that test. I lied to Lillian I know I better past that test or they will call me a stupid Nigga. Come on let me take you home. I walked her back to her house. I told her everything is going to be fine, so don't worry. Okay I hear that those test are real hard. Really how would you know that? Tony told me when he came over to see me that day. He said he barely passed it. You know those white folks think we are stupid anyway, but you make sure you do your best. I will. Well let me go I got to be over there at 6:00am in the morning. The test is at 7:00am. I'll come over when I finish okay. Okay. We kissed and she went into the house. I walked home thinking about what Lillian said about that I might get killed. That really scared me just the thought of getting shot send chills down my spine.

I got to the house Mrs. Hutchinson was sitting in the living room reading a book. Damn! I don't want to see her she's going to start asking me all these questions about Lillian and I. Oh you are home early. You spend the whole weekend with that gal? I sure did she's the love of my life. Must be from all that good loving she been giving you. I didn't say a word. Come in here and sit down and let me talk to you a bit. Now since you decided to join the Army you can keep her. Mrs. Hutchinson can I asked you a question?

Sure go ahead. Why is it so important to you that I join the Army to keep Lillian? She doesn't even want my to join. Well that's what she says now, but wait until those boys start coming home in those uniforms. Especially Tony. I told you that before you need to listen to me Jeffery. Come over here and sit next to me. I know you love this gal, but I seen you get hurt to many times behind some woman thinking they like you. A good looking gal like that will always have men chasing behind her. I just want you to be happy. Now she had me thinking. When tony was at the house I wonder if Lillian would have gone out with him if it wasn't my birthday? She told me her momma and daddy didn't like me and they wanted her to go out with Tony. I realize now I have to do well in this test.

Well I'm going to go to bed. I have to get up early tomorrow. I'm going to be praying that you do well tomorrow. Thanks Mrs. Hutchinson. I kissed her and went up to my room. I sat on the edge of the bed for a minute thinking about what she said about Lillian. I still think she is jealous of her. I took my clothes off and got into bed. I turned the light off and went to sleep.

CHAPTER TWENTY-FIVE

5:00AM CAME QUICK THAT morning. Maybe because I didn't sleep to well. I kept on tossing and turning I didn't fall asleep until around 2:00am. I dreamed Lillian went with Tony when she found out I failed the test. I was a nerves wreck. I got up cleaned myself up and got dressed.

I went downstairs Mrs. Hutchinson was cooking breakfast. Morning Jeffery. Morning. You hungry? Not really. Well you need to eat you something before you take that test. Now you sit down and let me fix you a plate it will come your nerves. I was so nervous I couldn't eat, but I needed to eat something. I finished my breakfast got my coat and headed out the door. Now you bundle up tight Jeffery it's cold this morning. Yes ma'am I will. I was about to leave when she stopped me. I pray for you to do well on this test. Your going to do fine. She kissed me on my cheek and I left. I opened the door to leave the wind was blowing so hard it almost knocked me down. Damn! She was right it's colder than a motherfucker out here. The wind was blowing harder than it usually does. I had my daddy's coat on it was big on me, but it was keeping me warm. The only thing that was cold on me were my hands. It was a short walk to the Recruiting Office. As I got closer to the Recruiting Office I could see two figures standing out in front of the office. I could make out that one was a man and the other was a

The Men that Time has Forgotten

woman. When I got to the front door I was shocked to see it was Lillian. Morning Mr. Ross.

Morning looking at Lillian. Hey baby(giving me a kiss). Hey...... what you doing here? I came down here to wish you good luck on your test. You two (looking at us strange) know each other? Yeah Sgt. Lampkin this here is my boyfriend Jeffery. Your boyfriend!The smile on his face went away when Lillian told him that. Yeah something wrong with that? He laughed and went into the office. Don't you worry about him he's just mad that I'm with you and not him. I didn't expect to see you here. Mrs. Hutchinson told Pam to tell me that you needed my support for this test. So here I am. Well this is real nice of you. I kissed her. Now I have to go in. You go on home and I'll come by when I'm finished okay. Okay I'll be praying you do well.

We kissed again than I watched her walk away until she was out of site. Than I went in to the Recruiting Office. When I walked in Sgt. Lampkin gave me this crazy look like how in the hell did you get a woman like that. Go into that room over there and have a seat. He said it in a mean voice to. I didn't care get mad all you want pretty boy. That my woman. The room was kind of small with about 10 desk in it. There was a podium in front and a big window in the back where you could see all of Maple St. There were about 8 other guys in the besides me. They all were looking at me when I walked into the room. That made feel uneasy. I wanted to say to all of them what the fuck are y'all looking at. I took a seat in the back. When I sat down a tall skinny white man with brown hair and eyes came in the room.

He was followed by Sgt. Lampkin who was carrying a shack of booklets. He stood at the podium. Good morning my name is Lt. Patrick Haas I'll be administrating this military exam to you today. You boys will have to pass this exam in order for you to enter into the U.S. Army. I want you to know the Army won't be taking any dumb Niggers. Everyone in that room tensed up even Sgt. Lampkin got mad. Now Sgt. Lampkin will be passing out a booklet to you. When you get this booklet you will fill out the information on the front. Ross why don't you move up here to this chair, so I can watch you. I move to the front chair than he gave me my booklet.

I'll give you boys 5 minutes to fill out the front. After we finished out the front he told us we had two hours to complete the exam. If any of you are caught cheating you will be disqualified you won't be able to enter into the Army. Does everyone understand, so boys don't cheat. He said that with a big smile on his face. He looked at his watch it's now 0700 hours you will have until 0900 hours to complete this exam. You can start now. I opened my booklet and read the first question I knew than it was going to be a long two hours. The palms of my hands started to sweat. I struggled with the first couple of questions once I got pass them I started getting into a groove. I breezed through the next 50 questions. Lt. Haas told us we had one hour left. One hour had passed and I was feeling pretty good about myself. Than they started asking some real dumb questions like one question asked how much water was in the Atlantic Ocean. How in the hell was I suppose to know. I know it's a lot. You have 30 minutes left. I finished the exam with 15 minutes to spare. I took it up to Lt.

Haas he took it from me and look though it. Okay Ross I see you have answered all the questions.

You can come back on Wednesday to get your results. What time on Wednesday? You can come around 0800 hours. Thank sir I will be here. When he told me that I left. I stood outside to catch me breath. I told Lillian I would come over when I finished, but I had a headache from taking that test. I decided to do home and take a nap.

When I got to the house there was no one there. I went upstairs and flopped down on the bed that test drained me. I was laying there and than I dosed off the next thing I remember someone was touching my head. I woke up to see who it was. When I looked up it was Lillian standing over me. Wake up sleepy head I thought you told me you were coming over after you finish taking the test? I waited for you to come over I even went down to the Recruiting Office they said you had already left. What time is it? It's 4:00pm. 4:00pm! I been sleep all that time? Yeah you have. I seen Mrs. Hutchinson downtown and she told me you were home sleep and you looked real tired. She told me to let you sleep and to stop by later. So here I am to wake you up. How do you think you did? I think I did real good. Really? Yeah I think I did well. What's wrong? I could see it in her eyes she had something to tell me. I grabbed her hand and she looked at me. What is it Lillian? I haven't gotten my circle yet Jeffery. I'm two days late and I have never been late. So what does that mean? I didn't even know what a circle was. That means I might be pregnant. I was speechless I didn't know what to say. Well Lillian it's just been a couple of days you will get it. What if I don't? I scared Jeffery. She started to cry a little. I held in my arm and told everything was going to be fine.

You sure? Yes I'm sure. Now go downstairs and see what Mrs. Hutchinson is cooking. She dried her eyes and went downstairs. I almost died when she left I fell flat on the bed. Please God don't let her be pregnant if she is I wouldn't have a choice but to go into the Army.

Damn! I picked myself up off the bed and went downstairs. When I got downstairs Lillian had made a plate of food. How you feeling Jeffery? I know you were tired from that test come and sit down and eat something. I sat down and started eating my food. Hey Lillian ain't you going to eat something? No I'm not hungry. What's wrong baby you sick? No I had already ate something before I came over here. Okay well I'm going to leave you two alone if you need me Jeffery I'll be in my room. Okay. We didn't say a word until Mrs. Hutchinson went upstairs and we heard her close her door. I don't know what I'm going to Jeffery if I'm pregnant. I know one thing if you are pregnant we are going to have to get married. A big smile came over her face. So you are going to marry? Yeah if you are pregnant. Well what if I'm not pregnant? I'm still going to marry you. She got up and came over and gave me a big kiss. You just made me very happy Jeffery. Let's keep this to ourselves until we find out if you are pregnant okay. This also go for my test score. I'll find that out on Wednesday than we will tell your momma and daddy. Okay. Okay. What about Mrs. Hutchinson? She don't need to know right now I'll tell her when the time comes. I finished eating my food and we went upstairs to my room.

CHAPTER TWENTY-SIX

THE NEXT COUPLE OF days we were walking on eggshells wondering if Lillian was pregnant or not. She told me her circle hadn't come. I could sleep that night I tossed and turned all night.

I got up early Wednesday morning around 6:00am. I got dressed went downstairs to get something to eat and walked to the Recruiting Office. When I went into the office Sgt.

Lampkin was at his desk talking to some woman. Well good morning Mr. Ross. Morning Sgt.

Lampkin. I guess you are here for you exam results? Yes I am. Alright hold on and I'll get them for you. He got up went into the room where we took the test. When he came out Lt.

Haas was with him holding a piece of paper. Jeffery Ross is your name. Yes sir. He stuck out hand to shake my hand. Congratulations. I looked at Sgt. Lampkin who had a smile on his face. You are the only one who past the test out of the 12 boys who took it. Are you serious?

Yes I am. I was in shock. You scored real high too. How high did I score? You scored a 80% on the test. You scored higher than most white recruits. That's officer material. You are kidding me. No I'm not kidding you. The Army could use smart boys like you. I wanted to punch him in his face for saying that, but I was to happy I wasn't going to let him steal my joy.

Now since you passed the exam Ross you will have to take a physical exam. You will have to pass this exam to get in. Okay so when do I do this exam? Come back tomorrow morning at 0500 hours. I will be here sir. Okay we will see you than. I turned to leave when Sgt. Lampkin shook my hand. Congrats Ross. Thank you Sgt. Lampkin. You know if you pass this physical you will be shipping out the next day. What! No I didn't know that. I know they ain't going to tell you that. I'm just letting you know, so you need to tell that pretty girl of yours. Okay I will thanks Sgt. We shook hands and I left. I was so happy I ran all the way home. I came running into the house. What's wrong with you Jeffery? Nothing. I ran upstairs to my room went to my closet and pulled an old coffee can off the shelf. I opened it took the money out of it was the money I had saved up from doing odd jobs around town. I counted it I had a little over $100.00 dollars. This should be enough to buy Lillian a ring. I closed my closet and Mrs.

Hutchinson was standing there. What you doing Jeffery? I passed that test. What! Yeah I did and I was the only one who passed it. That's wonderful Jeffery. She gave me a big hug. I'm not in yet I have to take a physical tomorrow morning I have to pass that then they will let me in. If I fail I won't get in. You will pass it. The Sgt down there told me if I pass the physical

They are going to ship me out to basic training the next day. She gave me this funny look.

What? She closed the door and told to come sit down on the bed. Come on sit down next to me. That gal is pregnant ain't she? I looked at her she might be. I know something was wrong, because I dreamed about fish last night. You dreamed about fish what's that got to do with Lillian being pregnant? She laughed a little. It's an old saying when you dream of fish someone in the family is pregnant. Your going to be a daddy Jeffery. Are you sure? Yes I'm sure. You don't have to get married now you can wait until you get back from training. I'll have everything ready for you when you get back. Now go tell her the good news. Thank you Mrs.

Hutchinson. Your welcome Jeffery. I kissed on her cheek ran

downstairs out the door headed towards Lillian's house. I ran all the way to Lillian's house. The closer I got I could see that Lillian and Pam were sitting out on the porch. Hey. Hey Popeye. Hey Pam. Why y'all sitting out here in the cold? We just sitting out here talking. In the cold? Yeah. Hey baby guess what. What? I passed that test. What! She jumped off the porch into my arms and almost knocked me down. That's good Popeye I'm happy for you. I'm not in yet I have to take a physical exam tomorrow morning at 5:00am, but they are going to ship me out the next day to basic training. What why? That's the way they do things. So we are still going to get married? Yeah when I get back from basic training. Well how long will that be? I'll be gone a couple of months than we will get married okay. Okay. Wait a minute Popeye you still have to ask our daddy. Oh yeah I forgot I have to ask him first. I'll go ask him right now. You going to ask him right now? Yeah. I don't think that would be a good idea now Jeffery. Why? I think you should wait until you get back from basic training. Why? He's not in the best of moods right now that's why we are out here we don't want to hear his mouth. No I'm going to ask him now. Okay don't let me tell you I told you so when he throws you out. I looked at Lillian and went in the house. Lillian and Pam came in the house behind me. Her daddy was in the living room listening to the football game. I stood outside the door first to gather my nerves and how I was going to ask him for Lillian's hand in marriage. Lillian and Pam were looking at me telling me go ahead. I knew I had to do this right or he was going to throw me out like he did Benny.

The one thing I had over Benny was I wasn't a lady's man. He had a bad reputation I didn't. I walked into the living room. How you doing Mr. Crawford. He looked at me I'm doing fine Jeffery. Who's playing? Texas and Houston. Who's winning? Texas is winning by 10 points.

You could come sit down and listen to the game with me. I sat down in the chair next to the radio. So how are you doing Jeffery. He gave me this strange look. I 'm doing good. I heard you took the test to join the Army. Yes I did sir. So how did you do? I passed sir. Oh you did well that's good. I was the only one who it. So when are you going to basic training? Well I have to take a physical exam first if I pass that than I will ship out the next day. So you telling me that if you pass this physical exam they're going to ship you out the next day? Yes sir that's what I was told. Damn! I gets up and turns off the radio. I sat there thinking what the hell is he going to do to me. He sat back down in his chair. He must have known I wanted to ask him something. So what's on your mind son? Well sir I came over here to ask you for your blessing. Blessing? Yes sir to marry Lillian. He looked at me and signed. Tell me why you want to marry my daughter? I love Lillian very much sir and I can't live without her. Is that it son? Yes sir. You sure this ain't got nothing to do with her being pregnant? I was shocked when he asked me that. How did he find out Lillian was pregnant? I bet it was Mrs. Hutchinson and her fish dreams. Who told you that sir? Who do you think told me? Mrs. Hutchinson? Hell no boy Lillian told me herself. What! I was shocked I didn't think she would tell him. I thought we were going to keep it a secret until we were sure. I taught my girls that they can come talk to me about anything with being scared. I couldn't say anything. I knew you would be by to come ask me for Lillian's hand in marriage and the answer is yes. You have my blessing Jeffery. A big smile came over my face he stood up and shook my hand.

Thank you sir. I trust you better than that sorry Benny. So you did you buy Lillian a ring? No sir I was going to buy nit when I got back from basic training. Lillian come in here. Yes daddy.

Jeffery just told me that he wanted to marry you. Do you love him like he loves you? Yes I do daddy very much. I gave him my blessing to marry you. Oh thank you daddy (she hugs him).

Jeffery since you are leaving soon you can go buy that ring now. You can go to Mr. Albert Jeweler's he doesn't close until 6:00pm. Okay I give Lillian a hug than I left. I wasn't planning on buy a ring now, but if I want to marry Lillian I better do what he tells me.

CHAPTER TWENTY-SEVEN

MR. ALBERT BERNSTEIN WAS a short fat bald headed Jewish man with a husky voice. He and his family fled Germany when the Nazis came to power. He came to Houston about 5 years ago and set up shop right outside of the black section. The white people thought he was crazy, but he didn't care. He was a very nice man. Most of us couldn't hardly understand what he was saying half the time. His shop sat at the edge of the well to do Negro section of Houston.

That section was in the 4th ward watch was right next door. I never come over here, because these so called upper class Negros look down on you thinking they are better than you. I think the reason they do that is because of of the Negros who live there are light skinned. It took me about 15 minutes to get to his Jewelery shop. When I walked in he was cleaning up. Hey Mr. Albert how you doing. I doing fine he said in his thick German accent. What can I do for you young man? I am getting married soon and I need to buy a ring. Well congratulations.

Thank you. So what kind of ring are you looking for? Well I really don't know this my first time. What kind of rings do you have? How much do you want to spend? I reached in my pocket and pulled out the $100.00 dollars I saved up. All I got is $100.00 dollars. Okay let's see what we can find you I think I got something you will like. He gets his keys opened up this small drawer and pulls out this little box. He opens it up and inside were six of the most beautiful rings I have ever seen. Do you like any of these? He takes one out of the box and hands it to me. Wow this is a beautiful ring. It was gold with a small white diamond in the middle. How much is this one? This is $225.00 dollars. Well I can't get that one I only have $100.00 dollars. Let me see that one. Yes this is very nice this is more in your price range.

The diamond was a little smaller than the first one, but it still was beautiful ring. Yeah this is nice how much is this one? He looks at the tag. This one is $160.00 dollars. Damn Mr. Albert all I got is $100.00 dollars. Okay I'll make you a deal. Okay I'm listening. What is your name?

Oh my name is Jeffery Ross. Okay Jeffery I'll give you this ring for $100.00 dollars. Really!

Yes I'm doing this is I know Mrs. Hutchinson. You know Mrs. Hutchinson? Oh yes she makes the best moonshine I have ever tasted. She also talks about you all the time. She says you are a good boy. I was shocked I didn't know he knew Mrs. Hutchinson. So do you want this ring? Oh yes sir I do. I gave him the $100.00 dollars. Do you want me to put it in a box for you? Yes please. He put the ring in a little black box and gave it to me. Thank you Mr. Albert I don't know how to thank you for this. Just thin of it as my wedding gift to you and your bride. I wanted to give him a hug, but we shook hands. Oh Jeffery. Yes sir. Would you please tell Mrs. Hutchinson that I'm going to need some more of that great moonshine of hers. I tell you what since you did me this favor for me I will bring you a couple of bottles by myself. Thank Jeffery I appreciate that. Now you take care and once again congratulations. Thank you. I left the shop and headed back to Lillian's house. When I got outside I wanted to take another look at the ring I brought. When I opened the box I was shock to see that Mr. Albert had switched rings. He put the $225.00 dollar ring in the box instead of the $160.00 dollar ring. I wanted to go back and think him, but I had to get back to Lillian's house I didn't want her daddy to think I had ran off. I will go by tomorrow after my physical and thank him. I was scared and happy at the same time. This was a big step for me I can't believe I'm getting married. Now I'm going to have a wife and a baby soon. That's a lot of responsibility for a young man like me. I took my time walking back to Lillian's house I was thinking about a lot of things. When I got back to Lillian's house her momma and daddy were sitting in the living room waiting on me to come back. Hey boy where you been I thought you had ran off. No I t didn't run off. Well did you get the ring? Yes sir I did. Well let me see it. I gave him the box.

When he opened it his eyes almost popped out of his head. Oh Jeffery this is a beautiful ring her momma told me. Lillian's going to love it. Yeah boy you did good for yourself. How much did you pay for this ring Jeffery? I only paid $100.00 dollars for it. $100.00 dollars! Yeah $100.00 dollars. They both just looked at each other. I didn't tell them that Mr. Albert switched rings that's none of their business. So Jeffery are you staying for dinner? Oh yes ma'am I am.

Well dinner will be ready in a few minutes. Where is Lillian at? She's upstairs she will be down in a few. I was looking for Mr.

Crawford to give me my ring back, but he didn't he just put it in his pocket. Now I wondered why he would do that. I guess it was his way of keeping me here just in case I would change my mind. Y'all go wash your hands and come on and eat. I washed my hands and went into the dining room. It was smaller then the living room with six chairs around a hand made wood table. The table was already set I sat down next to Mr. Crawford. Then Larry came in. Hey Popeye I didn't know you were here. So your Popeye.

Yes ma'am. So that's your nickname? Yes ma'am it is. Mrs. Hutchinson talks about you all the time. She does? Yeah. Why they call you Popeye any way. Well My auntie gave that name when I was a kid. She said my eye looked like they were about to pop out of my head. Your eyes don't look that big to me. Now they don't, but they were real big when I was a kid. Lillian came into the dining room followed by Pam and Patrice. Lillian had changed her dress. Y'all come on and have a seat I got some good news to tell y'all. Your sister Lillian is going to marry this fine young man here. So are they getting married now? No Larry they are going to get married when Jeffery comes back from basic training. You joined the Army Jeffery? Yeah I did. And he's a good man for doing it. Then he take my ring out of his pocket and gave it to me. Now go ahead and ask my daughter to marry you. I took the box from him opened it up got down on one knee. Lillian would you marry me. Yes Jeffery I will. I was shaking so hard I couldn't even put the ring on her finger. We kissed and everyone started clapping. Mrs.

Crawford came over and gave us both a hug. I'm happy for the both of you. Pam and Patrice help my bring the food out. I'm happy for you son your doing the right thing by joining the Army, because now you are going to have a lot of responsibilities you understand me. Yes sir I do. They brought the food to the table. Jeffery I cooked your favorite. My favorite what's that? Pig feet. How did you know I liked pig feet? Lillian told me it was your favorite. I looked at Lillian and smiled. Come on let's say grace. We grabbed hands and said grace and we ate. Mrs. Crawford cooked another good meal. Once again I ate until I was full. I told Lillian l let's walk around the neighborhood so I can digest my food. We held hands as we walked. I told Lillian about Mr. Albert switching the rings. It's a beautiful ring Jeffery you need to go by there and tell him thank you. I will after my physical. So what day will we be getting married on Jeffery. I don't know I'll have to let you know, because I don't know what day I'm be coming home after basic training. Mrs. Hutchinson said she will take care of everything, so you don't have to worry about that. That's nice of her to do that, but I want to have a say so in my own wedding. I know she will let you help her. Jeffery I love you so much. I love you to Lillian. We stopped and kissed. I'm going to miss you while you are gone Jeffery. I know Lillian, but it's only for a couple of months. Tears started to run down her face. It's going to be fine baby okay. Come on let me walk you back home. When we were walking back I started thinking about all the things that are going to happen once I pass this physical. I was scared, but I didn't want Lillian to know.

CHAPTER TWENTY-EIGHT

WHEN WE GOT BACK to the house Pam and Patrice were in the living room listening to the radio.
Where y'all been? None of your business. I laughed a little. Oh Jeffery I forgot to tell you Benny didn't go into the Army. He joined the Navy. Well good for him. I don't why she telling me this I could care less about Benny I never liked him. What y'all listening to? The Jack Benny Show. Jeffery you want to stay a little and listen to the radio? Yeah I'll stay and listen to the radio with you. We sat down on the couch together. This is nice she said. We kissed and held each other. I don't remember when we fell asleep, but when I woke up it was dark. I was confessed and didn't know where I was at. I could see neither. When I went to get up I couldn't when I looked down I realize Lillian was sleeping on my lap. Lillian baby get up I have to go home, so I can go home and clean up for my physical. What time is it? I don't know, but it is late. Come on get up. Where you going? I told you I have to go home. Know you don't. What? When you fell asleep my momma told Larry to go over to Mrs. Hutchinson house to send you over some clean clothes. Well did she. Yeah there over there on the chair.

Besides I don't want you to leave. I sat back down on the couch that's when she grabbed my dick. I instantly got hard. I looked at her now you know we can't do anything like that in your momma and daddy's house. I know I just wanted to see how fast he would wake up.

The Men that Time has Forgotten

Well you see how fast. I took my shoes off and we laid back down on the couch. Lillian put her head on my chest. This is nice I can't wait until we get married. We drifted back off to sleep. The next thing I remember is feeling someone shaking me. Jeffery baby wake up it's 4:00am go clean yourself up my momma is in the kitchen making breakfast. Okay baby. I got up got myself together put on the clothes Mrs. Hutchinson sent over. Then I want into the kitchen where Lillian had made me a plate of eggs, bacon, girts and toast. I ate my breakfast and got ready to go. Here baby I made you a little lunch just in case you get hungry while you are down there. Thank you baby I'm probably going to be down there all day. I put on my coat and gave gave her a kiss. You bundle up good it's cold out there this morning. You sound like Mrs.

Hutchinson. I gave her a kiss told her I love her and left. I waved at her as I walked to the Recruiting Office. It was cold and the wind was blowing harder than usual. When I got to the Recruiting Office it was a long line. Didn't know that many guys passed that test. Sgt. Lambkin was standing in front of the office. Good Morning Sgt. Lambkin. Morning Ross so you are here to take your physical? Yes I am. Okay than get in line. I got in the long line.

Alright everybody listen up we are going to walk to the old medical clinic where you will be given your physicals. Now in order for you to get into the Army you will have to pass this physical. Does everyone understand that? Yes Sgt. Okay lets go. The medical clinic he was talking about is the old 5th ward clinic. It use to be a hospital for the Negros who live in that area. They closed it down during the depression. It never opened back up, so the well to Negros got together and built a new one in the 4th ward over on 15th street. It took us about 10 minutes to get over there. When we got there I could see several doctors standing around waiting on us. Listen up when you go in you will be handed a piece of paper fill it out put your things in one of the chairs take off your shirt and get in line. I go in and they hand me this paper to fill out. I filled it out put my things down took my shirt off and stood in line so the doctor could see me. The old clinic was cold and it smelled old. This is where I was born. I haven't been in here since than. They did a good job of fixing it up. There wasn't any heat in there, so it was cold in there with no shirt on. When I got to the doctor my teeth were chattering. Stand here while I check your heart beat. He check my front than for some reason he started checking my back telling me to take deep breaths. I don't know why he did that my heart is in the front. When he finished he took my sheet and wrote something down on it gave back to me and told go into the next room. I went into the next room where they were checking eyes, ears, and mouth. I had to wait about 20 minutes to see him. I gave him my sheet he looked at it. Turn to your right. He stuck this tube down my ear it hurt like hell. He was pulling my ear everywhere. I wanted to ask him what the hell was he doing. After he finished checking my ears he told me to open my mouth. He stuck this stick in my mouth looking for what I don't know, but I guess it wasn't bad he told me I was good. He told me to turn around cover my right eye and read the first line of the chart on the wall. He told me to read several more lines. Then told me to cover my left eye and do the same thing. Okay Ross you are good to go now take your sheet into the next room where they are going to draw your blood. Draw my blood. Yes they have to draw some blood from you. Don't tell me you are scared of needles? Oh no sir I'm not scared of needles. I was lying to him I was terrified of needles I ain't never had blood draw before. I went into the room where there were two nurses drawing blood from other guys. Come over here and have a seat one of them told me.

    I sat down in one of the chairs. She came over and took my sheet from me. Gave me your arm and put it out straight. I did what she told me. Then she tied this rubber tube around my arm so tight my veins started popping out. Then she picked up this long needle. Now just relax you going to feel a little pinch. Than she shoves this needle into one of my veins I almost jumped out of my seat when she did that. When I saw my blood shoot into that tube my stomach started to feel funny. She pulled that one out and stuck another one in my vein. I started to feel light headed. The blood gushed into the tube I started to lose consciousness, but she caught me before I fell out of the chair. Okay now there you go we are finished. Now sit up so you can get some air.

Everybody was looking at me I was a little embarrassed by that. She helped me out of my chair into another room. You not the first boy to almost faint.

Now you sit here and catch your breath I'll be back to check on you. Okay. I sat there for about 20 minutes she was right I wasn't the only guy that fainted. While I was sitting there they brought in at least four other guys. One guy they had to carry him in. Are you okay Ross? Yes ma'am. Okay than take your sheet and go into the next room. I got up to go into the next room I was still feeling a little light headed. When I got in the room a private in a white coat took my sheet. Ross is that your name? Yes sir. Okay go over there and take off your pants. I looked at him what! Go over there take off your pants and get in line. I looked around and there were guys standing in line naked. I took off my pants than got in line. The doctor was checking their balls. I didn't know why he was doing that, but it made me nerves. I asked this one guy why was he doing that? There checking to see if you have any hernias.

What the hell is a hernia? It's when you have a bulge in your balls. Oh well I don't have that problem. Will you don't know that you could have it and don't even know it. Next the doctor said. I went in. Come on son I don't have all day. He took my sheet from me. The doctor was smoking a cigarette the smoke was killing me. Okay Ross go over there and stand on that scale. He adjusted it a little. Your 5'7" 140lbs. Now stand over here so I can check to see if you have any hernias. He went to touch one of my balls I moved. Don't worry son I'm not going to hurt you. He touched my right ball. Now turn your head to the right and cough. Than he did the same to the left. Turn your head and cough. Then he told me to lift up my feet so he could see the bottoms. After he finished he wrote something down on my sheet gave back to me told me to get dressed and go the room where I took my test. I grabbed my sheet and left. I get dressed fast I was freezing to death. When I got finished I went into the room where I took my test. Lt. Haas was sitting in the room when I got there. He took my sheet from me and looked at it. Jeffery Ross oh yeah I remember you. Your the one who scored high on the military exam. Yes sir I did. Well that's good, but I have some bad news for you that doesn't mean anything. Why you say that sir? Well the only jobs you boys can do are cooks, steward and truck drivers. You can pick one of these. I'll take truck driver. I took that, because I don't know how to cook and I didn't know what a steward was. It looks like your in perfect health Ross. Than he gave me this paper to sign. What's this? It for driving trucks in the Army this will be your job. Oh okay I signed it. All your paperwork looks good now all we have to do is get you sworn in follow me. I got up and followed him into this room where there was a podium and an American flag.

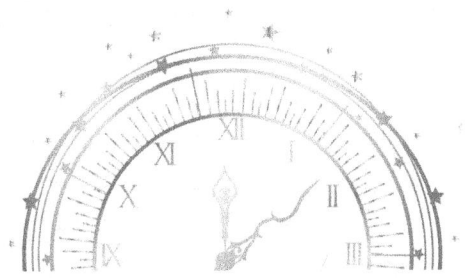

CHAPTER TWENTY-NINE

WHEN WE GOT IN the room it was full with men waiting. Okay Ross get in line. Lt. Haas stood behind the podium. My name is Lt. Haas you boys are about to be sworn into the U.S. Army.

When I tell you to you will raise your right hand and repeat after me. Now before we get started is there any one who doesn't want to be sworn in? Once you get sworn in you won't be able to leave, so if you don't want to be here leave now. No one left. Okay than let's get started. Raise your right hand and repeat after me. I want you to read the chart behind me word for word. Where the blank space is you will say your name. Now repeat after me. We said the whole oath which took all but 20 seconds. My heart was beating so fast when I was saying that oath. Congratulations boys you are now in the U.S. Army. We starting shaking each other hands and laughing. Now listen up boys you will be shipping out for basic training Saturday morning at 0500 hours. So you have one day to get all your things in order and say all your goodbyes. You will report to the Recruiting Office at 0400 hours. If you don't report you will be concerned a deserter and in the time of war that is punishable by death. Does everyone understand that? Yes sir. Your dismissed. I ran into the other room put on my coat got my lunch (which was cold by now) and left. I got outside It had warmed up a little the sun was shining and the sky was clear. I looked at my watch it was 2:30pm I had been down there all day. I started walking towards Lillian's house. As I was walking I was thinking to myself what the hell did I just get myself into. There's a war going on and I might get killed. I've sworn in now I can't change my mind. I got to Lillian's house it looked like nobody was home. I knocked on the door. Who is it? It's me Jeffery. Lillian's sister Patrice opened the door. Hey Jeffery. Hey Patrice where is Lillian? Oh she's upstairs sleeping it must be that baby making her sleep all the time. You going to let me in? She smiled and moved just enough for me to squeeze by. I knew what that was all about, but I didn't pay any mind to it. I walked upstairs to the room where she shared with her sisters. I knocked on the door and went in. It was a large room with three beds in it. Lillian was sleeping in the bed by the window. I walked over leaned over and kissed her in her lips. She opened her eyes. Hey baby how long have you been sitting there? I just got here. So how did you physical go? It went good I passed and than they swore us in. I'm now officially in the Army. I'm going to shipping out for basic training on Saturday, so we only have a day or so to spend together. A sad look came over her face. Oh don't be sad baby I'm coming back, so get up I'll take you out to eat. I didn't get a chance to eat the lunch you fixed me, so hurry up I'm hungry as hell, so hurry up. Okay give me about an hour. We kissed and I went back downstairs. It took her almost an hour to get ready. I had fell asleep on the couch. Hey Jeffery you sure you want to go out and eat? I know you are tired I can fix you something to eat here. Know I'm fine I want to go out and eat. Okay let's go. So where are we going? Let's go to Hattie's Place. We started walking towards Hattie's. Lillian I have something to tell you. Okay what is it. I'm scared. Why are you scared? This nurse today took my blood and I almost fainted. What!(laughing). Yeah my stomach started acting funny. If I can't handle them taking blood from me what I'm I going to do when I see some real blood. There's a chance I might get hurt or even killed too. She stopped me and looked at me Jeffery I don't know what I would do if that happened. If you are so worried about all these things happening Jeffery why did you join? I had to do something to take care of you and that baby Lillian. I can't take care of you on the money I make around here. Joining the Army my be a good thing. That means our baby will have a chance at a good education.

You understand? Yeah I do. Come on let's get something to eat I'm hungry. I love Jeffery. I love you to Lillian. We got to Hattie's Place and was met at the door by Carol. You two again? Come on follow me I'll sit y'all at y'all favorite booth. Y'all want the same thing y'all always order? Yeah. Okay I'll be back with y'all food and drinks. Carol brought our food and drinks back. We ate I paid the bill and we left. We walked to my house. When we got inside Mrs.

Hutchinson and Mr. Sutton was sitting at the kitchen table. I hear you two got engaged. Yes we did. So when is the wedding? There going to have it when Jeffery gets back from basic training Sunny.

Mrs. Hutchinson gave this look like I told you not to get that girl pregnant. Well I'm happy for the both of you Popeye. Thank Mr. Sutton. We went into the living room and sat down. Jeffery why did Mrs. Hutchinson give you this evil look? You saw that? Yeah and I didn't like it. I don't know why she's funny like that. I did know why, but I just didn't want to tell Lillian. Mrs. Hutchinson came into the living room and asked us were we hungry. No we are not hungry we just finish eating. We sat there talked, kissed and hugged each other when Lillian told me she was hungry. What! Lillian we just ate an hour ago. I know but I'm hungry baby.

Okay let's go see what Mrs. Hutchinson cooked. Mrs. Hutchinson had cooked baked chicken, macaroni and cheese, green beans and cornbread. Lillian fix herself a plate. Jeffery you better fix yourself a plate, because you know once to go to basic training you won't be getting any food like this. I know that I'm just going to sit here and watch you eat.

The next day we spend the whole day together, because I was leaving that next morning.

The morning of January 30, 1942 came quick. It was 3:00am in the morning I got up feeling like I didn't want to do this. I sat on the edge of the bed thinking to myself I said I would never join the Army. I looked at Lillian and told her to get up. I went into the bathroom to get myself cleaned up. When I came back Lillian was still laying in bed. Hey baby get up I got to go in a few. Come back to bed and hold me. I didn't even think I just got back in bed. Hold me. I held her so tight like she was leaving. Jeffery I don't want you to go. I know baby I don't want to go neither, but I have to. Than she grabbed my dick. Make love to me before you leave. We started making love it was so good I didn't want to stop. When I looked at the clock it was 3:30am. Hey baby I got to go I can't be late. Come on get up and get dressed. We went into the bathroom cleaned up got dressed ate something and than we left. It was 3:45am when we left the Recruiting Office was 10 minutes away. Where are they sending you to basic training? I don't know I'll find out when I get there. Will you be able to write me? Yeah I think so. Your not going to go there and forget about me are you Jeffery? No Lillian I'm not going to Do you like that. When we got to the Recruiting Office Mrs. Hutchinson and Mr. Sutton was out there talking to Sgt. Lampkin. How you doing Jeffery. I'm fine I didn't expect to see you here. Well we wanted to see you off. How you doing sweetie? I'm doing fine Mrs. Hutchinson.

Here Jeffery I made something for you to eat on your trip. Thank you Mrs. Hutchinson. I'm thinking to myself how did she find out I was leaving today. I never told her, but I realize there's nothing that goes on in the 5th ward Mrs. Hutchinson don't know about. While we were there talking an old school bus pulled up. The door opened up and a short stocky black man wearing an Army uniform smoking a cigar got off. He looked at us and we looked at him than he want inside. He was in there for a couple of minutes than he came back out. He looked at Sgt. Lampkin. Okay everyone let's get on the bus. Pvt. Ross say goodbye to you family. Okay Sgt. Well I guess this is good bye. I hugged Mrs. Hutchinson and Mr. Sutton. This was the first time in a long time I seen Mrs. Hutchinson cry. Lillian was a different story. She crying like I was never coming back. It's going to be fine (hugging her) Lillian. She was hugging me so tight she almost choked me. Mrs. Hutchinson had to pull her off me. Come baby he got to go. Everyone was on the bus but me. Pvt. Ross lets go. I kissed Lillian and got on the bus.

When I got on the bus the short black man looked at me. You know son that's a nice piece of ass you leaving behind you better get a good look, because where you are going you won't be getting no pussy for a while. Than he started to laugh. Now sit your black ass down. He made me mad, but what could I do. This is the first time I ever left the city of Houston. Then that Sgt stood up. You Niggas listen up. Your asses belong to the Army now. My name is Sgt.

Leroy Knox. They call me hard knocks and you don't want to find out why. You Niggas understand me? Yes sir. When I call your name you you better say yes Sgt.

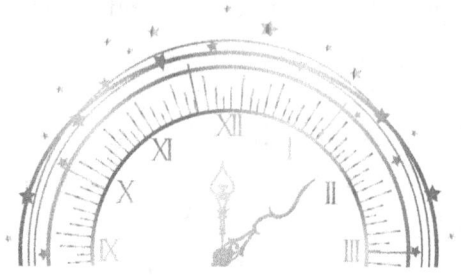

CHAPTER THIRTY

I HEARD MY NAME CALLED I said yes Sgt. Than I heard it called again, but when I opened my eye I saw this white doctor standing over me. Cpl. Jeffery Ross? Yes sir. Were you having a bad dream of something? I called your name you answered yes Sgt. Oh yeah I was sir sorry.

That's okay it happens in times of war. Would you mind sitting up so I could look at your wound. I sat up what day is it sir? It's Christmas Eve Cpl. What! Yes you've been out for the past three days. I looked at him. I've been sleep for three days? Yes looking at your chart according to this you came in on the 21 Dec 44 at 0800 hours. Your bandages need to be changed come over on and sit on the table so I can change them. Hold your arm up so I can cut these bandages off. The ones I had on were bloody. He cut the bandages off. Now this is going to hurt a little. He started taking the bloody bandages off it hurt like hell when he was doing it. When he took it off he pulled the scab off with it which made it start bleeding again. It looks good it's healing well. He put some fresh bandages on my wound. You know they are going to send you back out to the field after Christmas. Yes sir I know that, but can I ask you a question sir. Sure go ahead Cpl. Did we stop the Germans from advancing sir? No Cpl, but slowed them down a little. That's why we need men like you out there to stop them. Now I knew lying he must think I'm some kind of fool. If they have stopped the Germans in the

The Men that Time has Forgotten

three days I have been here. What makes him think I'm going to make a difference. There you go Cpl good as new. Thank you. He gathered up all the bloody bandages and left. I started thinking about Sgt and what's been going on with the company. I haven't heard from anyone since I been here. I hope they haven't forgotten about me. I could hear the bombing in the distant. I hope it doesn't come close I'm in no shape to be running. My arm was sore and stiff.

I put on my shirt and boots than I sat back down on the cot. I put on my jacket, but it was to big. I realize it wasn't mine it was someone else. Then Slim came into the room. I see you are up have a nice rest? Yeah I did I needed that. We all need a rest. Let me take a look at your wound. No need some white doctor came in and change my bandages. It looks good at least it's not bleeding. That white doctor told me it was Christmas Eve. Yeah it is. You know Popeye I forgot you were back here. I was so busy with the company I didn't think about you until Sgt mentioned your name, so I rushed over here to check on you. So how are things going out there? It's going good we had a few attacks from the Germans, but nothing big.

Anyone get killed? No but we got a lot of guys who are sick from the weather. You know most of us are from down south we ain't use to weather like this. Hey I got to get back out there.

You know they are going to release you after Christmas. Yeah I know that white doctor told me. Are you hungry? Hell yeah I'm starving Slim. Sit tight I'll go find you something to eat. Oh yeah here's a letter from your wife. I took the letter I was so excited to hear from her. I looked at the post mark. She wrote this letter about a month ago. Thanks Slim. No problem I'll be back. Okay. I could smell the perfume on the letter. I smelled it again and than I opened it.

Dear Jeffery,

I'm writing you this letter in hopes you are still alive. I haven't heard from you in over a month and they haven't come to the house to tell me that you are dead, so I'm figuring you are still alive. I pray everyday you come back to me alive. Our baby girl is getting bigger everyday. She's even starting to talk a little. She's starting to say momma to. I've been hearing about all the bad things going on over there. They say the war would be over by Christmas, but I don't see that happening. Everyday I see in the news paper the names of dead soldiers hoping one of them isn't yours. They been telling us that were are winning the war. Everybody back here is doing their part to help out. Pam, me, Patrice and a couple of our friends work in one of the factories they opened up in Houston a couple of years ago. It's long hours and hard work, but it's good money. Most of the people who work in the factory are women. My momma keeps Jennifer while I'm at work. I've been saving some money up, so when you get back we can buy a house of our own. The apartment we live is okay, but I want a bigger place. You will never guess who's getting married? Patrice. She's marrying this guy she met at the factory about a year ago. She's crazy about this guy and even my daddy likes him. Now you know he a good man if my daddy gave him his blessing. Pam is pregnant and you will never guess who the daddy is. Do you remember Raymond Peterson? You are probably thinking what happen to Benny. She haven't heard from Benny since he joined the Navy. Well anyway they will be getting married in a couple of months.

I miss you so much Jeffery I can't sleep at night knowing you are over there fighting. Please come back to me safe. Oh Mrs. Hutchinson said hello. She said she's going to bake you a cake and send it to you. She been real lonely since Mr. Sutton died. She been coming over to the house a lot getting on my nerves, but it's okay sometimes she even watches Jennifer for me. I got yo get ready for work I'll write you later. I love you. Write back soon.

Love You Always
Your Wife Lillian

I closed the letter a tears dropped from my eyes. I felt real bad that I haven't written Lillian a letter in a couple of months. I just haven't had the time. I better sit down and write her a letter before she thinks I'm dead for real. I miss my wife and daughter. I can't wait until I get back.

Now Pam marrying Raymond Peterson that's a shocker. Raymond was a bookworm all he did was read books. How him and Pam got together is a mystery. I feel sorry for Mrs.

Hutchinson I know she took it hard when Mr. Sutton died. Lillian told me about it when I was in England. She ain't been the same since Mr. Sutton got ran over by a truck. The rumor I had been hearing for years that said they were married was true. That shocked me I would have never guess they were married they never showed it. I guess it was their way of doing things. While I was sitting there thinking about home Slim came back with some food for me.

Here you go Popeye. He gave one of those tin pans with food in it. It's some what of a Christmas dinner. I looked at it. What is it? It's turkey, stuffing, green beans, cranberry sauce and this hard bun. I think that brown shit on your stuffing is gravy. We started to eat our food it wasn't like home, but it hit the spot. So let me get out of here I'll be back to check on you later. Alright Slim. Hey Slim was that Sgt? Than I heard him call my name. Hey Sgt he's back here. Popeye how you doing boy? I'm doing fine how you doing Sgt? What are you doing here? I came here to see how you were doing. They let me off line I told them I wasn't feeling good. Douglass told me to go get some medicine. He was still wearing that bloody jacket and he needed a shave. So how is your arm feeling? If feels fine, but it's stiff a little.

Aw you'll be aright. You know you are coming back after Christmas. Yeah I know. Did you get the letter from your wife? Yeah I did thanks, but I need a pencil and paper so I could write her back. You don't have to worry about that Popeye. Why? I already did that for you. You did.

Yeah while you were here I wrote her back. I got the address off one of your letters you left in your jacket pocket. So you don't have to worry. What about Benson's letter? I took care of that to. Slim told me y'all had a few attacks. Yeah, but there were small ones nothing big. We slowed those Germans down though. Yeah I was told that by this white doctor who changed my bandages. They want us now to start pushing those Germans back across the Rhine River into Germany. When is this suppose to happen? When Christmas is over. Now from what Douglass was telling me they plan on invading Germany and try to end the war by the end of February. So you better by ready, because those Germans ain't given up easy they are going to fight to the end. We have lost a lot of men, because of Hitler's final push to win this war. Sgt to be honest with you I really don't want to go back out there. I was blessed I just got shot in the arm. Next time I might not be so lucky. I know how you feel Popeye, but that's the chance we took when we sign up. Why you worried you got yourself a medal for just getting shot. I told you I got your back. How you going to do that Sgt? I got shot in my arm. I wasn't there that's why you got shot. I some what believed him every time he was around me nothing happen to me. Here are your other letters from your jacket. Thanks Sgt.

I got to get back Popeye I'll see you after Christmas. Come on Slim let's go. You take care Popeye. I will Sgt. Hey I'll be back after Christmas to come get you. Alright Slim see you than. You rest up now you are going to need it. I laid back on the cot thinking about going back out there. I was scared more than the first time. The thought about not seeing my wife and daughter weighed heavy on my mind. I closed my eyes trying not to think about it. It was Christmas Eve 1944.

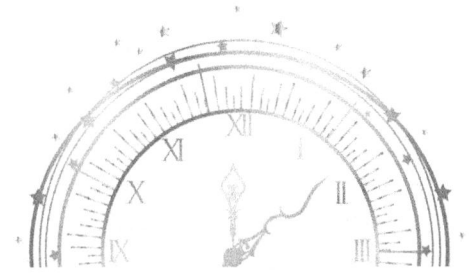

CHAPTER THIRTY-ONE

I SLEPT THROUGH CHRISTMAS I didn't even know it until Slim came in and woke me up. Hey Popeye get up and get dressed. I got up got dressed, but my mouth was dry. Hey Slim you got any water? My mouth is dry. He gave me his canteen I drink all the water in it. You need yo shave and brush your teeth. He handed me a tooth brush, tooth paste, a razor and some shaving cream. Get yourself cleaned up we don't have much time. We got to catch the last truck going back to the front. So hurry up we ain't much time we will be moving out soon. He gave me a helmet full of water. Here take this when you get finished meet in front of the tent. Okay. I put the helmet down on the table. I touched the water to see if it was hot. It was a little warm, but it would have to do. I shaved first so the water wouldn't get cold on me. Than I brushed my teeth twice so that I could get that nasty taste out of my mouth. Than put on my jacket grabbed my letters my helmet and went out to meet Slim. When I got out there he was standing near the entrance. Here is your rifle and gun belt I filled it with ammunition for you.

Thanks Slim. You ready to go? Yeah let's go. Come we're going to catch that truck over there back to the front. When we got outside the wind was blowing hard the snow was ankle deep.

There were soldiers moving equipment, the dead and wounded. We started walking towards the truck. Hey Slim why was I in that field hospital that long? The other doctors didn't want to treat you, so you became my responsibility. They wanted to patch you up and send you back out here. I told them you had the flu also. I told them it wouldn't look good for them sending a sick Negro soldier back out here if he dies somebody got a lot of explaining to do. I also forgot about you to. Than why did that white doctor come in and change my bandages? You know Popeye I really don't know why. Damn it's cold out here it Col. Conley get that cold weather gear for us. Slim laughed a little. What you got on is your cold weather gear Popeye.

I need some gloves for my hands they are freezing. If you want some gloves you better go over to those dead bodies (pointing to them) over there and get some off one of them. I needed a pair of gloves my hands were freezing, so I walked over to the dead bodies. When I walked over to the bodies I couldn't see any of them the snow had cover them up. I seen this one soldier who head had been blown clean off his shoulders. I turned away from him. I I would have gotten sick if I kept looking at him. After looking for a minute or so I seen what I was looking for. This one soldier had a pair of gloves on, but he was stuck between two other soldiers. The one who had his head blown off and another one who died with his eyes open. I could see the terror in his eyes. That sent chills down my spine looking at him. I moved them out the way so that I could get to the dead soldier with the gloves. There bodies were stiff as a board it was easy moving them out the way. When I got to the soldier with the gloves I found out he was a officer a Lt. Col. He had been shot in the head right between the eyes. I figured a sniper killed him. I grabbed one of his hands and started taking off the glove when it broke off in my hand. I was shocked that it happen I dropped the glove between a pile of bodies. Damn! Popeye come on the trucks about to leave. I got my rifle and headed back to the truck. Did you find yourself some gloves? No I didn't. We jumped in the back of the truck and it pulled off. There were six other Negro soldiers sitting back there. How y'all doing I asked them. We going good one soldier said. Where y'all coming from? We just got in from France we are to report to a Capt. Douglass. Oh yeah well he's our platoon leader that where we are going.

They looked real scared to me Popeye. Yeah they do. What is y'all names Slim asked them. I'm Cpl. Floyd Danson this is Pvt. John Jones we call him JJ. That's Pvt. Earl Seals, Pvt. Carl Hardin, Pvt. James Cole and Pvt. Freddy Lampkin. I knew a Sgt.

Lampkin back in Houston he recruited me are you two related? Yeah that's my brother. Your brother? Yeah. Okay. How is he doing? He's dead. What! Yeah he got killed on D-Day, so when we got the news he was killed I decided to join the Army. Now what's your name? My name is Jeffery Ross, but the call me Popeye. This here is Robert Brooks, but we all call him Slim. Well glad to meet y'all. I'm surprised he didn't ask you why do they call you that. After about 20 minutes the truck came to a stop that meant I was back here in this shit. Well here we are boys. We all jumped out of the truck. These new guys didn't have a clue what they were about to get their selves into. Popeye a voice said. I turned around to see who called my name. It was Staff Sgt. Hicks. Hey Hicks how you doing? You well rested? Hell yeah I am.

Where is Sgt? He's over there at the CP let's go see him. Hey you new guys follow me.

He's going to be glad to see that you are back. We walked though the ankle deep snow to the CP. When we got there Sgt, Douglass and some new NCO were talking about something. Well look who's back. Welcome back Cpl. Ross. Thank you sir. Yeah it's about time you got your ass back out here. So did you have a nice vacation Cpl. Ross? I wouldn't call it a vacation sir I was shot in the arm. Oh I see you know most guys who get shot are back out here in a couple of days. Yes I know this sir, but I also was running a fever to sir. I could see where he was going with this. He was making it seem like I was getting all the rest while they were out here freezing their asses off. I think he was just mad it wasn't his sorry ass. Col. Conley got his ass out here with and he doesn't like it. So Popeye how is your arm feeling? It's coming long Sgt. Good you are just in time to hear our plan to push the Germans back into Germany. Popeye I want you to meet Sgt. Henry Perkins he got here a couple of days after you got shot. Glad to meet (shaking hands) you Sgt. Perkins. Sgt. Perkins was a big man like Sgt. He was about

Michael Johnson

6'3" 240lbs dark skin with black hair and brown eyes. Glad to meet you Cpl. Ross I heard a lot about you. You did looking at Sgt. Sgt here are the new guys. Okay good. You guys go report to a Cpl. King he will tell you guys what squad you will be in. Okay Sgt. Okay since everyone is here let's get started. We got word from the Brass that the Germans are retreating back across the Rhine River into Germany. There are still small villages that they are defending stopping our advancement. Now need to take they small villages we were given the task of taking the village of Norberg.

It's a small village about 4 miles from here with one Panzer division guarding it. We have to go in there take this small village, so our troops can advance. Sir. Yes 1st Sgt. How do you know there is only one Panzer division there? That's what our reports are saying. Yeah I know that sir, but you know those reports can be wrong. You know what happen to us last time when they told us that. Yes I know and I understand your concerns 1st Sgt. I'll get some more information for you. Thank you sir. Douglass knew what Sgt was talking about the last time they told us it was small unit of Germans a lot of good men got killed. 1st Sgt. Banks will lead the attack with 1st Platoon and I'll lead 2nd Platoon. Staff Sgt. Hicks you will be in charge of second squad, Cpl. King you got 5th squad, Cpl. Taylor you got 4th squad, Sgt. Perkins you have 3rd squad, Cpl. Hill you got 6th squad and Cpl. Ross you got 1st squad. First squad? Yes 1st squad is there something wrong with that Cpl. Ross? No sir. I need to talk with you and 1st Sgt after this. Yes sir. I didn't like this I got a bad feeling in my stomach about this one. I just got out of the hospital and he is putting me in charge of some men. Now I'm responsible for these men lives. I didn't want that type of pressure on me. I wish I was back at that field hospital. Now does anyone have any questions? No one said a word. 1st Sgt. Banks and Cpl.

Ross I need to talk with you.

CHAPTER THIRTY-TWO

WE WALKED AWAY FROM the other to see what he wanted. You two have done a hellva job since you been out here. Thank you sir. So I got you two promoted. Cpl. Ross I got you promoted to Sgt. Sgt! You promoting me to Sgt? Yes is that a problem Cpl. Ross? No sir is this cleared by Command sir? Yes I talked with Col. Conley about it. You need to change your stripes now. Sir where am I gonna get stripes way out here from. Ask Sgt. Perkins he may have some extra ones. I didn't won't to get promoted to Sgt I was happy as a Cpl. 1ST Sgt Banks you have been promoted to the rank of 2nd Lt. I was shocked by this. He pulled a small black box out of his pocket and gave it to Sgt. Sgt took the box from him. When did this happen Sgt sir? We decided this a couple of days ago. You and Sgt. Ross did a hellva job defending this road from those Germans who tried to attack the depot. Sgt just looked at him. Now you are in charge of 1st platoon. I knew something was funny about all this. He didn't won't any responsibility, so he got Sgt promoted to Lt. If anything was to go bad he could blame it all on Sgt. It didn't make a difference to me Sgt was always in charge of the platoon any way. It was better this way Douglass was an fuck up anyhow. Now listen the plan for us is to back up the white troops they been fighting pretty hard these last couple of weeks. We slowed the Germans down a little, but there is some resistance. The 101st Airborne held the Germans off at Bastogne. Now the Germans are treating we want to push them across the Rhine River back into Germany. The Germans are determine to keep us out of Germany. The Russians are attacking from the east and we are coming in from the west. It's a race to see who can get to Berlin first. Get your squads together and brief them on what we are about to do. We going to be moving out at 1700 hours we got to link up with 3rd Army. 3rd Army ain't that Patton Army? I asked. Yes it is Sgt. Ross. I heard he was a crazy motherfucker. Yes he is, but he will lead us to victory. We saluted and we was dismissed. Sgt told the men to gather around. The men gathered around I saw a lot of new faces. They must have came in while I was gone it was about 50 new guys. Sgt divided the new guy between us. I got most of the new guys even the ones who I rode in with. I won't up for this. Sgt told us to brief our squads on what we was about to do and to meet him back at the CP. Okay 1st squad follow me I said.

I didn't know what the hell I was doing I have never lead anyone, but this is the Army and I better act like I do or I'm going to get these men killed. I have about 10 guys in my squad. We found us a spot where I can brief them on what's going on. I introduce myself. My name Sgt.

Ross I'm your squad leader. Say I thought you told me you was a Cpl. Pvt. Lampkin said. I was a Cpl I just got promoted to Sgt. Is that alright with you Pvt. Lampkin? No sir Sgt. I told them what was about to happen. Do anybody got any questions. Sgt. Y'all can call me Popeye I said. Okay Popeye Lampkin said are we going to see any action. I don't know, but be prepared for anything. Y'all get some rest you are going to need it. It's going to be a long night. I headed back to the CP when I got there Sgt, Hicks and Perkins was already there.

Sgt Ross now that's going to be hard getting use to saying, but you deserve it all the shit we been though together. You got that right. Where's Capt. Douglass at I asked? Where you think he at. He took his sorry ass back to the depot you know how scary his ass is. Soon as he made Sgt the platoon leader he got the hell out of dodge Hicks said. Why they let a man like that in the Army anyway? Because he will do what they tell him. We all started laughing.

Here Popeye these are the stripes you needed. Thanks Perkins. I ain't going to sew them on now, because my hands are cold. You heard what Douglass said you better sew them on now. Hicks was laughing when he said that. Don't worry about that right now Popeye you can do that later. Okay Sgt. I still called him Sgt even though he was a Lt now. Well since we are all here I can tell you the real plan. There's a village about 4 miles from here they want us to go in and take that village. They say there ain't nothing but Hitler youth, but Popeye and I know from experince that ain't the case. They been saying that ever since we been out here.

I believe these soldiers are seasoned fighters. We're going to have a hard time with these soldiers. Douglass told me if we were caught by those Germans they were told to shot us on the spot. Those Germans were told that we ain't soldiers and to show us no respect. So boys we are going in there to kick some German ass and ask questions later. When Sgt said that a chill went down my spine. I here that Sgt. When we get to that village this is what we are going to do. Perkins you are going to take your squad around the back of that village making sure nobody tries to escape. You understand. Yes sir. Hicks you going come in from the east.

Got you Sgt. Popeye, me and his squad will come in from the north. The map shows it's a small town, but let me tell you this. This map could be wrong Popeye and I been in a couple of battles where they told us that we won't have any problems and when we got there all hell broke lose. So keep your eyes open for anything. Perkins I know this will be your first don't panic you got to stay calm. If you panic your men well and they going to be looking to you for what to do if things get hot. Okay Sgt. Hicks you know what to do. Sgt always impressed me with his leadership skills. He won't to bad of a leader for a man who only had a 7th grade education. He was calm and not a worry in the world. Me, Hicks and Perkins was nerves as hell. The village we was going to attack reminded me of that mission we did a month ago which was all fucked up. A lot of men got killed on that fucked up mission. I got a feeling that this one going to be different, because Sgt was leading this one not Douglass.

Okay everybody knows their job. Yes Sgt. Good I don't won't any fuck ups. Hicks your squad going to stand watch. Okay Sgt. Y'all get some rest we going to be moving out in 5 hours.

There was some coffee made I got me a cup and sat down. The hot coffee in the cup warmed up my hands that was frozen. I should have got those gloves off that dead officer. The weather gear the Col promise us never came. The white soldiers didn't get theirs neither.

I sipped on my coffee thinking about all the men we lost these last couple of months. I was almost one of them. Popeye someone said. I turned to see who it was and it Perkins. Yeah Perkins. How you doing with all this? What do you mean? What I mean is this I just got out here a couple days ago. I don't know much about leading men into battle. I don't know how I suppose to do this. You and me both Perkins I ain't never lead no men into battle Sgt always done that. He save my life twice since I been out here. How many battles was y'all in? A couple the last one right here on this road I got shot in the shoulder. Sgt seems to like all this shit Perkins said. Yeah he do. You know the reason he likes this? Why? He can kill white people without getting in trouble for it. He smiled at me. Yeah I can understand that. He said.

Where you from Perkins? I'm from L.A. California. They got a lot of Negros in California? Hell yeah especially in L.A. Hey what y'all taking about Sgt said. Home. You two ain't got time to think about that go check on y'all squads to make sure they have enough ammunition. A truck load of ammunition just came in. We went out and told our squads to check their ammunition if they didn't get some off the truck that just came in. I walked back to the CP and Sgt was sitting down drinking some coffee. Hey Sgt you alright. Yeah why you ask that? You sitting here in a daze. I'm just worried about the young guys we have here that's going to die doing this attack on this village. I heard though the wire that Hitler has gone crazy he's starting to kill his own people. I knew that was going to happen people like that when they lose control they always blame everybody but them selves. You know Popeye people like that always kill themselves instead of paying the price for what they have done. That's the way those type of people are. I just sat there and listen to him. It's just like home those white folks can do anything to us and get away with it. They did my daddy like that living in Dolthan, AL ain't a nice place for Negros Popeye. He don't have to tell me that I live in Houston the most racist place in America.

CHAPTER THIRTY-THREE

WHEN MY DADDY COME home from the war he wanted equal treatment. One day he had got into an argument with some white man. He had gone to the store to buy some food for us.

My daddy paid for the food, but the white man who owned the store by the name of William Bates short changed him. He had a son name Billy Jr. who helped him run it. William Bates was a nasty white man who had know respect to Negros. He was also a member of the Ku Klux Klan and was proud of it. He would brag about what he did to Negros. I was told by my momma that he and some men burned down my daddy's friend Wilbur Johnson barn. When Wilbur went to complain about it they arrested him beat him and ran him out of town. I was 13 years old when that happen. One night we seen them coming up the road to lynch my daddy, cause Mr. Bates had lied on my daddy saying he had stole some money from him. When he seen them coming he told my momma to take my brothers and sisters to my uncle Charles house down the road. My momma didn't want to leave him, because she knew what was going to happen to him. He told them to go and they ran out the back door to my uncle Charles house. I stay with my daddy. Boy get your ass out of here now! I told him no I ain't going to leave you. Boy your the man of the house now you going to have to look after your momma, sisters and brothers. I ain't going to leave you daddy.

Then we heard them yell for my daddy to come out. My daddy had his two shot guns loaded ready to shoot who ever came in. He told me there ain't nothing you can do for me now boy get the hell out of here.

He pushed me towards the door. You better bring your Nigger ass out of there Willie. He asked them what you want with me. You stole some money from William Bates today and threaten his life and we are going to teach you a lesson about disrespecting white people boy. Go boy he told me. My daddy picked up one of his shot guns. I ain't stole know money from him and I ain't threaten his life he's lying. He short changed me today. That ain't what he told us Nigger. We if you want me you going to have to come get me, because I ain't coming out. Then a couple of torches came flying though the living room window. It caught fire quickly. My daddy looked at me and told me to hide. I hid in a little space we had under the house. The whole house started to burn. It started to fill up with smoke I could hardly breathe.

I crawled out the space on my hands and knees coughing and grasping for air. I went to lift my head up for some air that when I seen a shotgun pointed at my head. You a dead Nigger a voice said. I closed my eyes because I know I was dead. That's when I heard this loud bang. It was so loud it almost busted my eardrums. When I open my eyes it was blood everywhere I saw my daddy standing over this man's body. He had blew that Klansman head off. Get up boy and get out of here. I saw my daddy had been shot. Come on I told him grabbing his hand. No he I ain't going to make it tell your momma your brothers and sisters I love them. Now get boy. I ran out the back door towards the woods. As I was running they was shooting at me one of them bullets grazed my arm. When I got deep enough in the woods I looked back to see them drag my daddy to a tree where they had a noose hanging.

He was trying to say something, but one of them Klansman kick him in his face. I could see Sgt was mad a tear ran down his face. He was so mad he clutched his fist so hard you can hear his knuckles crack. Those crackers took my daddy tied his hands behind his back lifted him up put his head in that noose and let him go. When he was hanging there they kicked and punched him. Somebody even shot him. Then they set him on fire. I started to cry, because I couldn't do anything to help my daddy. They were laughing about what they just done, but one voice I heard that I remember hearing was of Billy Jr. He and I played together. I thought he was my friend, but I see he wasn't. So from that day on I hated him. I made up in my mind that he was going to pay for what they did to my daddy. My uncle Charles came and got me and we went to his house. When we got to my uncle's house my momma only saw me she knew what happen to my daddy. She fell to the floor and started to crying. The next morning my uncle, me and some other guys went to the house and cut my daddy down. We couldn't even recognize him he was burned so bad. We buried him a couple days later. My momma couldn't take it anymore, so she moved to St. Louis with my brothers and sisters a couple of months later. I didn't go I stayed with my uncle Charles. I was in town one day when I saw Billy Jr. Hey Willie how are you doing. You want to go swimming this afternoon. I started to say no, but I told him yeah. I told him to meet me at the lake at 3pm.

Okay he. I left my house at 2:45pm. I didn't live to far from the lake all I had to do was cross Mr. Baxter's corn field to get there. Where I got there Billy was sitting on the edge of the pier with his feet in the water. Billy and I were the same age, but I was bigger then he was. He was about 5'3 120lbs with brown hair and blue eyes. I was around 5'8 150lbs. I walked up to him and said hey. Hey Willie. I ain't seen you in a couple of days sorry to hear what happen to your daddy. Thanks I said. Billy wasn't bad people it was his daddy nobody liked. Come on he said just don't stand there lets jump in. He jumped in and I followed him. We was having fun until he said something that made me mad. What did he say Sgt? You know your daddy shouldn't have threaten my poppa life and maybe they wouldn't have lynched him. I looked at him and said what did you say? He said it again Popeye I tell I lost my mind. I mean I want crazy. I grabbed him by his skinny neck and pushed his head underwater. I held it under until he stopped fighting and kicking. When I let him go his body floated to the top and he wasn't moving. I called his name, but he did say nothing I realize then I had killed him. I was in shock I couldn't move. I looked around to see if anybody was looking. When I didn't see anyone I dragged his body out the water. I stood there looking at him I didn't know what to do. If those white folks find out I killed Billy they would lynch me to. I had to think of something quick. I said to myself I have to make it look like an accident. I saw a big rock in the bushes. I ran over and picked up the rock. Then I hit Billy a couple times in the back of the head until I saw blood to make it look like he hit his head on the pier. Then I dragged his body to the deep part of the lake. I let his body go and he just floated there. I got out of the water and throw the rock in the deep part of the lake. Then I ran all the way to my uncle's house. Later that night they found Billy. The whole town was upset. My uncle told me did I know that someone had killed Mr. Bates boy. No. Yeah somebody busted him in his head and throw him in the lake. People been telling that boy to stop going down to that lake by himself swimming he wouldn't listen. I didn't like that white motherfucker any how he got what he deserved. Tears started running down my face. He looked at me and said boy what the hell you crying for. I liked Billy Jr. he was a good friend to me. Well he dead now ain't know use crying over him now. My momma told my uncle to send me to St. Louis. I left a couple of days after they had found Billy's body. It wasn't until I joined the Army that my uncle found out I had killed Billy. How did he find out? He was the only one who knew I was at that lake with Billy. He was coming home and he seen me crossing Mr. Baxter's corn field. He knew where I was going, because I only go that way to the lake. He also found the shorts I was wearing that day. They had Billy's blood all over them. He burned them that same day. He told me they came looking for me to ask me questions, but he told them I had moved away. Did they do anything to your uncle you know how those white folks are if some white person get killed and they can't from the right person they will blame it on one of us. No they didn't do anything to him. He sold his farm and moved to St. Louis to. He was planning on moving anyway, but before he left he burned down Mr. Bates store for killing his brother. You see Popeye when I kill those Germans I see them as those Klansman who killed my daddy. I wasn't shock at what he was saying some white man had killed my daddy to. I told him that I understood how he felt you was a young boy who saw his daddy get lynched. It ain't right Popeye to done things like that. I have nightmares about what I did to Billy Jr. I'm going to tell you something Popeye when this is all over with I don't want to see another dead body or gun. I'm going to go back to St. Louis marry me a beauty gal have a bunch of kids and live happy ever after. I never heard Sgt talk like this before he was always laughing, joking and playing around, but not this time he was serious. It made me nerves. Popeye he asked me what time is it? It's 1400 hours. You get yourself some rest. Sgt you okay? Yeah Popeye I'm fine. You don't seem like yourself. I'm fine good buddy don't worry bout me. He smiled at me. Okay. I'll be back to wake you up in a couple of hours. Okay Sgt. He walked out the CP into the woods. I sat down in the corner of the CP to sleep a little. It was so cold I couldn't get warm. I had no gloves and the jacket I had on wasn't doing me any good. There was a blanket somebody left I grabbed and put it over me it helped a little, but not much. I sat back in took a deep breathe then I closed my eyes.

CHAPTER THIRTY-FOUR

I STARTED DREAMING ABOUT WHEN I came home from basic training I was so excited when the bus pulled up in front of the station. I had wrote home to tell them when I was coming home.

When the bus pulled up Lillian, Pam, Mrs. Hutchinson and Mr. Sutton was standing there waiting on me. When I got off the bus Lillian almost knocked me down when she hugged me.

Be careful child you know your pregnant Mrs. Hutchinson said. Yeah baby be careful we got us a little Jeffery in there I said. Hey baby how you doing Mrs. Hutchinson said. She gave me a hug. Hey Pam. Hey Jeffery you look sharp in that uniform. Thank you Pam. I did look sharp. How you doing Popeye? I'm doing fine Mr. Sutton. How you doing? You know me same old thing. I made you a nice dinner Jeffery Lillian said. You did! Well lets go eat I'm hungry as hell I can eat a horse. I got my duffle bag and we started walking. Where we going to eat at your momma and daddy's? No we going to the boarding house. The boarding house! Yeah I moved in when you left. I figured since we getting married I didn't want to live with my folks no more. How long you been living there? I moved in two months ago I help Mrs. Hutchinson around the house. She left me stay in a different room. I moved all your things in that room. It's a whole lot bigger then your old room. What room did you move into?

Mr. Larson's old room. What happen to him? He moved out right after you left. Where he go?

He moved to Los Angeles, California for those good factory jobs they have out there. Well good for him. How your momma and daddy doing? They won't you to come by to see them. I will do that after I eat. We got to the house and I could smell the food. I put my stuff down took my jacket off and took a seat at the table. The table was already set. Mrs. Hutchinson had broke out her best china. This had to be special she never uses her good china. Damn baby y'all really out did y'all selves. Lillian and Mrs. Hutchinson cooked a big meal. They cooked collard greens, rice, ham, green beans, corn bread, tea, peach cobbler, sweet potato pie, and my favorite pig feet. I made a pig out of myself. I ain't had a home cooked meal like this in 2 months. I food they feed us a boot camp was the nastiest food I have ever tasted. It made me sick to my stomach. When we finished eating we walked around the neighbourhood to digest my food. How was basic training Jeffery? I looked at her. Not to good baby. What happen? Well we (Negro soldiers) had to always wait on those white boys before we could do anything. They was always laughing and making fun of us like we was stupid. That made me mad. I didn't have it good myself. Why? I had this Sgt always on my back about everything. His name was Leroy Knox. He was from Little Rock, Ark. What did he do to you? Nothing really he just stayed on my case if I did something wrong he was on me.

Isn't that his job to keep you in line. Yeah but I think he went overboard with it. I found out after basic training he really liked me. He told me I was his favorite. So things wasn't that bad then. No the white officers treated us like dirt. Well what did you expect from them.

We would have to clean their barracks for them which they always left a mess on purpose.

Then they would laugh about it. One officer even took a shit on the floor in the head. You lying Jeffery. No I'm not Lillian. So you telling me someone shitted on the floor? Yeah that's what I'm saying. Well who had to clean that mess up? We had to clean that shit up. That was terrible Yeah it was. I'm glad it's over now I can spend more time with you. Did you get all my letters? Yes I did. Has Mrs. Hutchinson been charging you rent to stay here? Yeah she has, but not that much I understand why she does it. How long are you going to be home? I'm going to be here for 10 days than I'll ship out to some truck division in Iowa. Do you think they will send y'all to Germany? I really don't know Lillian they have been talking about it. I hope they don't. I don't know Lillian there are a lot of guys who want to go over there. Do you want to go. No, but If they do send us you know I have to go. We got to her folks house.

When we walked in her momma was sitting in the living room reading a book. Oh my God your (giving me a hug) home. Roscoe come down here and see your future son-in-law. You look sharp in that uniform Jeffery. Thank you ma'am. By this time Roscoe had come downstairs. How you doing boy? We shook hands he had this big smile on his face. Your looking good in that uniform Jeffery. Thank you sir. You can call me Roscoe now you will be family soon. Did Lillian tell you about the wedding? No (looking at Lillian) she didn't. They both gave Lillian this crazy look. I wasn't going to tell him until we got here. Tell me what?

Y'all are getting married on Sunday. Sunday that's tomorrow. Yeah tomorrow during church we figured it would be better. Oh okay I was caught off guard by that. I thought they would at least give me a couple of days. Lillian did write ma and tell me that everything had been taken care of. I didn't think we were getting married as soon as I got back. We are going to have our reception at Mrs. Hattie Place. Alright sounds good to me. Are you hungry Jeffery?

No ma'am Lillian just stuffed me. You stuffed yourself. Come on sit down and tell us about basic training. I sat down on the couch. It was alright I'm glad it's over. How did they treat y'all? They treated us like dirt. I knew they would. You know those white folks don't want us wearing those uniforms. They lynched a Negro solider a couple of days ago in Dallas for wearing his uniform. We heard stories like that in basic training. Our drill instructor told us that it was happening to Negro soldiers all over the country and to watch ourselves. He told us that those white crackers don't want you to wear these uniforms so watch yourself. I was going to take mine off when I got home, but Lillian wanted me to keep it on and besides I earned the right to wear this uniform. Jeffery I turned to see who called me. It was Patrice she came over and gave me a big hug. How you doing? I'm doing fine. Looking good in that uniform. Thanks Patrice. How long are you home for? I'm home for 10 days. 10 days! Yeah that's all the time they gave me. So are you ready for the big day tomorrow? Yeah I'm ready.

Well I just stopped to say hello. You take care. I will. She started walking towards the kitchen stopped gave me this look and disappeared around the corner. I knew Patrice liked me, but we knew we couldn't do anything. I knew what that look meant to. Lillian came back into the living room and sat down next to me. I put my hand on her stomach. It's going to be a boy.

you tell by just touching my stomach? I could feel it. How you know it ain't going to be a girl? I don't know. How come you didn't tell me we were getting married tomorrow? I'm sorry baby I was so happy to see you I just forgot. Did Mrs. Hutchinson know about it? You know she did Jeffery. She was the one who paid for everything. She really do love you Jeffery. While you were gone all she did was talk about you. She even told me how your daddy died. She did! So what did she say? She told me that your daddy got into an argument with this white man name George Clayton at the old sawmill. Yeah I heard that name before.

He told your daddy that he wasn't going to pay him his weeks pay. Your daddy got mad and threaten to go on strike. Mr. Clayton threaten your daddy's life and started calling him all kinds of names. Your daddy got mad and started cussing Mr. Clayton out. They got in each others faces and starting screaming and cussing each other out. When they were arguing they were standing by one of the saws. Mr. Clayton got so mad he pushed your daddy into that saw which cut him open on his side. He started bleeding real bad my daddy and some other men tried to help him, but he bleed to death right there. They told everyone at the sawmill to say it was accident or they were going to lose their jobs. My daddy and a few of the men got together and went on strike. The owner threaten their lives, but they didn't care they went on strike anyway.

Then other men joined the strike. The owner lost so much money from that strike he had to close the sawmill. I couldn't believe what I was hearing. Now why would Mrs. Hutchinson tell Lillian about what happen to my daddy, but she wouldn't tell me.

Why would she tell you and not me? I don't know baby maybe, because you were to young.

She always knew I wanted to know what happen to my daddy. My momma died of a broken heart over that. She got sick and she never recovered. Now I know why Mrs. Hutchinson never spoke to Mr. Clayton. He away had this smile on his face when he saw me. I was mad about it, but I feel a lot better that I know what happen to my daddy. Now as for Mr. Clayton they found him dead in the swamp with his head cut off. They never found out who did it, but I bet it had something with my uncle Johnny leaving Houston. Are you alright baby? Yeah I'm fine baby. She kissed me on my lips. You know we still can make love even though I'm two months pregnant. I know but let's wait until tomorrow. Okay. I better got going and get some rest we got a long day tomorrow. You better do the same. Okay I will. I'll see you at the church tomorrow. She walked me to the door. We kissed. You better not be late tomorrow. Oh I won't Mrs. Hutchinson will make sure of that. We kisseed again and than I left.

CHAPTER THIRTY-FIVE

WHEN I WAS WALKING home in my uniform I felt good. There were people smiling at me, shaking my hand and patting me on my back. It seemed like people had more respect for me now. On my way home I decided to stop by Mr. Bernstein Jewelry store. I didn't have a chance to think him for what he did for me before I left for basic training. When I got over there I could see Mr. Bernstein inside. I knocked on the door. He came and opened the door.

When he opened the door he was shocked to see me standing there in my uniform. Oh Jeffery come in. When I walked in he had all these pictures on his counter. I didn't catch you at a bad time did I? Oh no I'm just looking at some pictures. Please excuse the mess. I see you joined the Army. Yes sir I'm just home on leave. My son's in the Army also. Oh yeah what division is he in? None. None! What do you mean by none? You said he was in the Army right? Yes I did say that, but he's not in the U.S. Army. I don't understand. He's in the German Army. He's fighting for the Nazis. What! Now why would he do that? My son was part of the Hitler youth movement in the 1930's. He could he be part of that? You told me you were Jewish. Yes I did, but I'm Jewish and my wife was German. They brainwashed my son with all that Hitler crap, so when the war in Europe broke out he went to Germany to fight on the side of the Nazis. I haven't heard from him in months. The last time I heard from him he told me he was fighting on the eastern front against the Russians. I took these pictures out to remind me of what he looks like. I picked one of the pictures up and looked at it. He was this skinny white boy with blonde hair and blue eyes. Is there something you wanted Jeffery? Oh yes sir I came by to thank you for the ring you sold me. My fiance loved it. We are going to get married tomorrow. Well congratulations. Thank you. If you aren't doing anything why don't you stop by. Oh I couldn't do that. Why not? I'm Jewish. So what does that got to do with anything you are my guest. Okay if I'm not to busy I'll stop by. Good do you know where the church is right? Yes it's the one on top of that hill over there. Yes that's the one. It's starts at 11:00am. Okay Jeffery I'll be there. Well I better be going I got a long day tomorrow. I'll see you tomorrow. Good night. We shook hands and I left. When I got home Mrs. Hutchinson was sitting on the porch. How you doing Jeffery? I'm good how you doing? You ready for your big day tomorrow?

Yes ma'am I am. Sit down Jeffery and let me talk to you for a minute. You know Jeffery marriage is a big responsibility. Yes ma'am I know this. You being the man it's going to be your responsibility to take care of your family. You joining the Army you know that you might get killed. Well the way things are going they might not let us fight. All they want us to do is hard labor. Well it don't matter if you do or don't you love your wife with all your heart and respect her. My husband died in World War1 I never got a chance to tell him how much I loved him. Don't ever take what you got for granted. You love that girl and don't you let anyone come between y'all you hear me. Yes ma'am. When she was telling me all this she was holding my hand so hard she almost broke it. She had this serious look on her face when she was telling me this. Sunny is going to be your best man. Do you have the rings? Yes ma'am. Don't give those rings to Sunny until you get to the church he might lose them.

Now you go get some rest you got a big day tomorrow. Okay I kissed on her forehead and went in the house. I picked up my duffle bag and went upstairs. I started to go to my old room when I remembered Lillian told me she moved my things into Mr. Larson old room. When I opened the door I could smell Lillian's perfume. I cut the light on the room was spotless. I would have never keep this room that clean. The room was bigger than I thought you could fit my room in here. No wonder Mr. Larson paid more rent than everyone else. There was a nice size bed with a brass headboard, a long mirror dresser, a tall chest and there was a rocking chair in the corner. There was a fresh coat of paint on the walls. I was really impressed what Lillian had done with the little money I sent to her. I put my duffle bag down took my jacket off and unpacked my bag. I took the rings out and put them on the dresser. I took out a new shirt and pants for tomorrow. I took off my uniform and got into bed. The bed was real soft it was better than those hard bunks we had to sleep on in basic training. The scent from Lillian's perfume was all over the pillows. I took a long snuff of her perfume I smiled and went to sleep.

CHAPTER THIRTY-SIX

A KNOCK AT MY DOOR woke me up the Sunday morning. You up in there Jeffery? Yes I'm up. Okay get yourself together and come downstairs for some breakfast. Okay I'll be down in a few. I got up and walk to the window to see what the weather was like. It was a nice sunny day. I could see the flowers starting to blossom in Mrs. Hutchinson garden. I looked at my watch it was 0930 hours. I grabbed my ditty bag a towel and headed to the bathroom. I remembered in basic training we took showers not baths to my surprise Mr. Sutton had installed a shower head. I shaved, brushed my teeth and took a nice hot shower. That hot shower felt good the water in basic training was always cold for us, but those white boys always got hot showers. I didn't want to get out, but I had to. I dried off put on my uniform grabbed my cover and went downstairs. Mrs. Hutchinson was in the kitchen cooking breakfast. Oh Jeffery you look good in that uniform. Thank you. Cover over here and give me a hug. I walked over and gave her a hug. You got the rings? Oh no I ran back upstairs and grabbed the rings off my chest. You can't forget those Jeffery. I know. Now you sit down here and eat you something. I cooked this breakfast especially for you I cooked all your favorites.

She cooked biscuits, ham ,eggs, girts, bacon and pancakes. I didn't make a pig out of myself, because I knew there was going to be a lot of food at the reception, so I just put a little of everything on my plate.

Mrs. Hutchinson pour me a cup of coffee. I picked the cup up to take a sip my hand was shaking so bad I almost spilled my cup. I put the cup down. Mrs.

Hutchinson didn't see that she had her back turned washing dishes. I took a deep breath and picked the cup up again my hand was still shaking. I put it back down. This time Mrs.

Hutchinson saw it. You alright Jeffery you seem real nerves. I'm very nerves I can't hold my cup of coffee for my hand shaking so bad. You got what we call cold feet. I know how you feel my daddy had to stand by my husband with a shotgun to make sure he didn't run away.

What! Yeah he sure did. Your daddy wasn't going to shoot him was he? Yeah he was going to shoot him if he tried to run. Mrs. Hutchinson can I ask you a question? Sure baby go ahead.

Did you ever have any kids? Yes I did I had a daughter her name was Denise. What happen to her? She died when she was a baby. She from the Influenza pandemic. She was the only child I could have. I'm sorry to hear that. Oh that's okay baby it was a long time ago, but God works in mysterious ways. What do you mean by that? I always wanted to have children, but I couldn't. When your momma died God gave me you. You mean a lot to me Jeffery you are like a son I never had. I know I don't show you that I care, but trust me Jeffery I love you and I'm going to miss you while your gone. You will have your own family soon and you won't be needing me anymore. Oh don't say that (tears started running down her face) I'm going to need someone to look after Lillian while I'm gone. She has her family to do that. I know but she'll be staying here I want you to look after her like you looked after me when my momma died. I knew it was one of her guilt trips, but who could blame her I was her only child. Come on now finish up we got to leave in a few. I don't want you to be late I'm going to go upstairs and change I'll be back down in a few. Okay. I finished my food and drink my coffee. My hand had stopped shaking by this time. I grabbed my cover and waited for Mrs. Hutchinson to come downstairs. I looked at my watch it was 1015 hours. Mrs. Hutchinson came downstairs looking better than I have ever seen her. She was wearing a white dress that had different color flowers all over it a white hat with a big white bow on it, tan stocking, a white purse and a white pearl necklace around her neck. She was ever wearing makeup something I have never seen her wear. I was shocked when she came downstairs. Well look at you. You look beautiful Mrs. Hutchinson. Thank you Jeffery. Come let's get going. Where's Mr. Sutton? He's going to meet us at the church. When we walked out the door there was a taxi sitting in front of the house. A big heavy dark skin man was standing by the taxi and opened the door for Mrs. Hutchinson. Morning Mrs. Hutchinson. Morning Joe. It was Joe Dangle. He was the owner of the yellow cab company in the 5th ward. I didn't know him that well I heard Mr.

Sutton mention his name a couple of times. They would use his taxis to run moonshine. I how you doing young man? I heard you are getting married today. Yes sir I am. Well congratulations. Thank you and we got in the taxi and headed to the church. My stomach started to feel funny I know it's just my nerves. Mrs. Hutchinson grabbed my hand and told me it was going to be alright you are marrying a good woman. I smiled at her and said okay.

We got to the church it was 10:30am. The taxi stopped in front of the church there were a lot of people standing out in front. I didn't know Lillian had all these friends. I knew they weren't my friends. When I got out of the taxi Lillian's brother Larry came running up to me. Hey Popeye come on they are waiting for you in the church. Go ahead Jeffery I'll see you inside the church. Okay I kissed her and followed Larry into the church. Man I'm glad you are here Popeye. Why you say that? They thought that you weren't going to show up. Now why would they think that? I don't know, but my pops was going to come looking for you with his shot gun. What! Yeah. This was crazy Mrs. Hutchinson just told me how her daddy did her husband. Larry took me to the Pastor's office to meet him. He knocked on the door. Come in a deep voice said. When we walked in Mr. Crawford and some other man sitting on the couch was there. So you finally mad it Jeffery? Yes sir I did. How you son I'm Pastor (getting up off the couch) Fred Crawford. How you (shaking hands) doing sir. Jeffery this is my younger brother Fred. Oh really I didn't know you had any brothers. Yeah I got six brothers and we all were going to come looking for you if you didn't show up. Oh I was going to show up. When we were taking another man came into the room. Jeffery this here is my junior Pastor Bobby Joe Cole. How you doing Jeffery you are marrying a wonderful woman. Thank you. Than a little boy came and told the Pastor they were ready for y'all. Alright Sammy we will be out in a few minutes. You ready Jeffery? Yeah I'm ready. Okay than lets go. We all walked out the office into the church. Mr. Sutton was already standing there waiting on me. I walked over and stood next to him. You got the rings? Yeah I got them. I took the box out of my pocket and gave it to him. The Pastor waved his to signal to start the wedding. Mrs.

Mrs. Owens started playing the wedding music. She's been playing that old piano since I was a little boy. The church doors opened up and everyone stood up. A cute little girl with a basket full of flowers came walking in dropping flowers as she walked. A little boy around the same age came in carrying a pillow with nothing on it. It suppose to have the rings on it, but I had them. He was followed by Lillian's sisters Pam, Patrice and some other woman I have never seen before. Then Lillian came in escorted down the aisle by her daddy Roscoe. She looked beautiful in that long white dress and veil covering her face. I wonder where she got the money to buy a dress like that? The only person I could think of was Mrs. Hutchinson. The closer she got the more my knees started to shake. Mr. Sutton had to put his hand on my shoulder to calm me down. He whispered in my ear it's going to be fine Jeffery take it easy. I could feel the sweat started to drip down my forehead. The Pastor looked at me and asked me. Are you alright son? Yeah I'm fine. When Lillian got to me my knees stopped shaking, but I continued to sweat. I knew now that I was marrying the woman of my dreams. Everyone sat down and the Pastor started the ceremony. This went for about 5 minutes or so than he told us to face each other. Than asked me do I take Lillian and my wife? I said yes. He asked Lillian the same thing. She said yes. Than he asked for the rings. Mr. Sutton gave him the rings. Than he told me to say these words as I put the ring on

Lillian's finger. Than he told Lillian to do the same. Now I pronounce you man and wife. You may now kiss your bride. I lifted up Lillian's veil and gave her the biggest kiss of her life. Then he told us to turn around.

There was an old broom laying down in front of us. Now jump over the broom in God's glory as one. We jumped over it hand and hand. When we did that everyone started clapping.

Everyone started hugging and kissing us. Mrs. Hutchinson came up to me and gave me a big hug. You better take good care of my daughter you understand me Jeffrey. Yes sir I will take good care of her. We started walking out the church. People were lined up on both sides throwing rice at us. When we got outside there was a car waiting to take us to the reception.

We got in and headed towards Mrs. Hattie Place.

CHAPTER THIRTY-SEVEN

WE WERE ON OUR way to Mrs. Hattie Place when Lillian told me that we weren't having it over there. Why Not? Mrs Hutchinson and Mrs. Hattie got into an argument over the price to rent it out, so we are having it over my folks house. Okay no problem. She also told me that she was scared. Why? This is a big step in my life Jeffery. I know baby but we are going to be fine. You know my knees were shaking so bad if it had not been for Mr. Sutton I would have passed out. Really you were that nerves. Yeah. We both started laughing. When we got to the house they had everything set up. They put us at the bride and groom table. There was a huge cake on one of the tables. It had to be about four layers high. The local baker gave it to us as a wedding gift. There was lots of food. I can't tell you everything, but they had my favorite food pig feet. Even Mr.

Bernstein came like he said. Congratulations. Thank you Mr. Bernstein. You treat this beautiful lady like a queen, because you may never find anyone like her. I will. Patrice came up to me and hugged me while she was hugging me she whispered in my ear. Well I guess there ain't know chance of you and I getting together. No there isn't. I'm happy for y'all Jeffery. Thanks Patrice. I always knew she liked me. Brenda who I ain't seen in months came over and gave Lillian a hug. Hey Brenda (giving her a hug). Hey Popeye how you doing? You look good in that uniform. Thank you. Where you been? I been in Dallas.

Dallas! What are you doing in Dallas? I live there with my boyfriend. Oh yeah. Yeah when Mrs. Hutchinson went to Dallas to see her sister I went with her. When I was there I met this guy, so I decided to stay. We going to get married when he come back home. Where he at?

He in California now. He's in the Navy. Oh really well good for him. Yeah his ship going to be going to the South Pacific soon. What ship is he on? He on the USS Yorktown. What is his name? His name is Danny Holmes. I can't believe y'all got married. Popeye I can't believe how good you look in that uniform. Hey now you better watch yourself that my husband you talking to. We all started laughing. Who told you we was getting married. You know who told me why you ask me that question. I know who she was talking about Mrs. Hutchinson. When you going back to Dallas? I'm going back tomorrow. When I heard y'all was getting married you knew I had to come. Well I'm glad you came. Well I'm going to leave you two love birds alone I'm going to get something to eat. She ain't changed a bit I said to myself. When Mrs.

Hutchinson came over to the table. Y'all come on and let's cut this cake. I grabbed Lillian by her hand and took her over to the table where the cake was. We both grabbed the cake cutter and cut a slice of cake. Folks was taken pictures (pictures we would lose in a house fire) while we mashed cake in our faces. The reception went on for hours. Lillian and I were really enjoying ourselves. The guest started to leave around 9:00 the last people to leave was Mrs. Hutchinson and Mr. Sutton. They left around 10pm. I'll see y'all two tomorrow she said.

Okay see y'all tomorrow. Y'all be careful going home I said. Okay we will. I walked them to the door Fat Joe was sitting in his taxi waiting on them. Let me help you Mrs. Hutchinson. Fat Joe helped Mrs. Hutchinson put Mr. Sutton in the taxi. Mr. Sutton had gotten drunk off that moonshine they had made. They got him in and she waved at me and they left. I went back in the house. I told Pam I was tired. I'm tired to and I didn't get married. I'm going to go help momma clean up. Okay. I went in the living room and sat on the couch. Lillian had already went upstairs to bed. I was sitting on the couch thinking about the all the responsibilities of a family man I got now. I was also thinking what if I get killed who going to take care of my family. Now I'm wondering if I did the right thing by joining the Army. Then Mrs. Crawford came into the living room. You alright Jeffery? Yes ma'am I'm fine. Jeffery we are family now you can call me Mary. Okay Mary. I'm so happy for you and Lillian. Lillian needed a good man. These other fools out here wouldn't have treated her right all they wanted was to use and abuse her. To tell you the truth I didn't think much of you when I first saw you. I didn't think you was Lillian's type, but the more I got to know you I could see how happy you made her. All she did was talk about you while you was gone. I'm glad you're back, because she was getting on my nerves talking about you all the time. I grabbed her hand and told her thank you for everything. Oh you welcome Jeffery. Mrs. Hutchinson paid for everything. You make sure you tell I said thank you. I will. Well I'm going to go to bed I'm tired it's been a long day. You get you some sleep to. She kissed me on my cheek got up and went upstairs. I said goodnight to Pam. Goodnight she said. I started upstairs when I ran into Patrice. You going to bed now? Yeah. We was so close our lips was almost touching. She brushed up against me as she went downstairs. Goodnight she said. I almost got a hard on when she brushed up against me. I got upstairs and cut the light on Lillian was in bed already. I stood there and looked at her for a minute she look like an angel lying there. I walked to the bed leaned over and kissed her on her soft lips. She smiled and opened her eyes. You coming to bed she said. Yeah let me take off this uniform. I took my uniform off throw it on the chair turned the light off and got in bed. The bed was warm when I got in. I laid down next to my new wife, but I could feel she was naked. Why you still got on your boxers. We not going to make love in your folks house are we? Why not we married now. They are going to hear us. So what they ain't going to say nothing. I was surprise she said that, so I took my boxers off and she grabbed my dick I got hard as a rock. We made love all though the night.

CHAPTER THIRTY-EIGHT

THE NEXT MORNING WE were awaken by a knock on the door. Jeffery and Lillian y'all up? It was Patrice. No we ain't up leave us alone. She opened the door ans stuck her head in. Y'all need to get up. We up now closed the door girl. I was playing like I was sleeping. You ain't sleep Jeffery , so stop faking it. Get out of here Patrice. She just wanted to see if we was doing something with her nosie self. She leaned over and kissed me on my lips then started playing with my manhood. Alright now you know what going to happen. What going to happen? We got out of bed an hour later. We got up took a shower together (make love) got dressed and went downstairs. The house was empty. Where is everybody Lillian? They at work today is Monday. The only one who ain't at work is Patrice and Larry they in school.

Why ain't you in school? I graduated while you was gone. You did! Why you ain't tell me baby. I didn't won't to tell you until after we got married, so what are we going to our first day as husband and wife? First you can fix me something to eat and then we are going to go out and look for a place of our own. I don't won't you staying here and I don't won't you staying with Mrs. Hutchinson she will work you to death if you stay there. You need to take it easy with our baby on the way. I don't won't nothing to happen to that baby okay. Okay. We ate a nice breakfast of eggs, bacon, grits and toast. I got the apartment section of the paper her father was reading. We seen couple in the paper we liked and circled them. Let's start with the one's over on south street she said. I been over there a couple of times. How do the apartments look over there? They are brand new they were just built a couple years ago. My auntie and uncle live over there. Which uncle I asked? Pastor Crawford. Oh hell no I don't want to live by him. Why? He's going to want us to come to church with them all the time and he going to be in our business. Than he will start to get on my nerves. Yeah you right about that. He can really get on your nerves, so what do you want to do? Let's look somewhere else if we can't find a place than we will look over there by them okay? Okay. We left the house about 12:00pm It was a nice sunny day you can smell the spring in the air. We had to find a place quick, because I was leaving soon. We look all day and didn't find nothing. We didn't even bother looking in the 5th ward, because ain't nothing there. The upper 5th ward had all the good homes. That's where all the light-skin Negros lived. They thought they was better then anybody darker then them. They wouldn't even talk to you if you was darker than them.

The lighter you was the better chances you had. The white man didn't see it that way. A Nigga was a Nigga to him if you was high yellow or blue black it didn't matter. A lot of Lillian's friends asked her why would she marry a man like me. I didn't care what her friends think of me most of them didn't have a man. After about three days of looking we find this one place that wasn't in the paper. We were walking downtown when we saw this two story red brick building. We went to see if they had any apartments for rent. I ain't never seen this place before Jeffery it must be new. Yeah it must be. I knocked on the door to the office a tall light skin man with his hair sticked back came to the door. What do you need he asked us. My wife and I are looking for a place to rent. He looked us up and down and then told us to come in.

We followed him down this long hallway that was brightly lit. In here he said. We went into a room that was turned into an office. It had a wooden desk with papers all over it. A file cabinet in the corner. An ugly green sofa that sat against the back wall. There was a table with a coffee pot on it with a few cups. Have a sat he said. We sat in the two metal chairs in front of the desk. Can I get y'all some coffee he said? No thanks we said. He poured himself a cup and sat down behind the desk. Let me introduce myself my name is Earl Meekins. I own this this apartment building. It use to be an old warehouse, but my father fixed it up and turned it into these apartments. It took him three years to do it. How come it's not in the paper? The reason it's not in the paper is that we only want certain kind of people living here. Lillian and I looked at each other. What do you mean by certain kind of people? What I mean by that is this. We don't want anyone who are drunks, loud mouths, can't pay their rent on time, always getting into fights with their spouses. Well Mr. Meekins you don't have to worry about my wife and I we are not like that. Okay good. I'm sorry I didn't get your names. My name is Jeffery Ross. This here is my wife Lillian we just got married. Oh yeah I heard about that. You did.

Yeah news travel fast here. Well congratulations on your marriage. Thank you. So you looking for a place to stay. Yes we are my wife is having our first child and I don't want her living with her folks. I'm leaving soon and I want her in her own place. Where you going? I'm in the Army. Oh yeah I have know desire to fight that white man's war. He sounded like me about four months ago. So how many rooms you looking for? Just a one bedroom for now.

He picked up this book off his desk and turned a couple of pages. You in luck I got a one bedroom available. A tenant just moved out a couple days ago. He joined the Army to. Oh yeah well can we see the apartment. Yeah he got up and went over to this black box hanging on the wall. The box was full of keys and took one out. Okay follow me It's on the first floor. I grabbed Lillian by the hand and we followed him. We walked down the long hallway to the end of it. He it is 5A. He unlocked the door and we went in. It was much bigger then I expected. Wow Lillian said this is nice Jeffery. Take a look around. We walked around. It had hardwood floors, a gas shove, windows in each room and heaters to keep the place warm in the winter. How you like it Lillian? I love it. So you like the place? Yeah we like how much do you went for it? The rent is $60.00 a month. I'm going to need first month and next months rent. This that just to move in. Yes it is. I don't have that type of money right now, but if you give me a couple of months I'll have it. A couple of months it might not be here. Yeah a couple of months your not in the news paper how many people know about this place? Not too many. You also said you wanted certain type of people living here right? Yeah. My wife and I are good people. He looked at us. Okay how much do you have? I got bout $50.00 dollars on me now. I reach in my pocket and pulled the money out. If you can give me another $50.00 dollars I'll let you have it. Jeffery you can get the other $50.00 dollars from Mrs. Hutchinson you know she will do anything for you. I know she will, but I know I'm going to have to do something in return. Then your going to have to what you got to do I want this place. I hated asking her for anything, but if I wanted that money I had to shallow my pride and ask her after all she did pay for my wedding. I'm only doing this for Lillian. Okay Mr.

Mr. Meekins we going to take it. Okay good. Give me until tomorrow and I will have the rest of the money. Okay than I'll see you tomorrow. We shook hands then we left. When we got outside Lillian asked me, so your going to ask Mrs. Hutchinson for the money? Yeah as a matter of fact I'm going to ask her right now. Come on let me walk you home first than I will go over there and ask her for the money. I walked Lillian home. I'll be back in a little bit. Okay.

We kissed and I started walking towards the boarding house. On may way over there I kept thinking if she's going to want a favor from me. I hate asking her for anything, because I know she going to want something in return. When I got to the house there was no one around. I looked around and didn't see anyone. Now this was odd for Mrs. Hutchinson is always in the house or sitting on the porch. I walked to the back porch to see if she was there. I seen her coming out of the barn. Hey Jeffery how you doing? I'm fine what are you doing in the barn? I was checking on my moonshine we made some last night. I'm glad you here baby you can help Mr. Sutton and Larry. Larry! Lillian's brother? Yeah. Mrs. Hutchinson I don't think he should be doing this. If Roscoe found out he going kill you and Larry. He ain't going to do shit. Roscoe use to run moonshine to. I wish he would bring his big ass over here. I'll shot his ass and he knows it. I needed somebody to help move it. You ain't here no more. I was glad to I was tired of that shit. Who we taking this moonshine to? Y'all taking it to this guy name Bobby Joe Raines. Who's he? He one of my new customers. Have you ever done business with this guy before? No. So do you know what type of person he is? He a nice man he got himself this jute joint down in the 9th ward. He need some moonshine to get started. Mrs. Hutchinson the 9th ward is worse then the 5th ward nobody goes over there. I go over there all the time that's how I met him. My stomach started feeling funny I got this feeling this Bobby Joe guy ain't a nice person. Where is Mr. Sutton and Larry? They are in the barn loading the moonshine onto the truck. When they leaving? In a few minutes you go and help them finish loaded the truck. Okay.

CHAPTER THIRTY-NINE

I WALKED OUT TO THE barn where they was at. Hey Popeye. Hey Larry. How you doing Mr Sutton? I'm doing fine. What you doing over here? I thought you would be a much time with your new wife. I came by to see how y'all was doing. You sure you came over to see us or that you need something He gave me this look when he said that. Mr. Sutton ain't no fool he know I wouldn't come over here unless I needed something. Anyway Mrs. Hutchinson told me to help y'all finish loading the truck. Well we are finished now. She said y'all taking it to the 9th ward to some guy name Bobby Joe Raines. Mr. Sutton looked at me and didn't say anything. That look told me that he didn't like what they was about to do. Yeah we going over there. Well I'm going with y'all. Good I'm gonna need you he said. Okay let's go. We all get in the truck I sat in the middle since I was the smallest Mr. Sutton was driving. We were about to pull off when he stopped the truck got out went to the tool drawer and took out his .22. I didn't like this we never needed know gun when we delivered moonshine. We might need this where we going. Here hold this. He gave me the gun to hold I put the gun in my pocket.

Then we started on our way to the 9th ward. I don't like Sissy dealing with this Nigga Bobby Joe. Sissy who the hell is Sissy? Sissy that's Mrs. Hutchinson nickname Larry said. What!

Yeah it's true Mr. Sutton said. How come nobody ever told me? She

The Men that Time has Forgotten

didn't want you calling her that. So what's up with this Bobby Joe? He a shady motherfucker he killed a man a couple of years ago over two dollars. Two dollars! Yeah two dollars I told Sissy not to deal with this Nigga, but she won't listen. Now I was scared just my luck we go over here and something might happen and I get shot. What we are going to do is drop this moonshine off to this Nigga and get the fuck out of there. I don't trust this Bobby Joe motherfucker .

The 9th ward was on the other side of Houston. It was a rundown part of the city where all the people who lost hope during the depression live. It was the kind of place where you didn't go unless you lived over there or you came over there with someone who lived there. It had rundown shacks, pimps, whores, drunks, drug dealers and junkies. The 5th ward was a paradise compared to this place. I would never rise my family in place like that. I don't want Lillian living in the 5th ward upper or lower. I'm going to make sure my family gets the best and the Army going to do that for me. As we drove through the streets everybody stops and looks at us. I didn't feel good about this at all. Mr. Sutton I don't know about this. Don't worry Popeye it going to be alright. It didn't seem to bother Larry though. We turned down this dirt road and pulled up in front of this half-way deceit shack it looked better then the ones we passed though town. Before we got out Mr. Sutton asked me to check the .22 to see if it was loaded. I checked the barrel yeah it's loaded. Larry go knock on the door Mr. Sutton told him.

Larry gets out and goes knock on the door. A short skinny woman wearing a rag on her head came to the door. Whatca won't she asked Larry. We got this package for Bobby Joe. Hold on she said then she closed the door. After about 2 minutes she came back. He said to drive around back he's going to meet y'all back there. What she say Mr. Sutton asked Larry. She said go round back. She came out and opened the broke down gate and we drove to the back. There was two big men about Larry size standing there with shotguns. One of them put his hand out to stop the truck. What you got one of them asked. We got some moonshine for Bobby Joe. How much y'all got? I got about 5 cases 7 bottles in each case. He looked at the other man nodded and he went in the house. I don't like this I told Mr. Sutton. Be cool it's going to be fine. The big man came out followed by a short dark skin man wearing overalls.

He walked up to the truck I see you still running hooch Sunny. Yeah I still do it a little not as much as I use to. You got the money? He reached in his pocket to get the money, but before we knew it he had pulled out a .22 pistol and pointed it at Mr. Sutton head. It was so fast I didn't have time to pull out my pistol out. Get your motherfucking ass out that damn truck now. The two big men had their shotguns pointed at us. Mr. Sutton opened the truck door and we got out. Any of you Niggas move I'll drop you where you stand. You two Niggas (pointing at me and Mr. Sutton) get on y'all knees. Little Bow go get Skinny and Shorty to help unload this hooch. He went to the door and called for them to come out. The skinny girl and a guy with a limp came running out and started taking the moonshine off the truck.

Bobby Joe it ain't got to be like this. Shut up Nigga and he hit Mr. Sutton in the head with the gun. Mr. Sutton fell to the ground holding his head. I went to help him when Bobby Joe told you better not move Nigga. I looked at him and he had this smile on his face. I thought to myself if I could get my gun out I would blow his head off. I could see out the corner of my eye Larry reached in his overalls. One of the big men won't paying attention he was to busy looking at them unload the moonshine. Larry pulled out his .45 pistol and shot him in his head. He didn't have a chance. His brains and blood flew all over the truck. Bobby Joe was in shock before he could shot Larry. Larry shot him in his chest and he fell on top of Mr. Sutton.

Come on Larry said. Get in the truck and let's get the fuck out of here. I pushed Bobby Joe off Mr. Sutton and we got up and jumped in the truck. Mr. Sutton grabbed Bobby Joe gun before he got in the truck. Little Bow heard the shots and came running out shooting at the truck. Mr. Sutton put the car in drive and sped off kicking up dust everywhere. He lost control of the truck and Little Bow fired at us the bullets was ricocheting off the truck. When the truck spun around Larry shot Little Bow in his neck when he stopped to reload. The Big man went down holding his neck. Larry got out and started checking his pockets. What the FUCK are you doing? Get you're ass in this truck and let's get out of here. Mr. Sutton got control of the truck. Larry jumped in. Go, Go, Go, Go he said. Mr. Sutton floored the engine we busted though the gate. That's when the man with the limp came running out shooting at us. We was gone by that time. Popeye how come you didn't use that gun I gave Mr. Sutton said. Yeah you in the Army now I thought you was gonna shoot somebody Larry said. I couldn't talk because I was in shock. How you gonna fight in the war when you can't shoot nobody Larry said. Did you get the money Mr. Sutton asked. Yeah I got it he said. I knew that fat motherfucker had that money. How much is it Larry? Let me count it first. 20,40,60,80,100 it's $350 dollars here. I told Sissy that Nigga was a shady motherfucker. What about the police I said. What about them. They ain't going to say anything, because if they do they are going to jail. Sissy going to take care of that she have a way of taken care of stuff like this. This ain't the first time this has happen. We raced back to the 5th ward. I was so glad to be back there.

CHAPTER FORTY

WE GOT TO THE house Mrs. Hutchinson was sitting on the porch waiting on us. We pulled up in front of the house. What took y'all so long? We ran into some trouble your friend Bobby Joe.

He tried to rob us Mr. Sutton told her. What! Yeah I told you that Nigga wasn't any good, but you wouldn't listen. Larry had to kill two of them so we can get the hell out of there. Oh my God y'all alright? You alright Jeffery? Yeah he's alright he was scared to death. How much of the moonshine did they take? Popeye go see how many cases they took. I ran to the truck and yelled back 3 cases. They only took 3 cases that ain't too bad.. One of them had about $350.00 on him Larry told Mrs. Hutchinson. Oh yeah let me see it. Larry took the money out and gave it to her. This is will cover the 3 cases they took. I stood by the truck for a minute trying to understand what just happen. I was in a gunfight and I was too scared to fire a shot.

What going to happen when I get in a real gunfight with those Germans. I reached in my pocket and took out the .22. The last time I had a gun in my hand was in basic training and I barely passed that. I feel like a coward. That's what Mr. Sutton and Larry thinks I am. Mr. Sutton yelled to me to come over to the porch. Here you take this. He gave me the money Larry took off Little Bow. You take it go get that apartment you and your wife was looking at.

How did you know about that? Mr. Meekins told me you was over there earlier today. He and I go back a long ways. Now go home to your wife and don't tell her anything about what just happen. You understand me. Yeah I understand. What's going to happen to y'all? Don't worry about us baby I'm going to take care of it. Now you go on. She kissed me on my cheek and I left. I looked back to see her, Mr. Sutton and Larry go into the house talking about something. I guess about what happen. I started walking fast then I started to run. I was running so fast it only took me a few minutes to get to Lillian's house. I stopped at the front steps and sat down to catch my breath. I took out the money Mrs. Hutchinson had gave me to see how much it was. I started to count it and realize she had gave me all the $350.00 dollars. I didn't know if I wanted it two men had died over this money, but I knew we needed it. I was sitting on the steps thinking when the door swung open behind me.

I thought that was you. Why you sitting out here? I just wanted to sit out here for a minute and get some fresh air. Did you see Mrs. Hutchinson? Yeah I seen her. Did you ask her for the rest of the money? No I didn't for the money ask her. Why not? Because Mr. Sutton gave it to me. Oh that was nice of him to do that. How much did he give you? I gave her the roll of money. He gave you all this? Yep he told me it was a wedding gift from him. How much is this Jeffery it looks like a lot. It's $350.00 dollars. $350.00! where did he got all this money from? He told me he saved it up from running moonshine. I had to lied to Lillian if she knew where that money came from she wouldn't want anything to do with me or that money. I grabbed her hand and sat her on my lap. Now we can get that place we were looking at and some furniture too. Yeah we can. We kissed. What's wrong. Nothing I'm just happy we are going to get our own place. Me to. You hungry? Yeah what did you cook? Well I didn't cook my momma did. Okay let's go see what she cooked. We want in the house and Lillian fixed me a nice plate of food. I ate my meal I was full as usual. I walk outside to the back porch took a smoke. I started smoking in boot camp to calm my nerves all that yelling and cussing made me nervous. The first time I tried it was with this guy name Kenny Woods he was from N.Y.C. He told me it would calm my nerves. I almost choked the first time I tried it, but after a while I got the hang of it. Lillian came outside. Are you smoking Jeffery? Where did you pick up that nasty habit? It's not a nasty habit it calms my nerves. Oh ya I don't want you smoking around me and this baby. I got mad when she said that. I turned to her and said. Woman don't you tell me what to do.

Lillian had this shocked look on her face when I said that. You don't know what I'm about to get myself into baby. I seen pictures of that war and it's not pretty Lillian. They showed us pictures in basic training of men with their arm, legs, hands and even their heads blown off.

I'm scared baby for the first time I realize I could get killed in this war. If that happens I will never see you again. She put her arms around me as I started to cry. I have never cried in front of anyone not even when my momma and daddy died. It going to be alright. We going to pray about it and put it in God's hands. Yeah you are right. I felt a little better when she said that. My momma always told me when you feel bad pray that will make you feel better. It's getting late we need to get some rest, so we can go see Mr. Meekins tomorrow. Yeah I'm tired anyway. Jeffery would you do me a favor? Sure baby what is it? Would you please not smoke while you are here. Okay I took the pack out of my pocket and throw it in the trash. We said goodnight to everyone went upstairs to bed. I didn't realize how late it was. I didn't sleep well that night, because of what happen earlier that day. I finally fell asleep around 2:00am. As soon as I fell asleep good the alarm clock went off. We got up I was still tired from yesterday got dressed ate breakfast and we headed over to Mr. Meekins place. It was around 9:00am when we got to the apartment. Mr. Meekins was sitting on his steps when we got there.

Morning. he had this big grin on his face when he said that. I knew what that meant he knew we had the money. How y'all doing this morning? We doing fine I said. You here so that means you got the rest of the money. Yeah we got it, but I won't to see the apartment again.

The Men that Time has Forgotten

Why you want to see it again? You seen it yesterday. Yeah I know, but I want to see it again.

He looked at me funny. I thought you said you was coming back yesterday? We were, but I ran into some problems. Are you going let us see the apartment or do I have to take my money somewhere else. This big smile came over his face. He got up and open the door for us. Right this way. I made him show us the place again to let him know who was in charge.

So do you like it? Oh yeah we like it Lillian said. Now I'm going to need first and next months rent. How much did you say the rent was? I wanted to test him to see if he was going to tell us the same price. It's $80.00 a month. You said yesterday $60.00 dollars a month yesterday Lillian said to him. Are you trying to scam us Mr. Meekins? No. Then why are you asking for $20.00 dollars more? Well this is one of the bigger apartments. So you didn't tell us that yesterday. Do you know Sunny Sutton? Yeah I know him we go back a long way. Why you asking? He told me you were good people. Now if I went back and told him you was trying to scam us. What would he think of you as a person. He looked at us with this sad look. Alright then it's $60.00 dollars. So it's a deal? Yeah it's a deal. I owe you $70.00 dollars, because I gave you $50.00 dollars yesterday. We shook hands and I gave him the $70.00 dollars. I gave him next month rent also. When are you moving in? We are going to be moving in real soon. We walked down to his office we signed our lease agreement he gave us the key and we left. When we got outside Lillian started jumping up and down. We got our own place I'm so happy. Now we need to go look for some furniture for the apartment we have a enough to get some. The next couple of days we were running around buying things for our new apartment. Family and friends pinched in we they could. By the end of the week we had moved into our new apartment. I had one day left before I shipped out. That Sunday evening we spent it alone in our apartment. We were sitting on our couch listening to the Jack Benny show on the new radio her daddy gave us as a house warming gift. Jeffery. Yeah baby. I want you to come back to me alive. You are going to have a child to raise and a child needs it's daddy. I will baby I promise. I held her in my arms I love you so much Lillian I promise you I Will be back. We started kissing passionately. We went to bed we made love all through the night. I didn't care if I had to get up early I just wanted to be with my wife.

CHAPTER FORTY-ONE

I WOKE UP AROUND 3:45AM that morning. I woke Lillian up and told her to get up and get dressed. I told her I had to be at the bus station at 5:00am. Do you want me to fix you something to eat? You know I do, because this will be my last home cooked meal for a while.

She got up put on her robe went in the kitchen and started cooking breakfast. I could smell the bacon when I was getting myself together. All I could think about is what have I gotten myself into. I'm leaving my pregnant wife to fight a war I swore I wouldn't get involved with. I sat back down on the bed thinking this might be the last time I ever see her. Tears started to run down my face. I made up my mind that I won't getting on that bus. They are not going to miss me and besides they don't want us in this war anyway. I got up went into the kitchen and told Lillian that I won't getting on that bus I was staying with her. A smile came over her face. She came over and hugged me. You have to get on that bus you know those white folks are going to send some people after you and when they find you they going to shoot you or put you in jail for a long time. Than what am I going to do? Who's going to take care of me and this baby? You have to go Jeffery. Then she kissed me and told me she's going to be alright. She was right they will shot me. They told us in basic training if you try to desert. They will shoot you. Come sit down and eat your breakfast. I smiled at her sat down and ate me food. I ate until I was full, because I wanted to sleep on the bus all the way to Iowa. I finished my breakfast and packed the rest of my things.

Lillian was getting dressed while I was packing. I put on my uniform jacket then my cover. I looked at myself in the mirror. You look very handsome in that uniform. I turned around and kissed her it feels good for some who loves you to say something like that to you most of my life I felt like I was ugly. No one ever told me I was handsome. You ready to go? Yeah I'm ready let's go. We was about to open the door when someone knocked on the door. I opened the door and there was Larry standing there. Hey Larry what are you doing here this early in the morning? I came to drive y'all to the bus station. So daddy let you drive the truck Lillian asked to him? Yeah they know I can drive. Let me get that bag for you Popeye. He grabbed my bag and went downstairs. Lillian baby go get in the truck. I closed and locked the door and went downstairs to the truck.

He put my bag in the back of the truck. Larry pulled me to the side. Popeye you didn't tell Lillian what happen did you? Hell no are you crazy. Lillian would have had a fit if I told her something like that. It's good that you are leaving today. Why you say that? The police came around the other day looking for who killed Bobby Joe, Little Bow and that other man. What!

Yeah. So what are you going to do? Oh I'm going to be fine Mrs. Hutchinson took care of everything. It's you they worried about. Why they worried about me? You remember that girl skinny? Yeah I remember her. She told police what you look like. What! Yeah she did. So let's get you to the bus station and on that bus out of town. I started to feel sick to my stomach I almost throw up my breakfast. All I did was ride with them to deliver so moonshine and now I'm a suspect in three murders. How did that skinny bitch remember my face. Out of the three of us she remembers my face. Let me get my ass to this bus station. We got in the truck and headed for the bus station. What was y'all talking about Jeffery? I was telling Larry how much I was going to miss you and to look out for you while I'm gone. Lillian didn't say anything she just grabbed my hand and squeezed it. I didn't want to leave this morning now I couldn't wait to get the hell out of Houston. I seemed like it to for ever to get to that damn bus station. When we pulled up front Mrs. Hutchinson and Mr. Sutton was all ready there.

The bus was loading up. Larry parked the truck got out got my bag and gave it to me. Hey Jeffery. Hey Mrs. Hutchinson. She gave me a hug, but she whispered in my ear. You need to get you're ass on that bus now. The bus driver yelled last call for Iowa. Lillian gave me a hug and we kissed. Come on child Mrs. Hutchinson said he's got to go. Tears started running down Lillian's face. We kissed again Come on Popeye you better get your ass on that bus before it leaves you. I got to go I told Lillian. I'll write you when I get there. She blew me a kiss and I got on the bus. The bus driver wasn't to happy. He told me we ain't get time to wait on you get your black ass get your ass in the back of the bus with the rest of those Niggers. I didn't care what he said I was so happy to be on that bus. I also was hoping that trouble don't follow me. I waved at Lillian as the bus pulled away. She started to get smaller and smaller until I couldn't see her no more. I put me bag in the overhead bin and sat next to a guy who also was in the army. Hey how you doing I said to him. He looked at me first and spoke. I'm fine. He was a tall brown skin man with brown eye and reddish hair. What your name? Bryon Smalls. What's yours? Jeffery Ross. We shook hands. Where you going he asked me? Iowa I said. Where you going? I'm going to Seattle, Wa. Seattle is the where your post is? No. So are you going on leave? No. So why are you going to Seattle? I went AWOL. What! Yeah I don't want to fight in this white man's war. I ain't start it. If you were smart you would do the same thing. Are you crazy those white folks will catch you and when they do they going shoot you. They ain't never going to catch me. The part of Seattle I'm going to they ain't never going to look. I looked at him like he was crazy. Why you looking at me like that? You got more heart then me. I got a wife and a baby on the way I can't afford to do that. Where you coming from anyway? I'm coming from San Diego, Ca. If you didn't want to fight than why did you join? I joined, because my brother talked me into it. He likes this bullshit I don't. Where is he at? In San Diego with our unit. Does he know you are gone? No I just left last night and got on the first bus leaving town. I hope your brother don't get in trouble, because you know they are going to blame him for you going Awol. They might think he helped you. He dropped is head. I know, but I had to do what I had to do. Well good luck I hope you don't get caught. I didn't say anything else to him. We didn't talk much after that. I settle back in my chair and fell asleep. I guess all that food I ate made me tired. I was in a deep sleep when I felt somebody nudge me. Hey the voice said. I woke up yeah. Ain't this your stop? We are in Iowa. We in Iowa already? Yeah you slept the whole way. What time is it? It's 4:30 in the afternoon. Hey ain't this your stop boy the bus driver said. Yes sir it is. Than get your shit and get your black ass off this bus. I started getting my bag. Hurry up boy we ain't got all day to wait on you. This time he was making me mad. I got my bag. Told Byron to take it easy than I got off the bus. You take it easy to Jeffery. I well I said. As I left the bus I gave the bus driver this mean look. When I stepped off the bus he closed the door and drove away leaving me standing in a cloud of dust. When the dust cleared I could see a tall man standing next to a jeep across the street. What's your name Pvt he asked me. Pvt. Jeffery Ross sir, but my friends call me Popeye. The man I met that day was 1st Sgt. Willie Banks. Who would later become the best friend I have ever had.

CHAPTER FORTY-TWO

POPEYE A HEARD A voice say. I felt someone shaking me I woke up grabbing my rifle. It was Hicks. Popeye Lt. Banks want us to get our squads together, because we are moving out.

Okay I'll be there in a few minutes. I been trying to trying to wake you up for the past minute.

You are a hard sleeper that ain't good out here Popeye. How long have I been asleep? I say about two hours. Come on get your men together. Okay. I got up stumbled though the deep snow to my squad. When I got to them they were standing around bonfires they had made. Sgte one of them said to me. Why are you calling me Sgt? Well we were told by Lt. Banks that you were a Sgt. Than I realize I was promoted to a Sargent I just hadn't sew on my stripes yet. Alright men lets line up. They were moving to slow for me so I had to rise my voice to get them moving. LET'S GO WE AIN'T GOT ALL DAY. looked at my watch it was 2300 hours. the men lined up. I don't have to tell you what we have to do. Like I told you earlier there is a small village we have to take. I know this will be the first time y'all have been in battle. I know you will be scared, but stay calm and try not to lose control. Take care of each other. Does anyone have any questions on what we are about to do. No one said a word. I know they had questions, but they were to scared to ask. Alright than check your ammunition and make sure you have enough. Popeye. I turned to see who called me. Yeah Perkins. Are you ready for this? Yeah I'm ready as I can be. Are you ready? Yeah I'm ready.

Okay than good luck. You to Popeye. Move your men out. You heard the Lt let's move out.

We started marching through the ankle deep snow towards the small village of Norburg. The wind was blowing so hard it was blowing snow in my face I could barely see what was in front of me. My hands were freezing and I could hardly hold my rifle. The wind was cutting though my jacket like a knife cutting though butter. This reminded me of the raid we did about a month ago that was all fucked up. Good men lost their lives now here we are again being led to the slaughter like pigs. One of the Pvt asked me how far is this place. I don't know Pvt just keep walking we will find out soon. We walked what seem like for hours. Walking though that snow was like walking in mud. I was tried and I was trying not to show it. I knew I had to be strong for the other men. If they seen any weakness in me I will lose their respect. When finally got to the village my feet were frozen. We were told to stop at the end of these woods.

In the distant I could see the village. It look like it was deserted. Popeye come here Sgt yelled to me. I ran though the ankle deep snow to him. Yeah Sgt what's up? Douglass and Sgt was looking at a map. Look at this map he told us. We are going to attack this town like I told y'all back at the CP. Now 3rd squad and 5th squad going to come in from the south.

Cutting off any Germans trying to leave that village. 2nd and 6th squads you will be coming in from the east which is by the river. 1st squad 4th squads will come in from the north. What about the west Douglass asked. The map shows there's a lake there, so if those Germans start to retreat they have no where to run but jump into that lake. Now Hicks and Perkins take those radios and let me know when you are in place. Okay sir. That's a great plan Lt. Banks I want you to lead the attack. I was going to do that sir I'm just waiting for Hicks and Perkins to get in place. What time is it Popeye? It's 0200 hours Sgt. We are late

Douglass told Sgt. We need to get in place fast he said. Sgt got on the radio and called Hicks. Are you in place?

Yeah Sgt I'm in place. Good. He called Perkins and didn't get a response. He called him again. Damn! I can't get Perkins, so we are going to have to move without him. Lt. Banks we going in five minutes. Yes sir. I didn't know why Douglass was acting like he was going to lead the attack all he was going to do was hide. Popeye I want you to spread your men along this tree line. Already I want y'all to spread yourselves along these trees. Hurry up we ain't got much time. I ran back to Sgt and told him we were ready. Capt. Douglass we are ready Sgt told him. Okay Lt. Banks lets move in we don't have time to wait for Perkins to get into place. Let's go Popeye move your squad out. We started moving towards the small village. I surely hope Perkins is where he suppose to be. As we started moving slowly towards the village a window opened up and a machine gun started shooting at us. Everybody hit the ground. Get up Sgt told us and move forward. We got up and started running towards the village out the corner of my eye I could see men getting cut down by that machine gun. They was screaming and yelling for help. Bullets was flying passed and around me. Me and two other Pvt made it to a stack of wood and took cover there. I hadn't fired a shot. What are we going to do now Sgt? One of them asked me. I was scared to death and I didn't know what to tell them. I told them to start putting some fire on that machine gun. Sgt had joined us by this time. Popeye work you're ass around that barn. okay Sgt. I turned to run towards the barn when I saw all those dead bodies laid out in the blood soak snow. The site made me sick. I told one of the Pvt to come with me. What your name I asked him? Pvt. Cole. Okay Pvt. Cole on three you and I are going to run towards that barn over there. Pvt. Jones we are going to need you to give us some covering fire. asked Sgt. Sgte asked me was I ready?

Yeah I'm ready. 1…2…3 Pvt. Jones started giving us covering fire. Me, Sgt and Cole started running towards the barn. On our way to the barn two Germans opened fire on us. It cut our run to the barn short so we took cover behind another wood pile. I told Sgt and Cole to cover me while I worked my way around those Germans. They gave me covering fire as I worked my way around them and hide behind this old wagon. I saw two Germans hiding behind sandbags I pointed my gun at them waiting for one of them to stick their heads up.

One stuck his head up to fire at me and I shot him in his neck. I could see the blood fly everywhere. He fell on top on the other German. While the other German was trying to get his friend off him I ran over and pumped two rounds in his chest. The one I shot in the neck was still alive. He was laying there in a pool of his own blood struggling to live. I stood there for a second looking at him than I put a bullet in his head to put him out of his misery. I remember what Sgt said about if we was caught by the Germans and what they were going to do to us. That's way I did it and it didn't even bother me. Pvt Cole came running over to me. Did you kill them Sgt? I looked at him and pointed at them. When he seen all that blood he almost throw up. Get yourself together Cole we got to go. Where's Sgt? He and Jones want to take out that machine gun. I reloaded my rifle and we started across this field. We worked our way to this little house when all of a sudden the ground started to shake. What's that Cole asked me? I knew what that was it was one those Tiger tanks. When it seen us it fired off a round at us. The round flew pass our heads hitting the building in front of us and destroying it. The blast was so intense it blew us off our feet. Dazed from the blast we got up as quick as we could, because that tank was coming for us. We need to get the hell out of Cole. We started running toward this little house that tank let off another round. The house we was running to the tank destroyed it. We need to find somewhere to hide, because if we don't we are going to die Cole. Where are we going to hide? It was bullets flying everywhere out of all that smoke I could see two figures running toward us. I rise my rifle to shoot when I realize it was Sgt and Pvt. Lampkin. Don't shoot Popeye it's me. Sgt is that you? Yeah it's me. Man I almost shot you. Where you guys coming from anyway? I want to see how Perkins is doing. Did you find him? Yeah he and his squad walked right into a ambush. What! Yeah they were all killed only a few of his men got away Pvt. Lampkin was one of them. Sgt this place is crawling with Germans. There's a tiger tank over there. The reason this village looked empty is the Germans made all the people leave and they took over and hid in these houses.

The map they gave Douglass was wrong. This village is bigger then what the map shows. I should have known this was going to go bad. Where is Hicks I asked Sgt? He's on the other side of the village with his squad. They are holding on by the skin of their teeth. How many men do we have left do. It's only you, me and these four Pvt. That's it? Yep that machine cut most of them down when we was coming though those woods. We heard that Tiger tank getting closer. We need to stop that tank Sgt said. How we are going to do that sir we ain't got enough men. Don't worry about that Pvt me and this man here took down a tank by ourselves. Sgt was lying, but he needed to do that to encourage these young men. We were about to come up with a plan to stop that tank when the Germans started to bomb the village with artillery. Several shells landed next to us. We need to find better cover. I started looking around when I seen this farm house. Hey Sgt there's a farm house over there. We need to make a run for it. What about that tank Lt? Damn that tank Pvt that's the least of our problems if we don't find a place to hide we all are going to die right here. Popeye I'm going to go first than the rest of y'all follow. Y'all understand. Yes sir. It ain't time to be scared. Give me some covering fire Popeye. We gave Sgt some covering fire. He took off for that farm house. He made it there safe. Come on Cole you and I are going next. You two cover us. We take off for the farm house. Cole was right on my heels. We to the farm when we saw Lampkin coming right behind us. Where's Hardin Sgt asked. I don't know. Damn! He most have got scared and stayed. I got to go back and get him. Sgt you can't go back out there you are going to get killed with all those bombs dropping like that. We couldn't see Hardin from all that smoke. That tank had followed us to the farm house in minutes the farm house filled with bullets wood and hay was flying everywhere. We tried to shoot back, but the bullets from their machine gun overwhelmed us. Find some place to hide Sgt told us.

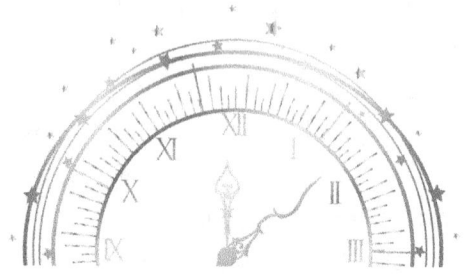

CHAPTER FORTY-THREE

WE HEARD THE TANK stop than the door of the farm house opened up. I could see them from where I was. I had ran upstairs and hid in the hay. I could hear a couple run around back.

They had us surrounded and we had know where to go. Than I seen Sgt throw a grenade at the Germans entering the farm door. The blast sent them flying back out the door killing them both. He started shooting at them like a wild man. The Germans that went around back started shooting into the farm house. Bullets, wood and hay was flying everywhere. I started shooting back at the Germans around back from where I was hiding. I don't know if I hit anybody I just kept shooting. Pvt. Lampkin came up where I was at. Sgt I'm out of ammunition

I gave him a clip. Sgt yelled to me Popeye let's get the fuck out of here. Before I could stand up a round came through the farm house the blast blew me and Lampkin out the back of the farm house. We went flying though the air and I came down hard on the ground. When I came to after about a second I couldn't see anything, because all the smoke and dust. I felt around for my rifle yelling for Sgt. When I got my rifle and the smoke cleared I saw Lampkin laying there. The blast had cut him in half it also killed those Germans also. I heard somebody call my name. Who is that? It's me Sgt come help me with Cole he's real hurt bad. I got my rifle and ran over to him to help him with Cole.

Come on Popeye give me a hand. I liked at Cole and he was shot in both legs. When I went to help Sgt with Cole that's when I notice he had been shot in the shoulder. Sgt you have been shot in the shoulder. I know Popeye, but we ain't got time to worry about that we gotta get Cole some help. We dragged him over to this brunt out house. Sgt he hurt real bad and so are you. Don't worry about me Popeye I'll be alright. Where is Lampkin? He's dead. The German were still shelling the village. Than out of nowhere here comes Hardin. We was shocked to see him. Hardin we thought you were dead.

No I was hiding. Hiding where? In the basement of that house over there. When y'all ran to that farm house I was about to follow, but those Germans were coming so I saw a window and climbed in. They sent a couple of men down there to check it out and I killed both of them. When I saw that Tiger tank blow up the farm house I climbed on the back of it and throw a grenade down in it. That's when I seen Lt. Banks helping Cole. Lt you bleeding bad.

We need to get y'all some help. Sgt was holding his shoulder with his hand it was covered with blood. I could see the pain in his eyes. Popeye. Yeah Sgt? Get them out of here and leave me some ammunition I will hold them off until y'all get somewhere safe. Are you crazy Sgt! I'm not going to leave you out here to die. He grabbed my by my collar do what I tell you Popeye. He had this serious look on his face. I looked at him yes sir. Do me a favor before you go. Yeah anything Sgt. Here take these. He gave me two letters. Don't open these until you get back home. You understand me Popeye? Yeah Sgt I understand. We hugged for the last time I knew he wasn't going to make it. Now get out of here those Germans are coming. I put the two letters in my pocket. Come on Hardin give me a hand with Cole. We started making our way to Hicks squad. I turned and looked at my friend for the last time. He winked at me and I smiled back at him. We dragged Cole to a safe spot. I could hear Sgt shooting at the Germans. Sgt. Yeah Hardin. Cole is losing a lot of blood. Yeah I know we got get him some help. You see that bridge over there. Yeah! Hicks squad is over there. We going to have to cross that bridge to get to them. We was about to run towards the bridge when an machine gun opened up on us. It was so intense it had us pinned down we couldn't move. We ain't going to make it pass that machine gun Hardin said. Yeah I know. What are we going to do Sgt? I had to think fast we didn't have much time. I realize I had a grenade on me. Listen Hardin give me some covering fire, so I could get close enough to take out that machine gun nest.

Okay Sgt. Cole hang in there man we are going to get you out of here. okay Sgt. He was bleeding bad, but we wasn't going anywhere until I took out that machine gun. I could hear gun fire in the distant. It must be Sgt I said to myself. I'm go on three you cover me. Okay Sgt. 1…2…3 Hardin started giving me covering fire. I started running toward this brick wall. The machine gun poured a hail of bullets at me. Bullets was ricocheting off the ground all around my feet. I make it to the wall safely. Hardin took cover when the machine gun started shooting at him.

I peeped over the wall to see where this machine gun was. I saw the machine gun was behind some bushes. I got on my knees and crawled to the end of the wall. I peeped around the corner and seen the machine gun was still shooting at Hardin. I seen a bush that I could hide behind I made a run for the bush. On my way to it I tripped over a hole on the ground where a shell had landed. When I fell the grenade fell out my hand and rolled into the bushes. SHIT! what the FUCK I'm going to do now? I hid in the hole to hide myself from that gun fire. I was trying to figure out what to do when I saw a dead German holding one of them grenade what we call a potato masher. I crawled over to him and pried that grenade from his dead hands. I crawled back to my hole I looked at it I remember they told us how to work this thing. I unscrewed the top when I did that it fell off with a string attached to it.

That was the pull string that would set the potato masher off. I got on my belly and crawled to the machine gun nest. I got right under the bushes. I gun was loud and the heat from it I could feel. I pulled the string and throw it in the machine gun nest. I covered my head and heard the blast it was so loud it almost busted my eardrums. The machine gun fall silent, but I could hear them moaning in pain. I took my rifle and put a couple of rounds through the bushes.

The moaning stopped I looked over the bushes to see six Germans dead. I seen one trying to crawl away I stood up and shot him in his back. In one swoop I killed six Germans I was shocked, but at the same time I was proud of myself. It started to become daylight I could see Germans running everywhere. I had to get back to Hardin and Cole. I wonder if they're still alive. I ran back to where I had left them, but they wasn't there. Now I was scared where hell could they have gone? I started thinking if they were taken prisoner by the Germans. I looked down on the ground and seen a trail of blood. That could only be Cole blood, because he was bleeding pretty bad. The trail of blood was going towards the bridge. I stood there for a minute then I heard somebody call my name. Popeye they said. I peeped around the corner to see who it was. I looked and it was Hicks. Come on across the bridge we will cover you. I looked around to see if there was any Germans around. When I didn't see any I started running toward the bridge. The bridge I had to cross was a man made bridge made out of timber wood. It looked like it was about 100 years old. As I was running towards the bridge the Germans were shooting at me. The bridge looked like it was about 50 yards long. When I stepped on to that bridge everything went black.

CHAPTER FORTY-FOUR

THE BLAST FROM A shell blow the bridge to pieces throwing me into the icy cold river. When I came to I was underwater trying to swim to the top to get some air. The water was freezing cold. The fast moving current was taken me down river. The Germans was shooting at me from the other side. Hicks squad was shooting back them as they tried to kill me. I could see them chasing me down the river bank trying to catch me before the current take me farther down river. If that happens I'm a dead man for sure. I felt like I was about to drown the water was getting in my mouth I was choking and my clothes was getting heavy from being in the water. I was trying to swim against the current, but the more I tried the more tired I got. I was thinking about all the shit I have been through and this is the way I was going to die. FUCK this shit I mustered up some strength and started swimming toward the river bank, but the current was to strong and I was really getting tired. The current started taken me farther down river I seen a tree branch hanging down I told myself to grab it, but the current was moving so fast I missed it. SHIT! Then somebody throw me a rope. Grab it a voice said. I grabbed the rope with all my might I almost lost my grip, because my hands were frozen. I held on for dear life. They pulled me up on to the river bank. Hold on Popeye we got you.

They struggled to pull me out of the water I was tired wet and frozen. After about two or three minutes they finally got out of the water they dragged me into the woods out of the way of the gun fire and laid me down on my back. I was so cold I shaking like a leaf. We almost lost you a voice said. I was so tired I couldn't see who was talking to me. Somebody get a blanket the voice said. As my eyes started to clear up I could see it was Slim. Popeye you got to get out of these wet clothes before you freeze to death. He started taking my clothes off in minutes I was butt naked. He took everything off drawers, jacket, shirt, T-shirt and pants. The only thing I had on was my boots. He wrapped me in a couple more blankets. The battle was still going on a shell landed a couple of feet from us. Let's move you to a safer place. Slim helped me to my feet I could barely walk I was still tired and dizzy from the cold water. We walked over to a tree and he sat me down. Sit down Popeye you are going to be alright. I didn't say anything I was to cold to talk. I'll be right back Popeye. Then somebody yelled we need a medic over here. Sit tight Popeye I'll be right back. I watched him as he ran in the direction of the man was yelling from. I sat there in the snow butt naked not knowing what was happen or where I was at. While I was sitting there I seen a blur figured coming towards me I started to panic then I realize I had no weapon. I picked up some snow and throw it at the figure. What the hell you doing Popeye? It's me man. Me who I asked? He came closer it's me Hardin. Oh Hardin I thought you was one of those Germans. If I was a German what were you going to do with a snowball? I don't know. What you doing here? Slim told me to come keep an eye on you. He said you won't in your right frame of mind. How is the battle going? We are holding our own against those Germans we taking a lot of casualties, but we are doing alright.

Where is Cole is he alright? Yeah he's going to be fine they took him to a medical station.

Have you seen Sgt? No I ain't seen him since we left him at that house. I should have not left him. I should have stayed with him. I'm sure he's alright Popeye he can take care of himself. You know how he is? Yeah I do, but he was wounded pretty bad. Who's that coming. A figure came walking toward us. Hardin pointed his gun at the figure.

Who is that? It's me Pvt. Simpson. Okay you can come forward. Slim told me to give these clothes to Sgt to put on. I grabbed the clothes from him and started putting them on. Thanks I said. No problem Sgt. After I put the clothes on I wrapped myself in the blankets I had. I was still cold and shaking. I told Hardin that I needed to change my boots, because these are wet. What do you want me to do Sgt? There's a dead Negro solider laying over there go take his boots and socks off him. What! Are you crazy I ain't taken know boots off no dead man. It ain't right to take a man's boot's when he is dead. Why he ain't going to need them. Hardin do this for me my feet are freezing. Hardin gave me this crazy look. Okay. But it ain't right. I knew he didn't want to do it, but who cares my feet were freezing. He ran over to the dead solider took off his boots and socks. He came back and throw the boots down at me. There you go Popeye. Thanks Hardin.

I'm going to go back to see what's going on. I'll be back. Okay. He took off towards the bombing. I took off my boots and those wet socks. My feet felt like they was frozen. I put on the dry socks and boots. The boots was a little too big, but they would have to do for now. The dry socks, clothes, boots and blankets I started to feel better. I sat there wondering what happen to Sgt. I shouldn't have left him there by himself. I would never be able to forgive myself if he got killed on account of me. Then the bombing and gun fire had stopped the forest got quite. Then I felt the ground start to shake. It sounded like a tank was coming. I got up and tried to run, but my feet was still cold I just sat back down hoping for the worse. Then I could see it wasn't Germans, but Americans. If it had been Germans they would've shot me by now. I sat back against the tree like I was hurt. A white medic came up to me. You alright buddy he asked me. No my feet are frozen and I can't move. I reached into his medical bag and handed me this plastic package. Here put these on they will warm your feet up he said.

He got up and left. I looked at the package what he had given me. It was a brand new pair of insulated boots. I put them on right away. After about five minutes my feet started warming up. Man this feels good I said to myself. My feet felt like they was melting. Slim came running up to me. Popeye you alright? Now I am. How you feel? Good some white medic then gave me these here insulated boots. He give you these insulated boots? Yeah. Damn! I need a pair myself. Come on we need to get you to the medic station. He helped me to my feet. My feet was still a little frozen, but I could walk. Slim you seen Sgt? No I ain't seen him. Come on lets go. He helped me to one of the trucks that had the wounded in it. He helped me on the truck.

Up you go Slim got in the truck with me. Oh before I forget here. He gave me the two letters that were in my jacket. The two letters Sgt had given me I had forgotten about them. I put them in my jacket pocket. I remembered what Sgt said to me not to open them until I get back home. I just hope he ain't dead.

CHAPTER FORTY-FIVE

WE GOT TO THE field hospital Slim had to help me out the truck. Slim what happen to Douglass? He got killed when those Germans started bombing that village. I didn't feel bad for him not all the bullshit he put us though. I hope he died like a man not like the coward he was. The field hospital was a bombed out building we had taken over after the Germans retreated. Slim took me inside and sat me down on one of the cots they had. There were a lot of wounded men at this station most of them were dead or about to die. They had legs and arm missing the loud screams from men in pain were deafening to the ears. One poor soldier was laying there with his guts hanging out. It was cold in that building the smell of death was everywhere. There was frozen blood all over the place they would take the dead outside and throw them in a pile with the rest of the dead bodies. I heard someone call me name. I turned around to see who it was. It was Cole. Hey Cole how are you doing. I'm doing fine, but my legs hurt like hell. What are you doing here? I was running across that bridge to get to the other side when a shell destroyed the bridge and blew me into that freezing river. I almost drowned. If it had not been for Hicks squad I would have died. Hey Cole have you seen Sgt?

No I ain't seen him. I have been asking everybody have they seen him. Why you worried about him Popeye we will be going home soon.

What do you mean we are going home? You mean you are going home I ain't going no where until I find Sgt. This war ain't over yet Cole.

It's over for you it ain't over for me. I heard from some of the wounded soldiers that the Germans are retreating back across the Rhine River into Germany. They say we might have to go into Germany to defeat Hitler. They said Hitler has gone crazy. Yeah I heard he even started killing his own people. I told I was going outside to get some fresh air, because I could no longer take that smell. I got up and went outside I was feeling better since I started to warm up. When I got outside I saw Slim standing against the building smoking a cigarette.

Can I get one of those. He gave me one and lit it for me. I took a long drag it felt good. Slim didn't say anything he was just standing there stirring off into space. What wrong with you Slim? I'm looking at the pile of dead Negro soldiers they just dumped over there about 20 minutes ago. Do you think Sgt is in that pile of bodies? Well there's only one way to find out let's go take a look. I took another drag of my cigarette and throw it down. I walked slowly behind behind Slim, because I didn't want to see my friend laying there among those dead bodies. The closer we got the faster my heart started to beat. The bodies were stacked up like firewood. We started looking over the dead bodies, but I didn't see Sgt among them which was a relief for me. A lot of the faces I have never seen before. Popeye help me lay them side by side. I started helping Slim lay them side by side. They were frozen solid I went to grab this one soldiers arm and it came off in my hand. We had to pull some of them apart, because they were stuck together from all the frozen blood. Slim would take there dog tags from them as we laid them down. Then we came across Lampkin the only part of his body they had was the upper torso. We didn't come across Sgt, but we did come across Douglass. He had been shot in the head by a sniper he even died with his eyes open. Popeye what do you think he was thinking when he got shot in the head? I don't know Slim. One thing he never showed us any kind of leadership. He got what he deserved. We stood there and looked at him for a minute. Slim closed his eyes and we laid him down next to the other soldiers. I came across a few guys from my squad. All

Michael Johnson

I could think about is Lampkin momma she's going to die when she finds out she lost two sons in this war. Well Popeye that's the last of them. No Sgt I guess he is still alive somewhere or the Germans took him prisoner or killed him. That made me feel good that Sgt was still alive out there somewhere. We said a prayer over the dead soldiers and than we went back into the field hospital. When we got back to the field hospital our division was rolling up. What you guys doing here? They pulled us off the line and told us to come here. Why? All they needed us to do was clear the way for those white boys, so they they could have a clear way to Germany. So what are they going to do with us now. I don't know Sgt. We are going to standby until they need us again. How many dead and wounded Slim asked? Hicks took out a slip of paper out of his pocket. We have 30 dead, 100 wounded and 3 missing that includes Sgt. So have y'all seen Sgt Popeye? No we ain't seen him. I'm pretty sure he's alright. Let's go get some coffee and get out of this cold. We walked over to this chow tent they had made for us. There was a lot of white soldiers standing around looking at us. I could hear them talking about us. Where did you get those insulated boots from boy?

Who me? Yeah you boy where did you get those boots from? What these. Yeah those on your feet. Those are for fighting soldiers. We are fighting soldiers too. Oh yeah since when all I hear about you Niggers is when you see the enemy you run. You stole those off some dead white man you know how you Niggers are you steal anything if it ain't nailed down. Than they all started to laugh. A white medic gave them to me. Yeah right now take them. A crowd started to gather us. I seen Hicks and Slim rise there rifles. If you don't take them off Nigger were a going to cut your feet off. NOW TAKE THEM OFF. Then one of those white boys grabbed me. GET YOUR FUCKING HANDS OFF ME CRACKER. Hicks and Slim pointed their rifles at them. If you white motherfuckers want those boots you are going to have to come though us to get them. If that's the way you Niggers want it then so be it. Then we heard a loud voice say WHAT THE FUCK IS GOING ON HERE? We turned to see who it was. It was Lt. Col Conley. We ain't seen his fat ass in weeks. Sir that Nigger over there stole them insulated boots off a dead white soldier. He turned to me and looked down at my feet.

Ross where did you get those boots from? Sir a white medic from another division gave them to me when I fell in the river. You fell into what river Cpl? The river near Norberg sir. My socks and boots were soaking wet my feet was freezing he gave me these to put on. The look on those white boys faces changed when I said Norberg. He was even shocked when I said that. You boys were the ones who took the village of Norberg? Yes sir it was us. Capt. Douglass was your Company Commander right? Yes sir. Where is he? He was killed during the attack sir. He didn't seem to concerned about that. So where is 1st Sgt Banks? He's missing sir. So who is running the division? No one sir.. You guys need a leader. Okay then Staff Sgt. Hicks you are now 1st Sgt Hicks you are now in charge of the division. Yes sir.

Those white boys didn't like that, because now Hicks out ranked a lot of them. I want you to get your whole division together and make sure they get some chow. When you all finish I want you and Cpl. Ross to report to me. Yes sir Hicks said. You men carry on. Sir. What is it soldier? What about those boots he has on sir? What about them soldier? Those boots are only for white soldiers. The Col walk back to him and got in his face. Oh yeah soldier these boys here just took a town that you couldn't, so he deserves to wear those boots. You understand me soldier? Yes sir. Now carry on. Yes sir. He gave me this mean look when he walked away. I just smiled at him. Come on Popeye let's get all the men together. We started walking over to where the men were at. Congratulations on your promotion to 1st Sgt. Thanks Slim. Popeye why was the Col calling you Cpl? I thought you were a Sgt. I am a Sgt I just haven't sew on my stripes yet. You better sew them stripes on before he change his mind. He was right I don't think the Col knew I was a Sgt. I better sew them on before I stay a Cpl.

When we got to the men they was stacking dead bodies. What the hell y'all doing Hicks asked them. This white Col told us to stack these bodies up. Why? He said he didn't want the dead bodies of the soldiers lying all over the roads. It didn't look good. Okay when y'all finish with

Michael Johnson

that y'all go over to that chow tent and get something to eat. Okay Sgt. Come on Popeye and Slim let's go get something to eat. I'm hungry as hell. When we got back to the tent all those white boys were gone. What do you boys need this Negro soldier asked us. We want something to eat we are starving I told him. Well we ain't got much those white boys ate up everything. What! Yeah you know how they are all they think about is themselves. So what you got Hicks asked? You got a lot of hungry Negro soldiers coming and if you ain't got anything for them to eat they are going to be real mad. Well let me see. We got some bread a lot of coffee and some beef stew what's left of it. How much of that beef stew you have left? I got this one big pot left. The pot was one of them long tall silver pots. I looked in it. That ain't enough to feed all of us. Well I'm sorry it's going to have to do this is all we got. Okay than gave on stoop of stew to everybody Hicks said. Okay Sgt. By the way what is your name Pvt?

Pvt Anthony Williams. I'm 1st Sgt Melvin Hicks this is Sgt. Jeffery Ross. We call him Popeye.

This skinny guy here is Cpl. Robert Brooks he's our medic we call him Slim. Sgt Ross if you are a Sgt why don't you have on Sgt stripes? I ain't sewed them on yet. Well you better sew them on quick you know those white folks need proof when it comes to us. Y'all get some utensils and a tray, so y'all can get something to eat. We grabbed some utensils and trays. He gave us bread and one stoop of that beef stew. I was so hungry I could eat the whole pot I wanted more but I knew the other men had to eat. The beef stew had very little beef in it. It was watered down with a lot of vegetables and know flavor. It was better then nothing I ate a lot of bread to fill myself up. The coffee was hot which was good, because it was cold as hell and it warmed me up a little. By this time the rest of the men had showed up. Popeye you finished we got to go see the Col. You ready to go? Yeah I'm ready. Slim get a count of all the men we have and their names. We will break them down into squads when I get back. Okay Hicks. Come on Popeye let go.

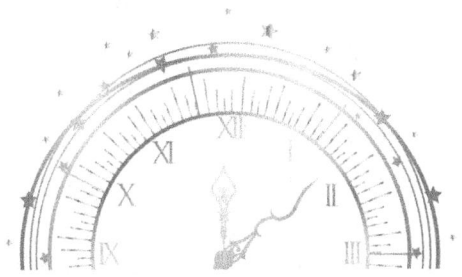

CHAPTER FORTY-SIX

WE STARTED WALKING TOWARDS the Col tent I was wondering to myself what the hell he wanted. I was hoping he wasn't going to send us on another one of those fuck up missions I was tired of them. Hicks what you think he want with us? I don't know Popeye. Whatever it is I hope it ain't nothing crazy I have seen a enough of this crazy shit to last me a life time. We passed the pile of dead Negro soldiers. We stopped, man look at at all those bodies. There is going to be a lot of sad families when they get the news their love ones are dead. We got to the Col tent. We knocked than we enter. 1st Sgt. Hicks reporting as order sir. I said the same thing. At ease boys. You boys have done a hell of a job out there taken that village. If it had not been for you boys we would have never got though there. Thank you sir. That village was a strong hold for the Germans and you boys captured it for us. I'm going to put your division in for a unit citation. I don't know if you are going to get it, but hell it's worth a try. I'm sorry about what happen to Capt. Douglass and Lt. Banks. They both were good soldiers. I doubt if he really cared about any of them that was just something for him to say. I'm also taking you boys offline and sending you back to the rear. Why are you doing that sir? Well we don't you anymore. The Germans are retreating back to Germany our forces are closing in from the west and the Russians are coming in from the east. The Germans are finished and the war will be over in a couple of months. He was lying I said to myself they said that this war would be over by Christmas and here we are still fighting. It didn't make a difference to me, because I was tired of fighting anyway I needed a break. So sir what are we going to be doing for the rest of the war? Well 1st Sgt. Hicks you boys will be helping out the wounded and guarding the prisoners we capture. Okay sir. Do you have a problem with that 1st Sgt. Hicks? No sir. Good.

Now I want you to report to a Lt. Caldwell he will be your new CO. Yes sir. I want again to thank you boys for a job well done. Your country is proud of you. Thank you sir. We saluted him and we left. Oh Cpl. Ross you can take those insulated boots off now you won't be needing them anymore give them to Lt. Caldwell he will know what to do with them. Yes sir.

Oh sir it's Sgt. Ross. Sgt .Ross! He said in a shocked voice. Who promoted you to Sgt? Capt. Douglass did a couple of weeks ago for holding off them Germans at that road we were guarding. He told me that he talked it over with you. He sat there and looked at me for a minute. Okay than if you are a Sgt where are your stripes? I reached in my pocket and pulled them out. Then you need to sew them on Sgt. Ross. Yes sir. We got outside and Hicks said to me. I told you're ass to sew those stripes on. I know, but I haven't the time. Well since we ain't going to be fighting anymore you can sew them on. You heard what he said we ain't going to be fighting anymore. I'm glad I'm tired of fighting. I'm happy about it. I'm not I was looking forward of going into Germany. What! Hicks you crazy you do know it's going to be worse if we go into Germany. I'm glad we going back to the rear. That's easy for you to say you been in a lot of fights. I want to do more. I want to kill me some more Germans. I want us to be part of taking Germany we earned it Popeye. I looked at him like he was crazy. They can have Germany as far as I'm concerned. Did it ever occur to you Hicks the reason he took us offline, because he don't won't us to be part of that. Yeah I thought about it and you maybe right, but it would be nice. Come on let's find this Lt. Caldwell. Slim had the men in ranks when we got back to our division with Lt. Caldwell. How many men do we have in our division

The Men that Time has Forgotten

Slim? We have 100 men. That's all we have is 100? Yep that's it. We lost more guys then I thought. We enter Norberg with over 200 men I was shocked to know we last that many. Okay then we got to report to some Lt. Caldwell I don't even know what this motherfucker looks like. Popeye go see if you can find this Lt. Caldwell. Alright Hicks. I started looking around to see if I could find this Lt. Caldwell I didn't know what he look like neither. It was so many white officers running around I didn't know who to ask. I was looking around when I seen this one white officer who stuck out. He was standing in the corner smoking a cigarette like he was hiding from someone. I walked over to him he was a little taller then me, very pale skin, brown eyes and hair. He looked at me. What do you need soldier? Yes sir are you Lt. Caldwell? Yeah that's me. I'm Sgt. Ross sir I was told by Lt. Col. Conley to report to you. Oh yeah you from that black division that took that village of Norberg. Yes sir that was us. We been trying to take that village for days and he you guys come and take it in hours. I lost a lot of men in that God forsaken village. He was a very nerves person he smoked about 3 cigarettes when I was talking to him. He looked at my arm. I thought you said you was a Sgt? I am sir. So where are your stripes? I ain't had the time to sew them on sir. Well you better do that you don't want to be walking around here being the wrong rank. Sir I will do that soon as we get back sir. So Ross where is your division? We just down the road sir. Well let's go see them. He put his cigarette out picked up his rifle and followed me. While we was walking to the division I got this feeling that he was shit canned this guy and I bet it got something to do with the village of Norberg. We always get the worse officers I'm glad we ain't fighting anymore this guy will get us all killed. I think he is worse than Douglass and I thought there wasn't anyone worse than him. So Ross how long you been out here? Oh since Aug of 44 sir. What were you doing? I was driving trucks sir. Driving trucks how did you get in the middle of this shit ? I don't know sir we just got caught up in it sir. He lit up another cigarette. So Norberg was your first time seeing action? No sir it wasn't. No! Really, so how many battles have you been in? I been in two plus Norberg makes three. You've been in three battles wow that's a lot. How many have you been in sir? One and that was Norberg I only been out here a couple of months. I joined during D-Day. I was only out here a day and they put me in charge of a company when their company commander got killed. I have never been in combat before and I was scary as hell.

They told us to go in there and capture that village, but what they didn't tell us was that village was heavy guarded by Germans. We want in there thinking it was going to be a easy time.

They cut us to fucking pieces. I got so scared I froze up one of my Pvt had to carry me out of there. I said to myself we are in big trouble if we had to go back on line with this guy. My stomach started feeling funny it hasn't been feeling funny in a couple of weeks. This mean something bad is about to happen. When we got to the division Hicks had the standing in ranks. Good morning sir 1st Sgt Hicks reporting. At ease 1st Sgt. How many men do we have?

We have 100 men sir. 100 is that it? Yes sir we lost a lot of men in that village sir. Sorry to here that Hicks. Sir I don't know if Col. Conley told you he took us offline. A stunned look came over his face when Hicks told him that. What! They took you guys offline? Yes sir Col Conley told Sgt .Ross and I we were going to the rear to help out with the wounded and guard the prisoners. Didn't he tell you sir? No! He didn't tell me anything. That didn't surprise me the Col never cared much about us anyway. So what are we going to do sir? I didn't know Col. Conley pulled you guys offline, so I guess you are here to support the other divisions. You guys won't be fighting anymore. That didn't sit well with the men. I acted like I was mad, but to tell you the truth I was happy as hell I didn't want to go back out there. I lost a lot of friends not to mention the best friend I ever had. So they want go back out there they can I'm staying in the rear. 1st Sgt. Hicks. Yes sir. Get the men ready to move out we moving out in 5 minutes.

Where are we going sir? We are going to Germany 1st Sgt. Popeye you need to get yourself a rifle there is a shack of rifles over there. Okay Hicks. I ran over to the pile to find me a rifle I looked around for a good one a lot of them were broken. I was getting mad, because I couldn't find one then I saw one that looked brand new. I grabbed it and I grabbed me two ammunition belts. I was about to walk away when I saw a Tommy gun it was the same gun Sgt carried. I dropped that rifle and grabbed that Tommy gun. I also grabbed the bag of clips that was lying next to it. When I got back to the division they were already moving out. What took you so long? I had to find some ammunition for this gun. I showed him the Tommy gun.

He looked at it. Ain't that the same gun Sgt carried? Yeah it is. So where are we going? To this city called Remagen to watch this bridge. The Lt. also said we are going to help the German citizens. Help the citizens! I thought the Germans were the enemy? Me to, but that's what he told me. I thought he said he didn't know what we were going to do? He told me the Col came to him last night while we were on our way here and told him what he wanted him to do, but he didn't know he was pulling us offline. He also said if the Russians get to Remagen before we do they are going to kill all the men and rape the women. Here we go again I said instead of us goin away from this shit we walking right back into it. To make matters worse we going back in with a leader who is worse then Capt. Douglass. How bad can our luck get.

We marched thought the ankle deep snow and wind for about 3 hours. I was really tired. I could barely stand up I hadn't slept in three days and I was hungry. The freezing cold made a lot of men sick. This was one of the worse winters in European history. Most of them were from the south and none of them had never seen snow that includes me. The closer we got to the city we saw people was running with all their belongs on carts, horses and some were even carrying their things. We were horrified on what we saw the roads were littered with dead bodies of German soldiers, civilians and burnt up equipment. It was a awful site to see.

You can smell the death in the air it really stunk bad. I have never smelled anything like that in my life. The site that really horrified me was the site of a woman holding her baby. They were both burnt to a crisp. The division came to a stop. 1st Sgt. Hicks I want you to get some men to check out those buildings to make sure their empty. Yes sir. Popeye you take third squad and check those building out. Okay third squad follow me. I told the men to go in two's to check out these buildings. Stay together and if you find anything come get me. Okay Sgt.

The buildings we was checking was bombed out and burnt up. I was saying to myself who in the hell would live in these building. We started down the street. The building reminded me of the row houses in Houston, but better. They was colorful building with fancy designs on them I pointed to which building I wanted them to go into. As we moved down the street I find myself in front of what use to be a apartment. The door was off it's hedges. I moved the door slowly.

There was a Cpl with me by the name of Shaw. I told him to go in. He went in and I followed him. The place looked like somebody was just there. There was cups, pots, pans, utensils, bowls and there was pictures still hanging on the walls. I guess they left in a hurry. Shaw and I started looking though the cabinets for some food. I got mad, because we didn't find anything.

I went into the bedroom and to my surprise it was intact. There was a bed in there with a brass headboard. It looked expensive it was better then the one I had. There was a nice looking wood chest in the corner. I bet Lillian would love that. I opened the doors to see if anything was in it nothing was in it. I was getting mad, because I wasn't finding anything. I opened the closet to see what I could find. It was empty to the only thing it had was this old box sitting on the top shelf. I went to reach it, but I was to short. I grabbed this stool that I find in the closet. I stood on the stool to try and get this box. My arms was to short to reach it. I stood on my toes to get it I still couldn't reach it. After about a minute I finally got it, but I lost my balance and fall. When that happen the box fell out my hand hit the hard wooden floor and broke open. I was shocked at what I saw. On the floor next to the box were diamonds shining back at me I picked one of them up. My eyes almost popped out of my head when I seen them I quickly put them back in the box I didn't know what to do. I couldn't take the box with me I had no bag to put them in. This must have been somebody's family stash they left in

The Men that Time has Forgotten

such a hurry they forgot them. I know they ain't coming back for them and I'm not going to leave them. I know if I don't take them somebody else will. I'm not going to gave them to Lt. Caldwell I'm going keep these diamonds and why not all the hell I have been though. Now the problem I had was where was I going to keep them at without nobody knowing about them. I had to think fast. My jacket had a hidden pocket on the inside of it. I could keep them in there I started taken the diamonds out the box and putting them in my pocket. I filled my pocket up and there was still more in the box. I started putting' them in my shirt pockets. I didn't have time to see how much I had, because somebody was coming. Sgt a voice said. Yeah I'm in here. It was Cpl. Shaw. Sgt we checked all the buildings and they were all empty. Okay lets get back to the division I got my rifle and we headed back to the division. Sgt did you find something? No. Why you asking me that Shaw? What was in that box on the floor? Nothing it was empty. Come on let's get back to the division. We got back to the division. Popeye did you find anything. No we didn't find anything Hicks. Okay well get your squad back in ranks we are moving out now. Okay Hicks. I was real nervous having all those diamonds on me if the Army found out I had them they will put me in the stockades. Then I will never see Lillian again, so I had to be careful that nobody finds out I got them. Move out the Lt told us. I notice Cpl. Shaw kept looking at me funny. I think he knows I found something what he doesn't know. He could look at me all he want to he won't be getting any of those diamonds. I know he's going to find out what I got. Shaw reminds me of one of those shady Niggas back in Houston. They always trying to con you out of something. I better watch myself around that Nigga. The walk to the next village was long and cold. They said this war would be over before Christmas and here we are still fighting the New Year will be here soon. I wonder if they are going to stop fighting so we can bring it in. I ain't wrote my wife in a couple of months. I'm glad Sgt wrote her while I was in the field hospital. I wonder how she and my daughter are doing. I have never seen my daughter I don't even know what she looks like. I don't know if she would even know who I am. It's going to take us some time to get to know each other. What if she rejects me that will break my heart. I can't blame her she's just a little girl. I had a picture of her, but I lost it when I got blow into that river.

CHAPTER FORTY-SEVEN

IT TOOK US ABOUT three days to reach this little village outside of the Rhine River. We had stopped at many towns searching for the enemy. They finally feed us along the way it wasn't much, but it helped a little. All the villages we passed though were deserted burnt out buildings, dead German soldiers and destroyed equipment along the roads. We were tasked with moving the destroyed equipment, so our troops can get though. The fighting on the way to Germany was bad. We didn't do any fighting and I was glad. Lt. Caldwell told us we were going to make camp in that small village. He told Hicks and I to set watches. Popeye third squad will have the first watch. Okay. I set the watches around the whole village. I told them they would be relieved every two hours and to stay alert and don't be asleep on watch. I got the rest of them together and told them the same thing. Popeye there is a small house over there where Lt. Caldwell is going to make his CP. He want us to meet him over there so he could tell us what we going to be doing while we're here. Okay Hicks I'll be over in a few. Shaw get all the squad leaders together and tell them to come to the CP. Alright Sgt. He ran and told all the squad leaders to come to the CP. What do you think he going to say to us Sgt? I don't know Shaw. We were all walking to the CP when we heard a shell coming. Take cover Hicks screamed. We all hit the ground the shell landed on the small house where the Lt. Caldwell had made his CP. The small house were blown to pieces.

When the shelling stopped we got up and ran over to the small house. When we got there all that was left of him were his boots and his feet were still in them.

Slim came running up behind us, but there was nothing he could do for him. The shelling started up again a couple landed where we had made our camp. I ran over to my squad and told them to stay down. As I was running I was saying to myself I hope I didn't lose any of those diamond I had in my pocket. I checked my pockets and shirt they were still there from what I could feel. Just as the bombing started it stopped. I met back up with Hicks. What are a we going to do now that Lt. Caldwell is dead?

We going to need to find somebody and tell them what happen. We ain't going to anyone a damn thing. We don't need damn officer. You, me, Slim and the squad leaders can run this division. We were running the division before Caldwell came anyway. Yeah you right even when Douglass was here Sgt was running the division we don't need them. Squad leaders go see if any of your men got hurt. Okay Sgt. So Hicks what are we going to do when they ask us for our CO. I don't know Popeye, but I will figure something out. Let's go find another place that we could make into a CP. We started looking around for place for our CP. How about that place over there Hicks. What place? That place over there (pointing at this little office) it looks like an office let's go check it out. We started walking toward the bombed out building. One side of the building was still intact. The door was still on it I tried to open the door, but it was locked. The door had glass windows I took the butt of my gun and broke them out. I reached my hand in and opened the door. When I opened the door we was shocked that it wasn't an office, but a store. We walked in and my mouth fell wide open.

Popeye do you see what I see? Yeah I see it. It was shocked with food. There was canned vegetables, flour, sugar, rice, beans, bread on one shelf. On another shelf was jars of different types of candy. I walked over to one of the selves and picked up a can of beans. Look at all this food Hicks. Oh yeah we then hit the jackpot Popeye. We need to take what we can before them white boys get here. You they don't give a damn about nobody but themselves. Do you want me to tell the rest of the division? No not yet I don't want them to come in here and take everything. What we can do is we can tell them to come in by squads. They can take a few items and leave. We need to keep men on watch. I was about to leave when Slim came in. Damn! Look at all this food. Popeye let Slim go tell the squad leaders to get their squads in ranks. Okay Hicks. Slim ran out to tell the squad leaders to tell their squads to fall into ranks. Popeye there's a door over here let's check it out. Okay. We moved slowly towards the door. Hicks whispered to me. On three I want you to kick the door in. I nodded my head okay. When he sad three I kicked the door in. Hicks went in with his rifle ready to shoot somebody. The room was empty, but you could tell that somebody had been living there. It had a old wooden bed in it and a picture with an old man, woman and a little girl. There was a tall old wooden chest in the corner of the room. A rocking chair sat next to the bed. A table sat in the middle of the room with a couple of chairs round it. The stove had teapot on it with hot water in it like somebody was making a cup of tea. I went over to the teapot and touched it. Hey Hicks this teapot is hot. There was plates, bowls, utensils and cups hanging on the wall over the stove. We started walking round the room when we heard something. Did you hear that Hicks? Yeah it sounded like it came from under the floor. We started to look around to see if we could find a door or something.

Then Hicks found something. Popeye come here help me move this stove there's a door under it. When we moved the shove there was a door. We looked at each other. Okay I'm going to open this door if anything jump out you shoot it. Okay I said. He opened the door. I stuck my Tommy gun down there and said Is there anyone down there come out with your hands up. Then we heard somebody say something in German. We didn't know what they was saying, because we didn't know how to speak German. Come out with your hands up I said again. Then we saw an old man come walking from the back. Get your hands up I told him. He kept saying something in German. We pulled him out of the hole. He was a short man with blue eyes with black hair and he was going bald. He was wearing some really old clothes. I guess these were the type clothes old people in Germany wore. Then this woman came out with her hands up. She scared the hell out of us. Popeye give me a hand in getting her out of here. She was wearing old clothes to. They look like they was married. Hicks asked them was there anybody down there (pointing at the hole with his rifle). They shook there heads no. I don't believe them Popeye go down there and see if there's somebody else down there. I'll cover you. The old woman was saying something, but we didn't know what she was saying. Hicks told her to shut up. I'll watch these two when you go down there. I walked down the wooden stairs slowly. It was so dark I couldn't see a thing. I told Hicks to throw me down a flashlight. What he said. I said throw me down a flashlight. I don't have one. Here use my lighter he throw lighter down to me. I flicked it on. At first I didn't see anything I started walking towards the back when I saw something moving in the corner. Who's there I said? I went towards the back and that's when I seen her. I pointed my lighter in the corner and she was balled up in the corner like a cat. I pointed my rifle at her and toward her to come out of there. Hicks yelled down Popeye did you find something. I yelled back yeah I did I found this girl in the corner. Well bring her ass up. A gave her a motion with my rifle and she started moving toward the hole. I yelled to Hicks that we were coming out. Okay. Hicks give her a hand getting out the hole. Come on girl we ain't going to hurt you. He helped her out of the hole. I walked out the hole back into the room. When I came up Slim and Shaw were in the room by now. Hicks and Slim was standing there staring at this girl. Damn Slim said. I couldn't see her, because she had her back to me. When I seen her I could see she was a full grown woman and she was very beautiful. She had long blonde hair, blue eyes and her skin was real white. She was the whitest woman I ever seen. Most of the white women back home were dirty looking to me. She was wearing a gray dress that came to her knees. Her breast stuck out like torpedoes though her dress and she was about 5'10. She was the tallest white woman I have ever seen. We all was looking at this woman in a amazement. What are we going to do with them Hicks? They are civilians we suppose to help them get out of here.

Yeah your right, but we need somebody who can speak German. Do we have anybody in our division who can speak German? Yeah we do there is this one guy in my squad who can speak a little German. Who is it Shaw? A Pvt. Stone. Who the hell is Pvt. Stone? You know the Pvt with the good hair. I ain't never seen him before go get him Shaw. Okay. Shaw ran out the room to go get this Pvt. Stone. The old man was saying something, but we couldn't understand what he was saying. I tried to tell them we ain't going to hurt them. They look scared. I would be scared to Popeye if I ain't never seen a Negro before.

CHAPTER FORTY-EIGHT

HICKS POINTED TO THE bed and told them to sit down. Damn where the hell is Shaw? I want to know what they are saying. Just than Shaw came in the room with Pvt. Stone. You Pvt. Stone? Yes 1st Sgt. You know how to speak German? Yes 1st Sgt. When I saw him I asked him you was he a Negro? Yes Sgt I am. Pvt. Stone was a tall (6'1) brown skin boy with straight hair and green eyes. His features didn't look Negro he looked more like he was Indian than anything else. Where you from Pvt? I'm from Oklahoma Sgt. So how do they consider you a Negro? Well my mother is half black and half Cherokee Indian. My father was white and he was Germany. So your daddy's white? Yes he is. What part of Oklahoma did you grow up in? I grow up on a reservation outside of Tulsa. Pvt how well do you speak German? I speak very well 1st Sgt. Good now tell these people we ain't going to hurt them. Pvt. Stone told in German what Hicks said. The old man started to talk to Stone we were amazed at how well Stone spoke German. They said okay, but the German soldiers told them that black soldiers were animals. I told them that we weren't animals we were here to help them not hurt them.

Ask them Stone how long they been down in that hole? They said they been down there a couple of days. They been hiding down there, because the German soldiers came looking for volunteers. They would only come up for food at night. Another reason they was hiding was they was afraid of the Russians they had heard the Russians were killing and raping German women. I heard the Col talking about that to Capt. Douglass one day. He told him that when the German invaded Russia the German soldiers was raping the women and killing the men.

He said the Russians were going to do the same once they got to Germany. Well Stone you tell them ain't nobody going to rape there daughter. I could see a smile come over there faces. They said okay. Ask them what are there names Stone. He said there names are Wolfgang, Ingrid and Audrey Kruger. Ingrid is their Granddaughter. Is this their store? Yes 1st Sgt this is their store. Well tell them we are going to turn them over to the Allied Forces it will be safer for them. Stone told them what Hicks said the old man wasn't to happy when Stone told them that. Wolfgang said this is all they have 1st Sgt. You tell him I said I understand, but if there is a lot of fighting going on here and if they don't leave they are going to die. He says he understands. He wants to know if he can take some food with them. Yeah he can take some food with them. Slim go out there tell the men don't take any more food until these people get their share food. Okay Hicks. Stone tell them to get their stuff together,so they can get ready to leave. 1st Sgt he wants to know if he could go down and get their things. Yeah he can, but you go with him Stone. Okay 1st Sgt. They do down to get their stuff. In few minutes he came back with two bags. The old woman walk over to the bed and took the picture down that was hanging over it. The girl took the blanket off the bed and put plates, utensils, bowls, cups. She dumped out the water in the teapot and put it in the blanket with the rest of the things. Stone ask her how old is she. She said she's 19 years old. She looks older then 19.

Okay y'all let's go. We walked back into the store and was shocked The guys had cleaned the store out. Damn! They didn't leave a damn thing for us Hicks and we are the ones who find the place. What the fuck happen to all the food? He was mad as hell I had never seen him mad. Did these motherfuckers think about me, Popeye and Slim. I guess not Slim said.

Wolfgang was very upset. What the fuck is he saying Stone? He saying my store my store.

What have you done to my store. Tell him to calm the fuck down. Stone told him to calm down and he did. What he saying now Stone? He saying that they don't have nothing to eat. Tell him we are going to get all their food back. Popeye go out there and tell everybody to fall the fuck into ranks, but not the ones who are on watch. I want outside and it was like a zoo.

WHAT THE FUCK IS GOING ON OUT HERE? I want everybody to GET THE FUCK IN RANKS NOW! They fell into ranks fast. What the fuck do y'all thing this is a party we still at war and your running around here like it's over. HAVE YOU MOTHERFUCKERS LOST YOUR MINDS? Hicks, Stone and the Kruger followed me to outside. Hicks walked up to the division. Listen up this store belongs to these people (pointing at the Kruger) I want everybody who took something out this store to bring it back Now. Pvt. Stone go get that car and bring it over here. Okay 1st Sgt. I want y'all to put anything you took out that store and put it in this cart. I won't y'all to do it NOW! The men fell out of ranks and put the goods in to the cart. To make sure they didn't have anything in their pockets I had all the squad leaders go around and check their peoples pockets. Sgt. Ross all the men pockets are empty. Okay Shaw.

The cart was so full of food it almost fell over. Stone tell them to take what they need and to follow those people to the Allied Lines. Before they left Wolfgang came over and shook Hick's hand. He's saying thank you 1st Sgt. You tell him I said he's welcome. The old woman came up to Hicks and wanted to kiss him, but he wouldn't let her. The young girl Ingrid just nodded her head. Then they started walking towards the Allied lines with the other Germans. I walked over to Hicks and whispered in his ear. Do you think we should have given them that food I ain't ate in a couple of days. I know Popeye I told Slim to put us some food up. Hold on for a minute. Listen up who here can cook. One Pvt raised his hand. What's your name Pvt. My name is Pvt. Harrison 1st Sgt. Okay Pvt. Corey Harrison you will be our cook for now on. Now I want first squad to take this food back to the store and put everything back on the shelf. I want you Pvt. Harrison to cook a meal for our division. There is a stove and oven for you to cook. Don't stand there and look at me Pvt let's get the cooking you got some hungry men out here. Now for the rest of y'all I want you clean up the streets up. If you have any question come ask me, Popeye or Slim. Squad leaders make sure it gets done. Come on Popeye and Slim let's go back to the CP it's colder than a motherfucker out here. Pvt. Harrison and first first squad was putting the food back on the shelves when we got to the CP. Pvt. Harrison what are you going to cook for the division? I don't know Sgt I can't read any of these labels.

Let me see. I took the can out of his hand. Oh this is beans. How you know that Sgt? Look at the pictures. Oh okay. Hey Pvt. Harrison make some stew. You got meat, potatoes, vegetables. Okay Sgt that sounds good I'll do that. While we waited for Pvt. Harrison to finish cooking the stew I asked Slim where did you hide that stash? He walked over to the counter.

He moved the counter and pulled out this blanket. He laid it on the floor and opened it up.

This the good stuff. In the blanket he had stacked it with can goods like beans, peaches, corn, candy, small bottles of beer and potatoes. The bread he had was bread I have never seen before. What's this I asked him? Bread he said. What type of bread is this? Don't worry bout it Popeye it's bread just eat it. We can boil these potatoes later. I picked up a can that look like meat, but I couldn't read it because it was in German. You got a can opener Hicks I want to see what this is. No I ain't got know can opener use your knife. I took my knife out and poked a hole in the top of the can. I worked my knife around the can until I got that top off. I put the tip of my knife in the can took a little out and tasted it. It tasted pretty good. It tasted like corn beef hash. I didn't care what it tasted like I was hungry it could have been dog food I still would've eaten it. Slim we can boil those potatoes now. How are you going to boil those potatoes with out water? When I was in that room I remember seeing a sink in that closet.

Slim found a pot put some water in it put the potatoes in it and let them boil. What are you eating there Popeye?

I don't know Slim, but it's good it taste like corn beef hash. Let me get a little bit of that. I gave him some of what ever I was eaten. Hey Slim see if they got any forks or spoons in there. Alright. When we were at that camp I over heard two white officers saying the war going to be over soon. Oh yeah. Yeah they say the Germans are finished. They been saying that bullshit for the past 2 months we will see. Hicks what do you think happen to Sgt? I don't know Popeye I find myself thinking about him sometimes, but I know he is doing fine knowing him. You think we are going to into Germany. You know Popeye I really don't care if we go into Germany or not. I'm tired of this war I want to go home. We was sitting there talking when all of a sudden the door flew open. We grabbed our rifles and stood up. It was Col. Conley. What the fuck are your doing he asked us? We just sitting here getting warm sir.

Where the fuck is Lt. Caldwell? He was killed in the last bombing sir. A stunned look came over his face. Why didn't you tell someone 1st Sgt Hicks? Well sir I didn't tell anyone, because I figured Sgt. Ross and I been running this division any way and we don't need an officer. He gave Hicks this funny look. Oh really? Yes sir. Well I guess you can run it now the war is almost over anyway. I want you to report anything that goes on to me you understand 1st Sgt.

Yes sir I understand. What the hell is that smell? That's Pvt. Harrison cooking a meal for the men sir. What is he cooking? He's cooking some stew sir. Alright carry on. We saluted him and he left. You can come out the room now Slim he gone. Slim stuck his round the corner.

We all started to laughing. We ate boiled potatoes and the stew Pvt. Harrison cooked. It was pretty good to. Then we got ourselves a good nights rest for the first time in months.

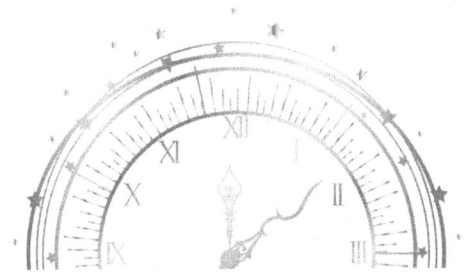

CHAPTER FOURTY-NINE

THE NEXT MORNING WE all were awaken by Cpl. Shaw. 1st Sgt. Hicks wake up. What is it Shaw? The Col wants to see you and Popeye right now. What time is it? It's 0500 hours in the morning. Okay come on Popeye get up we got to go see what the Col wants. Alright. We put on our jackets grabbed our guns and left. Where is he at Shaw? I'll take you to him. Damn! It's colder than a motherfucker out here. It had snowed a little that night and the wind was blowing hard. It was so cold I could barely walk. Shaw was is this motherfucker's CP at? It's in this house down this road. Is this the Col headquarters? Yeah this is it Sgt. Damn! This is nice. It was a beautiful brick house with different colors on it. It had a fence round it. There was wooden stairs going up to the front door. It look like one of those homes you see in those children story books. We got to the door when we were stopped by this white soldier. What the fuck do you Niggers want? We are here to see the Col Pvt. He wants to see us Hicks told him. He stood there and looked at us for a second. He seen the 1st Sgt stripes on Hicks shoulder. I'm sorry 1st Sgt you can go in. Thank you Pvt. He opened the door and let us in. We want in damn this is nice Shaw said. We walked into the living room there was marble statues, chairs, couches, tables made from the finest wood I have even seen. I know because I worked with a lot of wood and this is the best. We was standing there in with our mouths open when we

Michael Johnson

heard a voice telling us to come in. We walked though the living room to what I think was a den where the Col was sitting. He was sitting his fat ass behind a beautiful black lacquer desk. Have a seat. We sat down in these two beautiful custom made chairs. I seat down in the soft chair which was trimmed in gold. You probably wondering why I want to see you boys? Yes sir we were wondering. We're moving out he said we are making a final push into Germany. You won't be coming with us you will remain behind to guard this town. We are trying to get to Berlin before the Russians. What we are going to do while we here sir Hicks asked him. Help the civilians on what ever help they need. Hicks and I looked at each other.

We going to be move out in a couple of hours. Sir you going with them? No I'm going to stay behind, but I need you to keep division in line. I seen somethings I didn't like I'm counting on you two to kept things under control this war isn't over. We still have a lot of fighting to do.

Now you need to tell your division this. You understand. Yes sir. Now go tell your division what I said. We got up saluted and left. We got outside and I told Hicks I didn't like this. I know Popeye. Why we ain't going to Germany? I tell you why that motherfucker in there don't won't us to go. He want to keep us out of it. A lot of the guys are looking forward of going into Germany. I know, but that's the way it is. Let's go tell the men. We walked down the frozen cold road to the men. Slim had the men in ranks. Listen up I got some bad news for you. We ain't going to Germany we are going to stay behind and help out the civilians. We will be here until the war is over. So we ain't going to Germany Shaw asked. That's right Cpl. What you mean help out the civilians. What I mean by that is hand out food, water, clothes and help rebuild their homes. So what you are saying 1st Sgt is the war is over for us. That's what I'm saying Cpl. Shaw throw is rifle down in anger. I came here to fight not hand out food to know fucking Germans. Shaw I know I how you feel, but that's the way it is. I want y'all to take a look at all those dead bodies over for those who want to fight anyone of them would love to take your place. So Shaw if you want to fight go head. Go tell the Col you want to go to Germany. He looked over at those dead bodies picked his rifle and got back in ranks. Y'all should be thanking God you are alive. One day you are going to thank the Col for this. I know I will thank him. Now let's help out these German civilians put their lives back together. The next couple of days all we did was help the German civilians with food, water and medical attention. A lot of German prisoners came in also most of them had surrendered to our forces on our way to Germany. Popeye get some guys to guard these prisoners. Okay Hicks. I got a couple of guys to guard them they didn't look like they was going to run anyway. They looked glad and relieved they had surrendered. One German soldier came up to me and touched my face he looked at his hand he probably thought my skin color would come off in his hand. We all laughed at him when he did that. He looked at us and laughed to. He really didn't know we was laughing at him, because how stupid he looked doing that. I'm tired Slim I am go back to the CP. Okay Popeye I will see you in a few minutes. Before I want back to the CP I stopped at all the watch stations to make sure the men were standing proper watches. You guys make sure you stay alert, because if the Col catches any of y'all sleeping he's going to have you shot. So stay awake y'all understand. Yes Sgt. I started walking toward the store we made into our CP. This also will gave me a chance to look at all the diamonds I had. I got in put my rifle down took my jacket off and sat on the floor. We been here almost a week and I haven't had a chance to look at my diamonds. I reached in my pocket and pulled out took all the diamonds out of my pocket and spread them all out on my blanket. I started taken the ones I had in my shirt out. Some of them had falling down my pants leg. When I laid them all out I couldn't believe my eyes. It must have been about a million dollars in diamonds in front of me. Well it look like it to me. There was red, green, blue, purple, yellow all different colors. I'm rich I said. Then I got to thinking if the Army know I had all these diamonds they would shoot me for stealing them I need a place to hide them until we leave. I looked around to see where I could hide them at. I went into the bedroom to see if I could find a hiding place.

After looking around a few minutes I seen a small bag hanging behind the headboard. We must have missed it when we was checking the room. I took the bag off the hook it was on. It felt like it had something in it. I opened the bag and poured it out on the bed. It was nothing but shaving stuff for man. I left the stuff on the bed I'm going to need to shave later I ain't shaved in weeks. I put the diamonds in the bag. I was about to hang them on that hook when I heard Hicks and Slim come in. I quickly stuffed them in my pocket. Popeye what are you doing? Oh nothing was getting ready to shave. You get ready to shave? Yeah I find a shaving kit I was getting to shave. By this time he had walked into the room. I showed him the shaving kit. Well you get finished let me use it. Okay. I wasn't going to shave now I just told him that. got the guys on two hours watches and I want us to do the same. Shaw you going to do the first two hours. Okay Hicks. Slim I want you to stand watch over at the field hospital just in case we get some wounded men in. Alright. Popeye you and I are going to clean this place up. We are going to be running things until they get in another officer for us. Any questions he asked us. Well let's get to it. Hicks and I clean the store up the place was a mess from the guys coming in and taking stuff. It took us about two hours to clean all that shit up. We ate a little something (boiled potatoes) drink some coffee talked a bit and went to sleep.

CHAPTER FIFTY

I WAS WOKEN UP BY someone shaking me. I looked up to see who it was. It was Hicks. Hey man get up it's your time for watch. Alright what time is it? It's 0000hours. So how is the weather out there? It's colder than a motherfucker out there I'm glad my watch is over now I can get warm. I got up put on my jacket grabbed my Tommy gun. When I opened the door the wind hit me so hard it woke me up. The watches we had all Hicks, me and the squad leaders had to walk around making sure the men stayed awake and alert. The mud on the roads had frozen over and there were patches of ice everywhere. I had to be careful not to slip and fall in Houston we didn't have shit like this. I walked on two Pvt warming there hands over a barrel they had found. How are you doing Sgt? I stopped to warm my hands. How you doing Sgt?

I'm doing fine. Have you guys seen anything out of the ordinary? No Sgt we ain't seen nothing everything has been quite. Good let's keep it that way. If any thing happens to come get me I'll be walking around checking on the other guys okay. We will Sgt. I made my rounds to all the watch stations I caught a few guys sleep, but other wise than that everything was normal. I was heading back to the CP to warm up a little before I want on my next round when I saw this Pvt come out of this barn pulling up his pants. I figured it was the can, so instead of walking all the way back to the CP I'll just use that. I started walking towards the barn when I heard a women voices, but they were speaking German. I decided to go around back instead going though the front. It was a small crack in the barn I peeped though the crack and what I saw could get us all shot. I saw Pvt. Miller fucking some German woman and he wasn't they only one. There had to be a least 15 guys in that barn waiting their turn. Oh hell no. I knew if the Col found out about this shit he was going to blame Hicks and I. I started to run back to the CP and wake up Hicks, but I knew this was something I had to handle myself. I walked back around to the front of the barn and kicked the door open. WHAT THE FUCK ARE YOU NIGGAS DOING IN HERE? They were shocked when I did that one Pvt stopped in mid stroke. Nothing one Pvt said to me. So you telling me you don't have your dick in that woman? You Niggas suppose to be sleep are standing watch. You suppose to be sleep or standing watch not out here getting you some pussy. If the Col found out you motherfuckers were out here doing this shit he will have your asses shot. You motherfuckers know the rules don't you? Yes Sgt. Now you motherfuckers got 5 minutes to do what you got to do. I'm going to use the can you motherfuckers better be gone when I get back. All the German women were just standing there looking at me. I looked around the room and seen Ingrid the girl we pulled out that hole in the store. I was shocked to see her there, but than again I wasn't she got to make money to. I left to use the can I could hear them laughing when I left. I don't blame for getting a little pussy they been out here a long time with no women a man could go crazy. If I wasn't a married man I would be in there with them. I used the can did another round when I came by the barn they were gone. I looked at my watch it was 0145 hours it was time to wake up Hicks. I walked back to the CP and woke Hicks up. What time is it? It's 0200 hours. Is everything okay? Yeah I had no problems, but it is cold as hell outside you better bundle up good. He put his jacket on grabbed his rifle and headed out the door. When he opened up the door he said DAMN! You ain't laying Popeye it's colder than a motherfucker out here. I laughed at him as he left. I took my jacket off rolled it up into a pillow grabbed me a blanket laid down and went to sleep. The next three months we didn't see any action which was fine with me. All we did was help the wounded, guard the prisoners and help the German civilians help build their homes. The Germans had retreated back into Germany our forces had them surrounded. The Russians had defeated the Germans in the east and were closing in on Berlin. It was a nice day that day the weather had started to get warm most of the snow had started melt, but the bad thing about that was it all turned into mud which made it hard for equipment to move. So we had to make roads for the equipment move though. It was back breaking work I promise myself when this war is over I ain't going to do know more hard labor.

We had a lot of free time we spent most of it playing baseball. I had never played baseball before, but I found out I was pretty good. It also gave me time to write Lillian. She was glad to hear from me. She said she knew I won't dead, but she was still worried about me. I also thought about Sgt a lot by now I know he was dead. If he wasn't he would have turned up by now. I still had these letters he gave me I wondered why he didn't want me to open them until I got home. I was curious so I got one out my pocket. It was wrinkled up real bad and it had some of Sgt blood on it. I had to find out what it said I was about to open it when Hicks came busting though the door all excited. DAMN Hicks what you doing? Hitler is dead. What! What?

Didn't you hear me Hitler's dead he shot himself yesterday. Are you serious Hicks? Hell yeah I'm serious Popeye. Then the war's over right? Well they ain't said that, but it's going to be soon. I had to sit down when he told me that. You okay Popeye? Yeah I'm fine I just can't believe the war is almost over. I got to write my wife. What's that you got in your hand? Oh this it's a letter from Sgt. He give it to me back at that village we captured. Well what it say? I don't know he told me not to open it up until I get home. Well if he told you not to open it then why are you getting ready to read it? You know it's bad luck to open a letter somebody gave then you open it and read it. You know if you open that letter something bad is going to happen to you. I know what Hicks was saying was a bunch of bullshit I just put it back in my pocket. So what are they going to have us do now Hicks? We are going to continue to do what we been doing until they tell us otherwise. Why don't you come over to the barn with me Popeye we are going to celebrate Hitler's death. They are going to have a lot of those German girls over there. Oh yeah. Yeah come on man it beats sitting around here all the time.

You know since Hitler's kill himself those German girls started given that pussy away for free.

I know I'm gonna get me some I have had my fair share of that white pussy. Popeye these women love us. I got this one German woman name Gina man I laid this big dick on her one night the girl in love with me. It sounds good I don't think so Hicks I'm a married man and I love my wife very much. Popeye you ain't the only man married shit half the division is married that ain't stopping any of them from getting them a piece of pussy. I was shocked to hear all this I thought most of the guys was single. No thanks Hicks I don't care what they do to their wives I can't do that to mine. Okay I understand, but a least come over for a drink. I'll think about it. Well I'm going to head over here, because I'm going to get me some tonight. I'll see you later. Okay. He left to head over to the barn. I reached in my pocket and told out a picture of Lillian she had sent to me in one of her letters. I looked at the picture I had forgotten how beautiful she was. I can wait until I get home to have sex. I decided I would go over there and have a drink I ain't had a drink since we left England. A drink would be good I put my pictures in my pocket and head over to the barn. The sun was shinning a little the roads were full of trucks and vehicles. There were people everywhere fixing their homes trying to put their lives back together. I could see where all the guys were going so I just followed. I went into the barn it looked different from the last time I was here. They moved all the hay and equipment put in some tables and chairs. Thy ever had a bar it look like they stole it from somebody's house. There was a lot of people in the barn standing around, dancing, singing and drinking. They was singing something I couldn't understand. I saw Pvt. Stone talking to some German girl I want over and tapped him on his shoulder. Hey Sgt. Ross how you doing?

He had been drinking I could smell it on his breath. What are they

The Men that Time has Forgotten

saying? They are singing about how happy they are that Hitler's dead and the war will be over soon. You seen Hicks I asked him? Yeah he's over there in the corner. Okay I said see you later. I was on my way to see Hicks when I heard somebody call my name. I looked around to see who it was it was Cpl. Shaw standing behind the bar. Popeye you won't a drink? Yeah give me a beer. He took one of the glasses off the bar went to a barrel and filled my glass with beer. Here you go Popeye. To my surprise it tasted good and it was cold to. This is pretty good Shaw. I was talking to Shaw when I felt a hand on my shoulder. I turned to see who it was and it was Ingrid the girl we saved a couple months ago. How you doing Sgt Ross she said in her German accent. I'm doing fine? How you know my name? Your friends told me. Really I looked at Shaw. He just smiled at me. She was looking nice she was wearing this low cut dress that showed the top of her big chest. She had some big tits. Her blue eyes would make any man weak in the knees. You won't to sit down I asked her. Sure she said. We sat down at one of the tables and started to talk.

CHAPTER FIFTY-ONE

SHE STARTED ASKING ME questions about me and my family. In the back of my mind I'm thinking Hicks set this up. So I hear your married with a baby. Yes I am married. My wife's name is Lillian and my daughter's name is Jennifer. How long have you been married? I been married about two and a half years. Do you miss her? Oh yeah I can't wait until I get back to see her.

You must love her very much? I do she and my little girl mean the world to me. I wanted to think you and your friends for saving our lives. I don't think we would be alive if the Russians got to us first. Well I'm glad I got to you first. What happen to your momma and daddy? Well my father was in the Army he was killed fighting the Russians in the east. My mother worked in a ammunition factory in Berlin when she was killed during a bombing raid by one of your planes. I was 17 years old when that happen I was very angry about that I wanted all Americans to die. They told us that Americans was our enemies and they all such die, but as the war went on I realize the true enemy was right here in Germany. We had heard Hitler had gone mad. He wanted men, women and even children to pick up arms to fight. I take her hand and said I was sorry. Do you have any brothers and sisters? No. I'm the only child of my parents. How old are you? I'm 21 years old. How old are you? I'm 23 years old. I just turned 23 in January. I wasn't really listening to her story I was looking at her big titties the more I looked at them the more I wanted to fuck her. I started to get hard or maybe it was the beer or both. I know in my heart it would be wrong, but then Lillian wouldn't know I'm way over here. I started thinking to myself it ain't going to hurt to get me a piece of that white pussy or I could go back to the CP with a hard on hard enough to cut diamonds. I ain't got to worry about any trying to lynch me for having sex with a white woman. These German woman the enemy who going to care if I fuck one German woman my dick is hard as a rock. I was just about to ask her back to the CP when Hicks drunk ass tumbled over to our table. Popeye what's going on man? I knew you were going to come over here. Hey how you doing he said to Ingrid. I'm fine. He leaned over and whispered in my ear. What are you going to do with this white woman? I didn't say nothing I just looked at him. Well if you ain't going to fuck her I sure will.

Calm down man we just sitting here talking. What y'all talking about? You done had too much to drink Hicks I think you need to go back to the CP and sleep it off. I ain't going back to know damn CP I'm fine. He was falling all over me. Let me get you back to the CP Ingrid I'm sorry I got to get him back to the CP. You want me to help you? I looked at her yeah you can help me. She grabbed one arm and I grabbed the other. We walked out the barn and into the crowded streets everyone was looking and laughing at us. Sgt a Pvt asked me is 1st Sgt going to me alright? . Yeah he's going to be alright he had a little to much to drink. We struggled to keep Hicks on his feet. When we got to the CP Cpl. Shaw was coming out. What the fuck are you doing in our CP? I had to use the can. You had to use the can ain't there one in the barn? Yeah,but that one someone was using is 1st Sgt going to be alright? Get your ass out the way yeah he's going to be fine. I know that motherfucker was lying he was in there looking for my diamonds. He ain't never going to find them. I hide' them good, because I knew he was going to come looking for them. That Nigga think I'm stupid. We finally got Hicks inside and laid him down one of the cots we got from the field hospital. Let's lay him down on his stomach. Let him sleep that off. He was a hand full I'm tired. Yeah he was let's go back to the barn. No why don't we just say here I want to be alone with you Jeffery. I wasn't surprise I knew she wanted to do something. I could see it in her eyes. She kissed me on my lips and walked into the bedroom. You coming Jeffery. I started walking towards the bedroom, but my legs started shaking real bad. My heart was pounding in my chest and I started to sweat. I stood outside the bedroom door saying to myself what the fuck are you doing. She called my name again. Jeffery are you coming? What are you doing? I finally got the nerve to go into the room to my surprise she was sitting at the table with two tea cups on the table. I'm making some tea you want some? I stood there for a second. Yeah I would love some. Come on sit down it will be ready in a few minutes. I was kind of disappointed I thought she was in bed waiting on me, but I was wrong. What were you doing out there? I was checking on Hicks making sure he was alright. Are you sure about that ? She gave me this funny look. Yeah I'm sure why are you looking at me like that? I was thinking the reason you were taking so long is you might have thought I was in bed waiting on you and you didn't know if you wanted to make love to another woman that wasn't your wife. I smile at her she had me. Yeah I thought that. Why would you think that? You told me you were happily married and you truly loved your wife and daughter. Why would you go back on your word? I guess Ingrid it comes from being over here. I haven't seen my wife and daughter in 2 years. When a man gets lonely he does crazy things. That's really sad you haven't seen your family in 2 years I know that is hard on you. Come sit down. She poured me a cup of tea. You want any sugar? Yes please. She gave me two teaspoons of sugar. This is nice I ain't never had tea before. Oh really well tea is better than coffee. I don't like coffee it stains your teeth. I love coffee I got to have me a cup in the morning to function. We started to laugh. We sat there and talk about everything friends, family, both of our countries and the war. She looked at her watch. Well it's getting let and curfew is in a few minutes. Yeah curfew at 2100hours let me walk you to the door. She got up to leave when she turned around and said. I could stay if you want me to. I looked at her crazy thoughts started running though my mind. Do you really want to stay? Yes I want to stay. Okay. She walked to the bed took off her shoes and laid down. Come (holding out her hand). I took off my shirt, boots and laid down next to her. Move closer she said. She put my head on her soft breast. The perfume she was wearing smelled like roses. Are you comfortable Jeffery? Yes I am. Good now rest morning will be here soon. I felt good laying there next to her. I knew it was wrong, but it felt good. My dick was hard as a rock.

CHAPTER FIFTY-TWO

THE NEXT MORNING I was woken up with cold water thrown in my face. Wake up lover boy.

What the fuck. I look to see who it was it was Hicks standing over me with a bucket. You have a nice night. Where is Ingrid? She gone man she left early this morning. What time is it? It's time for you to get you're ass up. What time is it Hicks? It's 0600hours. Did you fuck that girl Popeye? No I didn't. Why not man she was primed and ready. I told you Hicks I'm a married man. Oh yeah I forgot you one of those faithful husbands. Is that a problem? No I'm just saying it couldn't have been me I would have fuck the hell out of her. Well that's you not me.

Come on get dress and let's go get some chow. He started to go out the room when he turned to me. There's something I wanted to tell you. Oh yeah when I woke up this morning I caught Cpl. Shaw going through your jacket pockets. What! Yeah I asked that Nigga what the fuck are you doing? He told me he was looking for a lighter to light is cigarette. I said Nigga you are lying you don't even smoke. I told him if he didn't put that jacket down and get the fuck out of here I was going to kick his black ass. What did he do? He dropped your jacket and left.

You know Popeye I ain't never trusted that motherfucker. He look like one of shady Niggas. I heard he was that type of Nigga that if you got in some shit he'll snitch on you to get his ass out of it. So why was he going though your pockets? I got up and closed the door. Do you remember that village we took a couple months back. Yeah. He thinks I found something valuable there. Like what? I found this box I thought it was something in it, but it wasn't. He came in and seen the box laying on the floor. He asked me what was in that box I told that Nigga nothing. He thinks I got something and he wants me to share it with him, but I ain't got nothing. Hicks just looked at me. I got me a couple of watches off a few dead German officers. Okay than we just have to watch out for that Nigga. You need to get in that Niggas ass for going though your pockets. Oh believe Hicks I will. Come on finish getting dressed, so we can get something to eat I'm hungry then a motherfucker. I lied to Hicks I wouldn't dare tell him what I found, because he might wont' me to share it with him. I finished getting dressed and we left. We left the CP and headed over to the chow tent. We was walking to the tent chow when we saw Shaw. There that Nigga Popeye. He didn't see us walking towards him.

He was to busy talking to some German girls. Cpl. Shaw. Oh hey 1st Sgt and Sgt hows it going? Hicks told me he caught you going though my pockets. What the fuck were you looking for? I was looking for a cigarette lighter. Nigga you lying don't even smoke. Did you find what you was looking for? Maybe he had this look on his face. He was trying to see what my response would be, but I knew he ain't find anything. You better kept you're ass out of my things Nigga. Or what? What your short ass going to do, but get you're ass kicked. By this time we was in each others faces. Hicks stepped between us. Now let me tell you something Cpl. I better not caught your ass at that CP even again or I will kick your black ass. You understand me motherfucker. Yes 1st Sgt. Now get the fuck out of here. He walked off saying something under his breath. Let's go Popeye. We walked over to the chow tent. Hey Pvt. Harrison what you got? Hicks asked him. We got bacon, eggs, grits, oatmeal, toast and coffee. Give me a little of everything. What you need Sgt? I'll have the same. We got our food and sat at the back table. Could you believe that Nigga. I wish it was me that caught that motherfucker going through my pockets I would've kicked his ass. He was caught going though your pockets and he gets mad at you. I wish it was me I would have killed that motherfucker. I wasn't listening to Hicks, because Ingrid had walked into the tent. Popeye you listening to me? Oh I see what you looking at your girl just walked in. She saw me and headed right for our table. Morning Jeffery, Melvin. Morning we said. Melvin I see you are feeling a lot better. I'm okay this morning thinks for asking. Can I sit down? Sure. Well I'm going get the men into formation so I could tell them what I need done today. Okay I'll be there in a few minutes. Don't worry about it Popeye I got this you take your time. You sure?

Yeah I'm sure. Okay. See you later Ingrid. Okay Melvin. He put his tray up and left the tent.

Where did you go this morning? I had to go help my grandparents with the morning chores.

Oh yeah. Where you are living at now? We are living at our little farm house. I thought the store was your home? Oh no we have a farm to. The store was something my grandparents owned to make extra money. I went to your CP but you won't there. Then I seen Cpl. Shaw he told me you was here. So what's on your mind? I came to ask you would you like to come over to my house for dinner. At first I didn't know what to say. Sure I would love to come over for dinner. What time do you want me to come over? 1900 hours is that okay with you. Yes that will be fine. Okay I will see you then. She got up to leave she turned and said don't forget 1900. I won't I said. I watched her as she left. I notice a big difference between American women and European women. European women are more open to who you are. Where in the U.S. all they see is your skin color. If Ingrid was living in the U.S. she wouldn't say a word to me and I wouldn't dare speak to her. If I was ever caught with a white woman I surely would get lynched. I put my tray up and rushed to formation. When I go there Hicks was finish telling the men what he needed done for the day. Y'all understand. Yes 1st Sgt they said. They hand saluted and was dismissed. Well how did it go with Ingrid? She asked me over for dinner. For dinner! Yeah what wrong with that? Nothing I mean if a woman ask me over for dinner it must mean she likes me. It also mean she gonna give you some of that pussy to. Oh it ain't nothing like that. Come on man she would have given you some last night, but I was there. I would be trying my best to get me some of that. You could see she likes you. I tell you Popeye it couldn't be me. Let's go over here and see what these fools are doing. We walked over to this brunt out German truck. They are suppose to be stripping it for parts, but they was playing around. What the fuck are y'all doing? Get the fuck to work and stop bullshitting around.

Popeye we need to keep an eye on these fools if we don't they are going to start to slack off, so we have to stay on top of them. Y'all better stop fucking around and get to work. That better be done by 1600 hours like I told y'all. Hicks I'm going to walk over to the field hospital to see what Slim is doing. Okay if you need me I'll be walking to see if I can catch any one else fucking around. When I got to the hospital Slim was sitting down at his desk. Hey Slim.

Hey Popeye how you doing? I'm good. What you doing over here? I just came to see how thing were going with you. I'm fine got a lot of wounded men, but other wise then that I'm good. I hear you got yourself a hot date tonight. Who told ya that? News travels fast here. I wouldn't call it a date she just ask me over for dinner. He looked at me with this funny smile.

Popeye if a woman asks you over for dinner that's a date to me. Let me tell you about what's her name? Her name is Ingrid. Yeah Ingrid everybody and I mean everybody has been trying to get some of that pussy. She ain't given nobody nothing but she's been given you all her attention you are the only black soldier she talks to the rest of us she could careless about.

So you must be special. I don't see it that way. Alright well that's not the way I see it. Let me get out of here and check on these guys. Alright then I 'll see you later. He said that with a smile. The rest of the day Hicks and I walked around checking on the men making sure they were doing their jobs. I thought about not going I didn't feel right. I looked at my watch to see what time it was it was 1545 hours I had a little time left. We were going to form up in 15 minutes I walked over to the place where we are going to form up and I seen Hicks talking to some white officer. Popeye come over and meet our new CO 1st Lt. Brad Sutherland. I walked over to them slow. Lt. Sutherland this is Sgt. Jeffery Ross. How yeah doing sir. We shook hands. Popeye Col Conley sent him here. He just got here a couple weeks ago. Damn a green horn. I said that to myself. He's going to try to show us who the boss is. The new ones always got to try and prove themselves. They always send us the new ones who ain't got any experiences. This could mess up my plans for tonight. The men started falling into formation.

Let's go men line up. Attention. He went on to introduce the Lt. Sutherland. Lt. Sutherland was about 6'3 brown hair and eyes medium build. I can tell he was from up north. He talked a little like them English people in England. It him about 20 minutes to tell us what he had to say. Which was a bunch of bullshit. Hicks came over to me while he was still talking. Popeye this motherfucker ain't staying at our CP we are going find him somewhere else to sleep.

Where? You remember that house where Lt. Caldwell got killed? Yeah. A couple of guys fixed it up and they been using it to fuck those German girls. I smiled at him yeah he can stay his ass over there. I got a date tonight like you and I be damn if I'm going to let this bastard mess up some pussy for me. 1st Sgt Hicks. Yes sir. Where will I be bunking at? I'll take you over there now sir. Pvt. Mason get the Lt. Sutherland's bags and follow me over to his quarters. I started walking towards the CP when the Lt. Sutherland called me. Sgt. Ross I want you to come to my quarters I have a few things I went to discuss with you and 1st Sgt. Hicks. I looked at my watch it was 1630 hours.

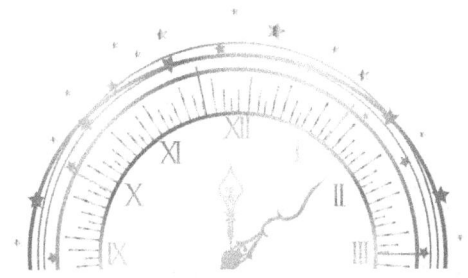

CHAPTER FIFTY-THREE

WE WALKED LT. SUTHERLAND to his CP. Hicks open the door and he walked in. The guys didn't do a bad job fixing the place up. It had a couple of cots they got from the hospital. The windows had curtains on them and there was and desk in the corner. They fixed the side of the house that was destroyed by the bombing. Well here you are sir this will be your CP. He looked around and turned to Hicks. I expected better looking quarters than this 1st Sgt. Well I'm sorry sir this is the best you are going to get. The place we stay in is no better than this one. Well I guess it will have to do. He put down his rifle took off his helmet, jacket and gloves and laid them down on one of the cots. We'll try and find you a chair for that desk sir. That will be fine 1st Sgt. Okay the reason I wanted to talk with you two is that I was told you boys were out of control. That's why the Col sent for me to put you boys back in your place. What! Sir who told you that? The Col did. Hicks and I looked at each other. He also said you and Sgt. Ross haven't been doing your jobs keeping these boy under control. Now this is what I want you and Sgt. Ross to do. I want the division in ranks every morning at 0500 hours with clean shaves, shined boots and clean uniforms. Also liberty will end for all you boys at 2400 hours.

I'll leave that responsibility up to you and Sgt. Ross if I catch any mean out after 2400 I will hold you two responsible and that person will be court-martial. You understand? Yes sir we understand. Now that we understand each other where can I get a nice hot meal? There's a chow tent down the road sir. Okay I will see you two at 0500 in the morning. Yes sir we saluted and left. Popeye did you hear that sorry motherfucker? Yeah I heard his ass. He must be out of his motherfucking mind thinking we such be in at 2400 and Col. Conley he ain't about shit. That motherfucker all he do is lie. You know he don't know what we are doing his fat ass ain't here half the time. You know Hicks I knew he was going to come in here and throw his weight around to show us who was in charge. He ain't in charge shit Popeye. His ass ain't never been in a fight, so fuck him. I got me some ass lined up for tonight and I'll be damn if he is going to fuck it up for me. You got that date with Inger and I know you are not going to be back by 2400. I just thought of something. What? Does your girlfriend have any sisters? Hell yeah she got seven sisters. Why don't you do this take Lt. Sutherland over to the barn tonight and hook him up with one of her sisters. Let her get his ass nice and drunk so we stay out a little later. He might even get lucky if you know what I mean. Yeah that ain't a bad idea Popeye and you can spend more time with Ingrid. I'll talk you Jeri about it. Who's Jeri?

That's my girl's name Jeri. What time is it? It's 1800 hours what time you got to be over Inger house? She told me to come at 1900 hours. Than you need to get ready. I ran back to the CP and started getting ready. I took off my dirty uniform washed up in the small sink put on a clean uniform. I shined my new boots I got off a dead officer. I looked at myself in the mirror I was looking sharp. I my ammunition bag, Tommy gun, put on my jacket and grabbed my cover and left. I looked at my watch it was 1830 hours. I started walking and realized I don't know where Inger lived she never told me. I know she live on a farm, but which farm is hers. I saw two German girls that I remember seeing with Ingrid one day. I asked them did they know where Ingrid lived? Yes she lives down this road and her house is on the right. It's the brown little house with the black roof. Thank you. I started walking down the dirt road which reminded of the dirt roads in Houston. It was getting dark and I needed to find her house soon. The houses were smaller than the ones in the village. There were a few someone was trying to rebuild from all the bombing. I was thinking about all those people who were killed. I wasn't paying attention I almost walked pass Ingrid's house. I walked down the small path her house looked like one of those houses in those children story books. I knocked on the door.

The old woman from the store we saved answered the door. Yes. Yes is Inger here? Yes she is come in. I could understand her German a little. Come she said. I followed her into another room. The inside was smaller than the outside. We walked into the small kitchen she there was a small table with four chairs I figured the fourth chair was for me. They didn't have a shove, so she was cooking the meal in the fireplace. There was a rusted sink in the corner.

The table was already set. Sit down Ingrid will be down soon. I looked at her. I thought you didn't speak any English? I never told you that I speak good English it's my husband who doesn't speak any English. But when we asked y'all if you spoke any English you sad no. No you asked my husband you didn't ask me you assumed I couldn't, so I didn't say anything.

She called Ingrid and her husband to come to the table. Her husband came in smoking this stinking cigar that filled the room with smoke. She told him in German to put the cigar out. He said something to her and than he put it out. Than Inger walked in she was looking beautiful she was wearing a dark blue dress that looked like one of those dresses the women in Switzerland would wear I thought the dress was ugly. Hello Jeffery. Hello Inger. She came and sat down next to me and grabbed my hand. Her hand was soft like a baby's ass. Her grand momma put two pots on the table. Now we can eat. Her grand daddy said something.

Okay. What did he say? He said we should say grace before we eat. We bowled our heads he said a few words in German and we started to eat. Do you like lamb Jeffery? Yes I like lamb I was lying I have never had lamb I didn't want to be rude and say no. So what's in that pot there? Oh it's vegetables potatoes, carrots, peas and onions. So this is a slew? Yes it's a slew. You don't like slew. Oh no I love slew. Her grand daddy cut off a piece of lamb and put it on my plate. I tasted the lamb and it was pretty good. Inger put a stoop of slew on my plate.

You like the lamb and slew Jeffery. Yes it's very good. Her grand momma smiled at me. Her grand daddy tore off a piece of bread of a loaf and gave it to me. So Jeffery what part of America are you from? I'm form the state of Texas ma'am. Texas that's where all the cowboys come from like John Wayne right? I laughed a little yes ma'am. What city in Texas are you from? I'm from the city of Houston ma'am. They ride horses in Houston. Yes ma'am they do in some parts,but must of the time we drive cars. How long have you been in Europe I've been here since August of 1944. So you were not part of the invasion of Normandy? No ma'am I came a couple of months later they didn't want us mixing with the white soldiers. Why not?

The same reason the Nazis don't want y'all mixing with the Jews. Than we heard a knock at the door. I'll get that Inger told her grand parents. I thought I heard Hicks voice. Inger came back and told me that Hicks was at the door. I got up to see what he wanted. Popeye you need to come back to the base. Why? We are moving out tonight. What! Tonight? Yeah tonight. Why are we moving out tonight? The Lt told me they have been finding camps all over Germany with dead and starving people in them. I turned and looked at Inger I can tell by the look in her eyes she known I had to leave. I got to go Inger we are moving out tonight.

Are you coming back? I don't know, but I have to go. I told her grand parents thanks for the dinner I grabbed my gear and left. When I got outside I asked Hicks what the fuck is going on? Why are we moving out tonight? The Lt came to me about 30 minutes ago and told me they have been founding death camps all over Germany. Death camps? What kind of death camps? These camps are where the send the Jews to die. How many of these camps have they found? I don't know that, but the Lt told me we were moving out tonight. Was the Lt looking for me? No he was to busy trying to get him some pussy. Damn! She had that motherfucker in the palm of her hands until that fucking Pvt came in and told him that bullshit.

When we got back to base the men were already loading up on the trucks. Popeye let's get our gear packed before they leave us. We started packing our gear. You Popeye I caught that motherfucker Shaw in here again. You caught Shaw in here again? Yeah. Did you kick his ass? No, but that motherfucker keeps coming in here looking for something. I don't why he keep coming in here. I wanted to tell him so bad, but I couldn't. Come on hurry and get your gear before they leave us. Okay I'll meet you out there. Okay hurry up. I watched him as he left before I got my diamonds. I went over to the counter moved it reached down and grabbed my bag of diamonds. I looked in it to make sure all of them were there. I knew what Shaw was looking for. I put them in my duffle bag. Come on Popeye Hicks yelled. I grabbed my Tommy gun and went out to the truck. When I got outside the truck was already driving away, so I had to run to catch it. I throw my duffle bag on the truck give my Tommy gun to Hicks. Give me your hand. He pulled me on to the truck. What the hell took you so long? I was making sure we didn't leave anything behind. I sat down next to Hicks I could see Shaw looking at me. I just smiled at him. That made him mad. How far is this camp we going to? The Lt told me it's about 40 miles from here. We had no idea what we were about to find, because for the first time in a while my stomach started to feel funny. I knew it wasn't going to be anything nice.

What we would find would horrify and shock the world.

CHAPTER FIFTY-FOUR

IT WAS ABOUT 3 hours into the ride before the smell hit us. What the fuck is that smell Shaw said? The closer we got the worse the smell got. Look at that Sgt. When I looked I seen dead people laying all over the road. People were coming up to the truck asking us for food looking like skeletons. There was men carrying dead boys and women carrying their dead babies.

There people looking like they ain't ate in months. Walking skeletons we called them. We were all shocked at what we were seeing I almost throw up when I seen all that. I had to sit down when I seen all that mess I couldn't believe what we was about to get into. I took out a my scarf and put it over my nose to kill the smell, but it didn't help. The truck stopped in front of the main gate the smell was unbearable when we stopped. 1st Sgt get all the boys off the trucks and fall into formation. Alright you heard the Lt let's line up. We formed up and he told us what we had to do. Listen up boys we are here to help the sick, hungry and to bury the dead I know the smell is unbearable, but we got a job to do. 1st Sgt Hicks I want you to take 1st platoon and round up all the sick and hungry. Sgt. Ross I want you to take 2nd platoon and gather up the dead and bury them. I knew he was going to give me that task my stomach was already feeling bad and now he wanted me to go around burying dead people. This ain't going to be nothing nice. Alright you got your orders let's move out. Sgt Ross yes sir. There are some shovels in that truck over there get some boys to get them. Yes sir. Like I didn't know that. What did he think we were going to do bury them with our hands. I told a couple of Pvt to go those shovels off that truck. As we walked to the camp there were dead people lying everywhere it was worse on the inside then the outside. There were dead bodies shacked up like firewood I was to shocked to move. What the fuck happen here who would do should a horrible thing to these people. Popeye. Yeah Hicks this is some fucked up shit. I ain't never seen any shit like this in my life. Those Nazis are some fucked up motherfuckers. Yeah you are right. I told the men to started burying the dead bodies. A lot of them had already started rotting away. I saw a dead woman holding her baby it made me think about Lillian and my daughter Jennifer. I walked over to this long building I opened the door the smell almost knocked me down. I couldn't see anything so I took out my flashlight to see I flashed my light to see a long row of people in these little spaces packed in like sardines. When I flashed light most of them put their hands up to shield themselves from the light. It reminded me of how they packed the slaves on ships like that a tear fell from my eye. How could somebody be so cruel? I heard those Nazis were cruel, but I didn't think they were this cruel. Now I see they ain't know better then those redneck motherfuckers back at home. Then I started to get mad.

Who in the fuck are they to treat these people like this? I called some men in and told told to help these people out of here. Every building I went to was the same thing people living like dogs. I went to help one poor soul he was so scared I might hurt him, because I was black. I told him in German I wasn't going to hurt him I was here to help him. When I did that all them started crawling out of those little spaces. We helped them out of those small smelly space into fresh air this was just the beginning the worst was yet to come. I continued walking though the camp helping and burying the dead when I came cross two Pvt trying to open up this big steel door. What the hell are you two doing? Sgt we have been trying to open this door, but it's hot as hell. What you mean hot? I walked over touched the handle of the door and damn near burned my hand off. Damn this hot. See we told you it was hot. What is this?

We don't know Sgt. Get a cloth or something so that we can open this door. One of the Pvt pick up a shirt off the ground. Go ahead and open it I told him. they opened the door the heat was so intense it almost burned our faces. What is this Sgt? I don't know it looks like an oven. I couldn't tell at first, because of all the smoke. But when the smoke cleared I get sick to my stomach. This was a big oven the Germans used to burn the Jews in. All the bodies were burned to a crisp they were shacked up on top of each other like they was baking bread. The smell from the burned bodies was unbearable I use my scarf to cover my nose from the smell.

What's your name Pvt? Pvt. West Sgt. Pvt. West I want you to go get Lt. Sutherland. Okay Sgt then he took off running to go found him. What kind of people would do this to another man Sgt? These ain't men Pvt these people are animals. The Lt. Sutherland and Hicks came running over to us. They stopped in their tracks the Lt walked over to the oven. Watch yourself sir it hot. What the fuck is this? It's a oven with burnt bodies in it. He stood there for a second. Where is the photographer? Right here sir. A short white man with glasses came walking up to him. I want you to take pictures of this, so we can get a record what has happen here. Yes sir. Is this the only oven? I don't know sir. 1st Sgt Hicks I want some men to go around and find out if there are more of these. Yes sir. I want you 5 to go around and count all the ovens in this camp. Yes Sgt. We had the grim task of pulling those bodies out of those ovens. We had to let them cool down first before we could do that. One of them Jews told the Lt that the German had been burning bodies for days and burned these bodies last night before they left. A Pvt came back and told the Lt that there were over twenty ovens in the camp and all them had burned bodies in them. After seeing all that I find myself a little corner and cried like a baby. Hicks came looking for me. Popeye what are you doing hiding in this corner? I looked at him. He seen the tears in my eyes he sat down next to me. I know this is some fuck up shit Popeye, but you can't let your emotions

The Men that Time has Forgotten

get in the way. You just here to free these people you ain't never going to see these people again, so don't take it so hard. This don't bother you. Why? The reason I feel like this Popeye is if it was you or me how many of these white folks would care about us. He had a point, but I didn't feel the same way he felt. I never thought I would cry for a white person not because they are white, but what was done to them. Come on let's go see what this Lt want. I put on my helmet grabbed my Tommy gun and followed him. Slim came running up to us. Where you been they have found some more bodies. What! How many more bodies? I don't know, but from what I saw it was a lot. They found them in some railroad cars behind those barracks over there. Damn how many people did these motherfucker kill? Well let's go see what they want us to do. By this time the camp was crawling with top brass even Gen. Bradley was there. When we got to the Lt he was talking with Col. Conley fat ass 1st Sgt. Hicks, Sgt. Ross I was just telling the Col what a tremendous job you boys are doing. We just looked at each other we knew it was all a bunch of bullshit trying to make himself look good. I'm going to put you boys in for a unit citation. The Col told us. Keep up the good work. We saluted him and he left with Lt. Sutherland behind him. That's a lying motherfucker he ain't going to put us in for know citation that was something for him to say. Come on let's give them a hand with these bodies. It took us about three weeks to clean and clear that camp out. We had to dig these big holes to bury all those dead bodies. They told us to gather up all the German civilians in the village to help bury the bodies. A lot of them were horrified at what they saw. A lot of them were saying they didn't know all this was going on. I didn't believe them I believe they did they just didn't care. The smell from all those dead bodies you could smell a mile away they didn't think there was something wrong. All the Jews they set free most of them went looking for love ones they were separated from during the war. We buried over 15,000 bodies that was the most dead bodies I have ever seen in my life. We set up our CP in that camp it still smelled a little, but it was our home until the war ended. A couple of weeks later The Russians captured Berlin after we liberated this camp. There was also a rumor going around that the war was over, but we haven't heard anything. I was tired that day , so I want back to my barracks to get some rest. I was looking at some pictures of my wife and daughter when I heard loud cheering. I went outside to see what the cheering was all about. I got outside and Slim came running up to me.

Guess what Popeye? What? The war is over the Germans surrendered to our forces this morning. What! Are you serious Slim? Yeah I'm serious now we can go home. I was in shock I leaned up against the door. I can't believe it I made it though the war alive. I don't really sink in until a Pvt came and told me again. THE WAR IS OVER SGT. I went back into my barracks closed the door got on my knees and started thanking God for getting me though this mess. I looked at the picture of my wife and daughter and started to cry. Than Hicks came in. Popeye don't tell me you are crying again. Damn! So I guess you already heard the news? Yeah I have. Come on dry your eyes the Lt wants to fall in to ranks in the yard. Okay. I got myself together and followed him into the yard.

CHAPTER FIFTY-FIVE

THE MEN WERE LINING up when we got to the yard. Alright y'all let's line it up. The Lt came out. Attention At ease. Boys as you have heard the war in Europe is over the Germans surrendered unconditionally to the Allied Forces this morning, but the war in the Pacific is still raging on. Now saying that all the soldiers in Europe won't be going home yet. The plan is to send all the white wounded soldiers home first. Than the soldiers who were on the battlefield.

Then the ones who have families and than you boys will be last. There will be a small amount of men left here to make sure all the Germans surrender. Now all colored soldiers who have families won't leave until all the white soldiers with families have left. That's it does anyone have questions for me. Yes Sgt. Ross. Sir how long will is this going to take? It might take one or two months from what the Col was telling me. One or two months. Yes Do you have a family Sgt. Ross? Yes sir I have a wife and child. Well you are going to have to be patient.

You will see them after the war. Then he smiled at me. That's easy for him to say he only been out here a couple of months. I been out here for almost a year and I ain't seen my family in almost two years. Any more questions for me? Good than you are dismissed. Staff Sgt Hicks and Sgt Ross I need to talk with you in my quarters. We walked over to his quarters which was an old German officer's barracks. Come in boys have a seat. He didn't much in his barracks room but a bunk, a desk and a night light. There was a small table with a coffee pot on it. He poured himself a cup of coffee. You boys want some coffee. No sir. Then he down at the desk took a big sip of his coffee. Now since this war is over it's going to be you two responsibility to keep these boys in line. We can't have them running around here out of control. Staff Sgt you and Sgt Ross need to pick some responsible MP's to watch over these boys. The Army will court-martial any one who is doing any misconduct. The village a couple miles away is off limits to colored soldiers at 2400 hours. Anyone is caught over there after 2400 hours that person will be court-martial and thrown in the stockades then they will be shipped back to the U.S. with a dishonorable discharged. You boys understand that? Yes sir.

If any of those boys get in trouble I'm going to blame you two. Do you have any questions?

Yes sir. What is it? When will we start using MP'S sir? You can start tonight. How many do you want to patrol the village sir? I'm going to leave that up to you boys anything else? Yes sir with all do respect sir the men would like for you to start calling them men not boys I think we all deserve that for all the things we have done for our country. He looked at us okay I'll do my best not to call the men boys Staff Sgt. Thank you sir. Is there anything else? No sir. Then you are dismissed. We stood up and saluted him and we were about to leave when he stopped us. Oh one more thing Staff Sgt if you want me to start calling you guy men not boys than you better act like that these Germans have never seen a Negro before, so y'all better be on your best behavior. Your representing your whole race one fuck up and that can go all down the drain. You understand Staff Sgt. Yes sir. Okay carry on. We walked out slamming the door behind us. Who the fuck do he think he is talking to us like that. He's right Popeye we got to be on our best behavior, because you don't know what those white boys told those German girls. I thought about what he said and he was right if we go out here acting like fools they going to make an example out of one of us. Let's get all the men in ranks, so we can tell them what the Lt said. Okay Hicks. I called all the men to get in formation. Listen up men we have a few rules we have to tell you. As Hicks was telling them what the Lt expected out of us. I started day dreaming about how nice it's going to be to get back home. Lillian had told me in one of her letters that my baby girl was starting to talk. When I heard my name called it broke me out of my daydream. Popeye you listening to me? Yeah I'm listening. You are going to be in charge of the MP's. Okay. You are going to have to pick which squad is going on patrol tonight and which squad is going to stand the watches. I want 1st squad to patrol the village tonight. That was Cpl. Shaw's squad he wasn't to happy when I said that. I really didn't care that Nigga shouldn't been looking though my stuff. I also want 3rd squad to stand the watches tonight. Cpl. Knight. Yes Sgt. You are in charge of three squad right? Yes Sgt. This is what I want I want two men at the front gate and one man in each tower I want you to rotate the watches every four hours. You got that Cpl? Yes Sgt I got it. The rest of you men can get clean up and hit that village is there any questions? Then you are dismissed. Cpl. Shaw came up to me. I know why you picked my squad? I just smiled at him. Then he walked away. I know what that Nigga wants those diamonds, but his sorry ass ain't getting shit. I got them hid out in a secret place where that Nigga can't find them I better watch my back when it comes to that Nigga. Hicks came over to me. Cpl. Shaw was madder than a motherfucker when you picked his squad for MP duty. Why does he got a problem with you? I told you he think I found some thing back in that village we were in and he wants me to share it with him.

Popeye fuck him. Oh yeah I forgot to tell you since you are in charge of the MP's you got duty tonight to. Good I didn't want to go into village anyway. Will you know me I'm going to try and find me some German pussy. Well good luck if those white boys ain't got it all first. Well I'm going to clean up a little and head out to the village I'll see you at 2400 hours. Okay I'll see you then. I walked back to the CP. I was a little tired from all the good news, so I decided to take a nap before all the men started coming back. It was 1700 hours.

CHAPTER FIFTY-SIX

I WAS AWAKEN BY SOMEBODY shaking me. What, what I said. Sgt come quick something has happen. What I said. Just come. I didn't see who it was they left so fast. I got up put my shirt and boots on. I ran out to see what was going on. When I got outside I seen a crowd of men standing around something. I ran over to see what was going on. What's going on? When I got to the crowd I seen a Pvt laying on a stretcher. His face had been smashed in. I kneel down what happen to him? Those motherfucking white crackers beat him up. What!. Yeah they beat him up. How did this happen? Slim came running up to us. Move out the way. He looked at the Pvt for a minute then he looked at me. Is he alright I asked? No he's dead.

Dead! Yeah he's dead they killed him Popeye. I was stocked. Where is Hicks Slim? He is on his way. What is this Pvt name? His name is James Greer he's from Tennessee. We need to tell the Lt about this. What are you going to tell him Popeye he ain't going to do nothing. How did this happen? He was at one those cat houses when he got into a fight with this one white boy over some woman. He was kicking that white boy's ass when his friends jumped him.

How do you know all this Pvt was you with him? Yes Sgt I was with him I stepped outside to smoke that's when I seen him come flying out the window. They throw him out a window?

Yeah they did. What your name Pvt? Pvt Henry Sims. Hicks had joined us by this time. He was stocked.

What the fuck happen to him? Some white boys beat him up over some woman in some cat house I told Hicks. Who was with him? I was with him Staff Sgt. This is Pvt Sims Hicks. Which cat house was you two at? The one behind the train station. The one behind the train station that one is on the other side of town. What the fuck were y'all doing way over there? I told y'all to stay on this side of town Pvt. Well Staff Sgt we met this German girl and she took us over there. Hicks looked at him and shook his head. Damn! What are you going to do Hicks? We got to go tell the Lt about this anybody seen him? Yeah I seen him he in some bar drinking with some other white officers. What bar is he in Slim? He's in a bar called the 81/2. I know where that is. Come on Popeye we got to go tell him what happen. Slim I want you to stay here with Pvt Greer take him to medical. Wait a minutes Hicks let me get my cover. I ran to the CP got my cover and we started walking towards the village half the guys were with us. We were a crowd of mad black men looking for revenge for killing Pvt Greer. I was really mad, because I was tired of these white folks killing our people and getting away with it. The road to the village was about a mile long, but we didn't care all we wanted was somebody to pay. It didn't take long for us to get to the bar when those white boys seen all those black soldiers they got real scarred. The 8 ½ was a small hole in the wall bar. It had a few tables and chairs with a bar that sat in the corner. It reminded me of the jute joints in Houston. Everybody stopped when they seen us this fat white officer was standing out front when we got there. What do you Niggers want? We are here to see Lt Sutherland Hicks told him. What do you want with him? Is he here? He went inside and yelled. Hey Brad your Niggers out here looking for you. Then he looked at us what this smile on his face. I wanted to kick his teeth down his throat fat motherfucker. Hicks and I want inside the Lt was sitting at the end of the bar talking to some ugly woman. What do you boys need? Can we go outside and talk Hicks asked him. Sure we can. He downed his drink and told some officer he will be back to order him another. We went outside. When he got outside he was shocked to see half the division standing out there. He looked at us what is all these boys doing out here Staff Sgt? He turned to Hicks what is this all about? A Pvt in my division was beating up by some white soldiers and killed. What! When did this happen? It happen about an hour ago. I haven't heard anything about that. I know you haven't sir, because ain't nobody saying anything. Who was this Pvt? It was a Pvt. Greer from 2nd platoon. He walked away a little bit from us. Where is this Pvt at now? He's in medical with Slim. Wait here he said and ran in back into the bar. What the fuck is he doing? He came back out with two other officers Staff Sgt Hicks this is Capt. Scottie Drummond and Capt. Douglass Moss they're both medical doctors they are going back to the camp with us to examine the body. If this Pvt. Greer was killed by these white soldiers as you say they will be able to tell. Sir with all do respect Pvt. Greer is dead we know this why would we need them. We want to make sure Staff Sgt, because if he is dead you going to need a medical doctor to write up the report not a field medic Capt. Moss told Hicks. You understand. Yes sir. Now Staff Sgt you know there won't be a investigation right away. Why not sir he was a soldier to he served this country he deserves some justice. I understand how you feel Sgt Ross, but the war just ended and nobody going to care about some Negro soldier who got beat up. Not beat up sir he was killed! Who's going to tell his family what happen to him sir, because I tell you what I'm going to write his family and tell them the truth.He looked at all of us. We will talk about that when we get back to the camp.

We walked back to the camp nobody said a word. When we got to the camp we walked right to medical. Slim had put Pvt. Greer on the table and covered him with a sheet. Capt. Drummond who was a medium built man with brown hair and blue eyes walked over to the body took his glasses out of his pocket. Is this him? Yes sir. He pulled the sheet off Greer and when he seen what they did to Greer he said my God. Capt. Moss walked over to take a look.

They bashed his face in? You say white soldiers did this the Lt asked Hicks. Yes sir. Who was with him? Pvt. Sims was with him sir. Where is this Pvt Sims at? Hicks told this one Pvt to go get Sims. Your sure it wasn't German civilians. No sir it was white American soldiers. Pvt. Sims came in. Lt this is Pvt. Sims. Pvt tell me what happen? We were at this cat house. Wait which cat house? The one behind the train station. Wait that's on the other side of village.

What were you boys doing way over there? We met this girl and she took us over there sir. So tell me what happen. He was telling the Lt what had happen I was thinking to myself we need find a white boy and bash his motherfucking face in. Okay Pvt. Sims your going to have to tell that to the investigators. Yes sir I will sir. Alright then your dismissed. So Brad what are you going to do? This can't go without somebody looking into this. I know we got to tell the Battalion Commander Brad. This is a serious matter a man has been murdered. The Lt was not to happy about all this. If he could sweep this under the rug he would. I'll go tell the Battalion Commander The Lt said. Capt Drummond are you gonna write up the report? Yeah Brad I'll handle it. I'll help him out Capt Moss said. 1st Sgt I want all the men in ranks in 5 minutes. Yes sir. Hicks and I ran out and told all the men to get in to ranks. Did you hear what he called us Hicks? Yeah he called us men. We both smiled at each other thinking it was some sign of respect, but we would find out later it didn't mean shit. The Lt came out and told them what had happen to Pvt. Greer. I'm going to have to put the village off limits to you boys until farther notice. This didn't sit to well with the men. If anyone is caught in that village from this division you will be subjected to court-martial. Is that understood! Yes sir. Your dismissed 1st Sgt, Sgt Ross I want all these boys in there barracks and tomorrow morning the Battalion Commander will be here. So have the boys in ranks at 0700 hours make sure they're looking sharp. Yes sir. What the fuck is the Battalion Commander going to say to us? I don't know Popeye I don't know.

CHAPTER FIFTY-SEVEN

THE NEXT MORNING THE Battalion Commander arrived to talk to us about what they were going to do about Pvt. Greer's murder. He was with our Division Commander Lt. Col. Conley. You know by now that the village is off limits to your division. There will be an investigation into this killing. If any of you are caught in that village you will be shot. What! Shock came over everyone's face including the Lt. Now does anyone have any questions for me? Okay than you are dismissed. I could see Lt. Sutherland taking to Col. Conley about something. I don't know what it was about, but he had this worried look on his face. Come on Popeye let's go back to the barracks. You know the real reason they don't want us in that village is they know who killed Greer. They ain't going to do nothing all they are going to do is cover it up. If it had been one of us killing one of them there would be an investigation. They don't care about us to them it's just another Nigga dead. I'm not going to let this go Hicks everyday I'm going to go over to the Lt office and ask him have they found Greer's killers. So now we can't leave the camp until further notice. We are stuck here doing nothing. Since we couldn't leave the camp all they had us do is busy work. If you weren't doing anything the Lt would get mad at Hicks and I asking why aren't we doing anything. I was beginning to hate the Army all the things I did for this fucking country and this how I get treated. I almost lost my life twice for these white motherfuckers.

A lot of good men lost their lives including my best friend. I'll be glad when I get the fuck out of here. A rumor was going around that they were going to send some of us to the Pacific to help out the troops there. I was praying that I wouldn't be going over there I been hearing they have been having a hard time trying to beat those Japanese. I movies I have seen of the Pacific are nothing nice. They also been telling us that the Japanese treat their prisoners bad they torture them and even kill them. Hey Popeye. Yeah Hicks. Are you hungry? Yeah I was just about to ask you that let's go get something to eat. We started walking towards the chow hall. You know Popeye they still ain't found those two white motherfuckers that killed Greer. Well that don't surprise me Hicks. They thinking about sending me to the Pacific. What! Where did you here that from Hicks? This Pvt. Name Timmons told me. He said that the Lt got a list of name and he seen my name on that list. Did he see my name on it. I don't know Popeye he didn't say. Well I hope not I don't want to go over there. I don't want to go neither Popeye, but I ain't got know choice. We are going to have a meeting with the Lt soon about who's going to the Pacific. We got to the chow hall they feed us the same thing we had yesterday. After we finish eating we went back to our Barracks we talked and laughed a little and than Hicks went to sleep. I stayed up and wrote my wife Lillian a letter. Since the war in Europe been over I been getting letters from her on a regular basis. All I could think about is what if they send me to the Pacific and I got killed I would never see my family again that weighed heavy on my mind. I didn't want to tell her that they might send me to the Pacific. I didn't want to worry her with that. I finished my letter and went to sleep. When I got up the next morning Hicks was gone. I knew where he went. I got up and got myself together for morning muster. Hicks came in with this piece of paper in his hand and lgave it to me. What is this? Take a look at it. What do you think it is? I took it from him this must be the list of names who are going to the Pacific. Yeah it is. I dropped it on the floor I was to scarred to see if my name was on that list. Hicks picked it up and gave it back to me.

Look at it Popeye. I looked at it and looking at the names my heart sink when I saw my name on the list, but it was crossed out and Hicks name was in my place. I looked at him. Why is my name crossed off and your name in my place? I did that, because I want to go to the Pacific. Why? I ain't got nobody back at home. What about your momma and daddy? They dead and I ain't got no brothers and sisters. Besides Popeye you have a family. I see the way you look at the pictures of your wife she must mean the world to you. She does. I had to convince the Lt to take your name off he wanted me to stay here to help find Pvt Greer's killer.

Now that I'm leaving Popeye that going to be your job. You can't let this go Popeye things have got to change and it's got to start with us. We have got to start standing up for ourselves.

We also got to stop letting these white folks run all over us. I will stay on top of this Hicks. h Now finish getting dressed and I will meet at muster. Okay. I'm gonna let you give them the bad news. Thanks I said. He laughed then he left. I finished putting on my boots grabbed my cover and went to muster. Attention Hicks told them. Popeye got some news to tell you. I got a list of names here that will be going to the Pacific. I read off their names. Pvt McDonald, Sims, Carson, Pepper, Milton, Carr, Parker, Pearson, Brooks, Sheppard, Wells, Brown, Ellison, White, Bates, Peale, Barton, Page, Fisher, Edwards, Cpl. Shaw, Dillon, Pickett, Mincey, Sgt Howe, Morgan, Lawson and 1st Sgt Hicks. That was just a few names I read off in all there were about 100 men that went to the Pacific that was over half of our division. If your name was called you will muster in the yard at 1800 hours with me for your orders Hicks told them. Is there any questions? Know one said a word. Good let's go to work your dismissed.

Hicks that's a lot of men. I know and there might be more. Why you worried Popeye you ain't going. Yeah I know Hicks, but those Japanese are crazy and some of these men are young.

They are going to be alright Popeye. So when are y'all leaving? Saturday morning. To bad we can't go into that village I would pay you a drink. Thank you Popeye I would like that, but you know that's out the question. I heard a rumor somebody made some Hooch. Hooch! Yeah Hooch you know what that is don't you? Yeah I use to run it for a woman I lived with back in Houston her name was Mrs. Hutchinson. He looked at me get the fuck out of here you ain't never ran no Hooch. I just looked at him I was going to tell him the story about how I almost got killed one night. You ran Hooch for real? Yeah I did. Well let's go find this Hooch. Do you know who made it? No I don't know that. We was on our way to find this Hooch when this Pvt came running up to us Staff Sgt. Yeah. The Lt want to see y'all in his office right now. Okay.

Now what the fuck do he want with us now Popeye. I don't know Sgt, but you better get up there fast. Come on Popeye let's go see what this motherfucker want. We walked over to the Lt quarters. We knocked on his door. Come in. I opened the door and we walked in. Staff Sgt Hicks, Sgt Ross reporting as ordered sir. Sit down. The Lt wasn't alone Col Conley fat ass was sitting there with him. You are probably wondering why I called you here. Yes sir we were. We found the two men who killed Pvt Greer. You did Hicks and I looked at each other.

Where are they.? Their being held at the stockades the Col said. What's going to happen to them? There going to be shipped back to the U.S. for trial. Why are they getting shipped back to the U.S. can't they stand trial here. We don't have the proper facilities to trial them here.

Well if you gonna do that don't Pvt Sims need to be there? But y'all sending him to the Pacific and we leave in a couple of days. When the trial starts we will send for him. What if Sims gets killed what happens than. If he dies then there's nothing we can do the Col said. Then those white boys get away with murder. They didn't say anything. You two boys don't worry about that we got everything under control. The Col told us. These two boys who committed this horrible act will be punished for it. Well since you caught these two killers does that mean we can go back into the village sir? They looked at each other. The Lt said sure why not. Thank you sir. We got up to leave when the Col said to us. This conversation stays between us nobody else you understand. Yes sir we understand. Good your dismissed. He had this shit eaten grin on his face. We hand saluted and left. When we got outside we were mad as hell.

Those motherfuckers ain't going to do nothing they are going to let those white boys get away with murder. That's why they sending them back to the states. Let's muster all the men, so we can tell them they can go into town and then you can buy me that drink. I'm gonna need it after that. We mustered the men together and told them they could go out into the village, but had to back at 2400 hours and stay out of trouble. What is the news on those two white boys that killed Greer. They still looking. That's what that meeting was for we will let you know when they tell us. Now remember men you have to be back at 2400 hours. You understand?

Yes Staff Sgt. Okay then y'all are dismissed. Come on Popeye let's go buy me that you promise me. We went to some hole in the wall bar Shaw took us to. I can't remember the name of the place, because Hicks and I got so drunk I don't even remember how we got back to our barracks.

CHAPTER FIFTY-EIGHT

I WOKE UP THAT MORNING with a bad hang over I have never gotten drunk like that in my life if Lillian had seen she would've been a shamed of me. I look over at Hicks he was still asleep.

He and I were still in our clothes I got up to use the can. I was still feeling like I was drunk I was walking to the can when I stumbled over a floor board. My boot had got stuck in the hole where the board use to be. After I stopped cussing I got my balance. I had to focus my eyes to see where this hole was. When I got my focus I could see it was where I had hide my diamonds at. I quickly got down on my knees and stuck my hand down to see if I could feel the bag was still there. It was gone. I sat on the floor puzzled trying to figure out who would have known where I had hid them. I started thinking about who would know this than it came to me Shaw! I do remember one thing he was in here with us last night. That Motherfucker stole my diamonds he must have found them when Hicks and I passed out. I picked up the floor board and throw it when I did that I woke up Hicks. Popeye what the fuck are you throwing around? I looked at him. Where is your .45 at Hicks? Why? What wrong Popeye? It's over there in my gun belt. What you need it for? I didn't say a word I just walked over to it and took out his .45 out of his gun belt checked the clip to see if it was loaded. I put it back in the gun and cocked it and headed for the door. Hicks jumped up and grabbed my arm.

Popeye where the fuck are you going with that gun? What the fuck are you going to do? I turned around and looked at him I'm going to kill me a Nigga. I swung the door open to walk out the sun was so bright it almost blinded me I got my focus and headed for Shaw's barracks. Wait up Popeye I'm coming with you. I was walking across the yard looking like a wild man carrying an loaded .45 in my hand. When other guys saw that they got the fuck out of my way. Where Sgt going with that gun one Pvt said. You better not get your ass in my way or you will find out When I got to Shaw's barracks two Pvt were sitting in front of his door. You better get the fuck out of the way if you don't want to get shot. I kicked the door open. I scarred the shit out of Shaw when I did that. He was sitting at the table looking at my diamonds with some other Pvt.

I walked right up to him and put that .45 in his face. Nigga what the fuck are you doing with my diamonds? Hicks came in after me and closed the door. All these diamonds are yours Popeye? Yeah Hicks they are mine. He brought us all those drinks, so he could get me and you drunk that would give him time to look around our barracks for Hicks put my diamonds back in my bag for me. Okay Popeye. Hicks started putting the diamonds back in the bag. I should blow your motherfucking brains out for stealing my diamonds. Nigga if you ever put your motherfucking hands on anything that belongs to me again Nigga I'll kill you. Shaw had this real scared look on his face thought I was really going to shoot him. If you two Niggas tell anyone about this I'll kill the both of you. I didn't know that these diamonds belong to you Sgt he told me that he had found them and he was going to split them with us if we didn't tell anyone. What about those two Niggas sitting outside they in on this too? Yeah Sgt that's why they are sitting out to watch out to let us know when someone is coming. Hicks tell those two guys to come in here and check their pockets. Hicks opened the door and two the two Pvt to come in. Y'all two Niggas empty y'all pockets out. They ain't got nothing Popeye. You got all the diamonds Hicks? Yeah I got them all. Hicks open the door, so we can get the fuck out of here. When Hicks opened the door there was a bunch of

Pvt standing at the door. Move the fuck out the way and go about y'all business. I pointed the gun at Shaw and left behind Hicks.

They was looking at me like I had lost my mind. Y'all all heard with Staff Sgt said go about y'all business. Come on Popeye let's go back to the barracks. We ran back to our barracks. Popeye where in the hell did you get all those diamonds from? In one those German villages we had passed though I found them in a closet on top of a shelf in a box. Okay, but what does all this got to do with Shaw? He asked me did I find anything in one of those houses I told him no. He didn't believe me,because he had seen the empty box on the floor. That's way he was in our CP that morning when you caught him saying he was looking for a light. Okay now I understand that Nigga wanted to steal them for himself? Yeah! Thieving motherfucker I told you I didn't trust that motherfucker. You know you can't trust those Niggas from New York City.

Well here he throw the bag at me. You don't want half? No Popeye. He walked over to the cabinet pushed it aside move this brick put his hand in this hole and pulled out this small bag.

What's that? He throw the bag to me. Open it. I put my bag down and open it and I looked at him. He had a bag full of diamonds just like me. Where you get these from? I got them from one of those German woman I was missing around with. She wanted to hide them from for her,so she gave them to me. We left so unexpectedly I never had a chance to give them back.

Are you going to give them back to her? Now how am I going to do that Popeye? Well the war is over here maybe you can go to that village and give them back. He just looked at me. You going to give yours back? Hell no! We both started laughing. What about Shaw? What about him? He might go tell the Lt. About the diamonds. Popeye he ain't going to do shit if he do I will go kill that Nigga myself. You know that Nigga than stole more s hit hen you and me he ain't going to tell nobody. If he got all that shit then why is he after my diamonds? He's a greedy motherfucker Popeye. I tell you what Hicks if that Nigga touches my shit again I'll kill him. Let me get your bag Popeye I will hide it in here with mine. I throw both bags to him. Hold up I said let mark my bag, so I don't take the wrong one by accident. I got a black marker and put my name on it then Hicks put them in the hole put the brick back and slide the cabinet back in front. I looked at my watch it was 1030 hours. Hicks how did we get back to the barracks? I think Shaw and a couple other Pvt. Brought us back here. Shit Popeye I can't remember. My head is killing me. Let's go get something to eat Hicks. Okay. I put the .45 back in Hicks gun belt and we left to get something to eat. The breakfast was pretty good today they had eggs (real eggs not the powdered ones) bacon, grits, hash, toast and coffee. We sat down to eat when Slim came in. Hey did you hear? Hear what? They have captured most of the islands in the Pacific. What! Yeah General MacArthur has taken back the Philippines Islands now they are planning to invade mainland Japan. Where you hear all this shit from?

Capt. Moss he's getting this information from one of his buddies. He also told me that the guys who are going to the Pacific might be leaving soon. How soon? Like tomorrow morning.

What! The Lt said we wasn't leaving until Saturday. I'm just telling you what he told me. Look I said. The Lt. walked in the chow hall. Here he comes I'll see y'all later. Good morning sir Slim as he passed him. We stood up when he got to the table. Staff Sgt Hicks/ Sgt Ross at ease.

Yes sir. I guess you already heard the news I figure that's way Doc Slim was here. Yes sir he already told us. So there no need for me to tell you then you will muster the men at 0500 hours we will be shipping out at 0600 hours to the Pacific. Will you be going sir? Yes unfortunately I will be going. Who'll be taken your place sir? Doc Drummond will be taking my place. Sgt. Ross you will find him a little easier then me most medical doctors are laid back people. Do you have any questions for me? No sir. Okay then I better get back to command.

Oh Staff Sgt you can give the men the rest of the day off. Yes sir I will. He left after that. That was strange. Yeah it was. He looked like he was scarred I seen it in his eyes. I seen it to Popeye he doesn't want go, but they are making him go. I bet he thought he was going to stay here. I bet your right. Well I better get back to the barracks and start packing he give us the rest of the day off. You know why he said that? No. It's Friday Popeye and we're leaving tomorrow. Yeah it is Friday. When you finish packing we can go to the village and I can by you a drink before you ship out. Okay cool. I took him about two hours to pack. Why it took him so long to pack we were laughing, talking and he was telling me about his family. Hicks is a very well educated man. He went to college and got a degree in education. He joined the Army to get out of Kentucky the Army wanted him to become an officer, but he turned them down. He was going to marry his high school sweetheart, but when he joined the Army she married someone else. We even talked about Sgt. I ain't talked about him in a couple of months I do think about him a lot still. We got dressed and went to this little bar that this Pvt told us about it wasn't what we expected, but it would have to do. I couldn't remember the bar we got drunk at, so we went there. We drink and we even played dominoes. which shocked me I didn't know the Germans played dominoes. Some German guy asked us if we wanted to play. Hicks didn't say much that night. We left around 2300 hours. When we got back to the barracks he just jumped in bed and went to sleep. I could understand he had a lot on his mind. I felt bad, because he was taking my place I'm the one such be going, but he was thinking about my family. I wish there was a way I could pay him back. I couldn't sleep that night I laid there wide awake staring at the ceiling. I must have dosed off some time later, because Hicks was shaking my telling me to get up. Popeye get up man damn you are hard to wake up. Come on we got to muster in 15 minutes. I got up got myself together went and mustered. The whole division was out there. Attention Hicks told us when the Lt came out. Staff Sgt is all the men here? Yes sir. I'm not going to get into what's happening today most of you are shipping out to the Pacific to help out with the over there. Doc Drummond will be taking my place as your Company Commander he's a good man treat him with respect like you did me. It was a pleasure serving with you even though this is my first time commanding Negro troops you're the best I have ever seen I wish you the best of luck in the future. Now Staff Sgt get all the men on the truck who are shipping out. You hear him if your name was called yesterday load on to those trucks. Let's move out. Popeye it's been nice knowing you man. You to Hicks your a good man. You take care of yourself Popeye. I will we shook hands and hugged. I walked him to the truck. Oh yeah I left you half my diamonds you are going to need them more then me he jumped on the truck. We shook hands again. You take care you hear. The truck pulled off. I waved to him as it drove away. Hicks was a good friend he saved my life I will never forgot that. That would be the last time I ever saw him I never knew what ever happen to Hicks, but I will never forget him. Now as for Shaw I heard he was killed in New York City for of all things stealing. I run into a Pvt name Miller I served with during the war told me what happen to Shaw.

CHAPTER FIFTY-NINE

THE LAST MONTH OF the war was very boring I didn't do nothing. It was May the war in the Pacific was still going on. I thought about how Hicks and the other guys were doing. Doc Drummond left me in charge of everything he was always in the village drinking. So Slim and I ran the division. Doc promoted Slim to Sgt for all the work he did with the sick and wounded. I listened to the radio all the time keeping up with the fighting in the Pacific. The fighting there was real bad a lot of men were killed. The Japanese ain't given up that easy even though they know they have lost the war. That would all change on Aug 6, 1945 that's when we dropped an atomic bomb on the city of Hiroshima. It destroyed the whole city killing over 140,000 people. That still didn't stop the Japanese they kept on fighting. A couple days later they dropped another bomb on the city of Nagasaki killing 70,000 people this time. I didn't know a bomb could kill that many people at one time. I was writing a letter to Lillian when someone knocked on my door that evening. Who is it.? Pvt. Young Sgt. Come in. Sgt. Ross Doc Drummond wants you to muster all the men in the yard. Okay tell all the squad leaders to muster all the men. Okay Sgt. He left I put my boots on got my cover and went to the yard.

The men was falling in ranks when I got out there. Let's go line it up. All the men here Cpl. Bonner?

Yes Sgt. Attention. I saluted Doc Drummond when he came up.

Michael Johnson

Men I have some good news. As of this evening the Japanese has surrender to our forces this morning. The war is over. Everybody stood there for second looking at each other. Than we broke out into a loud cheer, jumping around, hugging, shaking each other hand. I couldn't believe it was over.

It was really over four long hard years has come to an end. Alright men settle down I have more info to put out to you. Settle down I yelled. When will we be going home sir? I'm getting to that Sgt hold your horses. Like Lt. Sutherland told a couple months ago all the white troops will leave first and then the black troops. Now if you are married you will be leaving tomorrow morning. I was speechless when he said that. What time tomorrow sir? Early as possible Sgt.

They want to get all the married men home to their families. How would you know who's married and who's not? I have a list right here and he took out this piece of paper from his folder. I have a list of who is married and who will be leaving tomorrow. He called off the names on the list. My name was the first one called. If your name was on this list I want you to muster tomorrow at 0500 hours to ship out to go home. If you are leaving tomorrow I would start packing now. Sgt. Ross I want you to get all the men who are leaving together, so they can turn in all their equipment. Yes sir I will sir. Good your dismissed. Listen up I said all the men leaving tomorrow I need for y'all to muster in my barracks now. We ran to my barracks now listen you need to hand in your rifle, bullets, helmet, gun belts, canteen and anything else. You can't take those things back with you, so go to your barracks and I will meet at the ammunition cage. Yes Sgt they ran to their barracks. I got all my equipment together and took it to the ammunition cage. When I got there it was closed. A Pvt was walking by. Hey Pvt who is in charge of the ammunition cage? I think Cpl. Taylor is Sgt. Well where he at? I don't know Sgt. Well go find him and tell him to get his ass over here and open this cage now. Yes Sgt.

He took off and ran to find Cpl. Taylor. I waited about 5 minutes before Cpl. Taylor came running to the cage. I'm sorry for keeping you waiting Sgt they had me doing something else.

That's okay Cpl. He opened the door and we went in. I handed all my equipment to him. Cpl. Taylor. Yes Sgt. Make sure when these guys hand in their equipment you inventory it don't let them leave until you get all their equipment. Yes Sgt I will. I went back to my barracks and started packing. I put all my things in my duffle bag except my uniform. While we were here they issued us new uniforms I lost mine whole duffle bag somewhere between France and Belgium. I wanted to look sharp when I get off the bus in Houston. I took the diamonds out of the hiding place where Hicks had them and stuffed them deep down in my bag. I took out a picture of Lillian and my baby girl I sat down and and looked at that picture a tear dropped out my eye. I was finally going to see my family for the first time in almost two years. I kissed the picture. Thank you Jesus. I heard a knock at my door. Who is it? Doc Drummond stuck his head in. Can I come in? Sure sir come in. He had this sad look on his face. What wrong sir? I have a bit of bad news and it has something to do with us going home. I looked at him funny.

What do you mean by that sir? I must have miss read the message it didn't say you guys was leaving tomorrow. It said you guys won't be leaving until the camp has been closed. How long is that going to take sir? I don't know Sgt a couple of days or so. Well that ain't to bad sir I can handle a few days. Now if you would've said something like a couple of months than I would've had a heart attack. He smiled a little. So when are you leaving sir. I'm leaving tomorrow morning. So you are married? Yes Sgt I been married over 8 years now our anniversary is next week. So they going to get you home just in time so you can spend your anniversary with your wife that's nice sir. Yes it would be nice I haven't seen my wife in two years. He had this worried look on his face when he said that. Well I better get going I got a lot of packing to do. Sir who's going t take your place? Lt. Ray will be taking my place. Is he a doctor to? Yes he is Sgt. Okay sir you have a safe trip home sir. I will Sgt you take care. I will sir. We shook hands then he left. DAMN! They always fucking with us. The ways things are going I ain't never going to get home. Now I got to muster all those men together again and tell them the bad news. I grabbed my cover muster all the men together and told them the bad news. They didn't take it to well they got the cussing throwing their hats down. I told them to calm down it's going to be fine we going to go home soon just be patient. I would find out later why they wanted us to stay. Col. Conley fat ass wanted us to stay, because he wasn't married and they wasn't going to let his ass go home yet. So he wanted us to stay even the married guys.

CHAPTER SIXTY

IT TOOK US A lot longer to close the camp down then I excepted it took us almost two weeks to do. What made it take longer is every time we thought we was finish they would come up with some more bullshit for us to do. It was Aug 20, 1945 and I was tired of this fucking place I wanted to go home. That morning we got the news we were finally going home not just the married guys, but all of us. I was happy I didn't want nobody to be left behind. We fought hard we did I jobs. We deserve to go home. We left the camp that afternoon around 1400 hours.

We got to the air station it was so many guys there trying to get home. I thought most of them was gone by now. People was pushing and shoving each other to get on the few planes leaving. They was loading the planes by company. They gave us a ticket back at the camp which told us what plane we was getting on. My ticket said C-130-85. That was the plane and flight number I was getting on. When I looked at the flight board wouldn't you know it my flight was leaving last. I took a seat and waited my turn. To make the time go faster I grabbed my a stars and stripes paper off a chair some soldier left. There wasn't nothing worth reading the same old bullshit how we win the war and what we going to do next. I was about to throw the paper away when I seen a article that caught my eye. It was information on the GI Bill. It was taking about how veterans can get loans, buy homes and even go to school. This shocked me I didn't know this. I bet all them white boys knew it. I tore the article out of the paper and put it in my pocket. I went to lay back when this Pvt came up to me. You need something Pvt? Your name Jeffery Ross, but they call you Popeye. Yeah who what's to know? Did you know a Lt by the name of Willie Banks? I sat up when he said that. Yeah I knew him why? Is he here? I stood up to see if I could see him. Nah he ain't here he's dead. I sat back down in my seat I looked at the Pvt. How you know him? He was brought to a field hospital about four months ago. I was working as a medic than that's where I met him. It was on the outskirts of the Rhine River. The Rhine River they didn't let Negro soldiers go that far. I was part of a tank unit that crossed that river. So how did you come to know Sgt? Me and this other Pvt were driving some wounded soldiers to the field hospital when he jumped out in front of our truck we almost ran him over. We got out to see if we hit him he was shot up real bad. We put in the truck with the rest of the wounded soldiers. He kept on saying where is Popeye find Popeye.

That's all he kept on saying all the way to the hospital. Then we asked him who is Popeye. He said you was a friend of his that help captured some village in Germany and y'all was part of a truck division out of Iowa. Yeah we came over in Aug of 1944. I thought he was lying and he was loosen his mind. I started asking people did they know about this truck division from Iowa. Nobody knew what I was talking about until I ran into this Pvt name Edward Rollins.

Yeah I know Eddie he got left behind in Iowa he mysteriously got sick before we left to come to Europe. I asked him did he know this Lt. Willie Banks. He said that he knew a 1st Sgt name Willie Banks. I asked him did he know you. He said he knew you. I told him there was this Lt. Banks in the medical tent and I needed him to come see if he knew him. We went over to the tent and when he saw him and he said yeah I know him. They talked a little and he told him to find Popeye. He told us you was somewhere in Germany. I asked him how are we going to find you in a big country like Germany. He told us we couldn't miss you. You was the only Negro in Germany with eyes that look like they going to pop out his head. So when I saw you sitting over here I knew it had to be you. Your eyes don't look like they are about to pop out. I laughed a little no there are not I got that name when I was a kid. He told us when we find you don't forget about the letters he gave you. Yeah I got them right here in my pocket did he say anything else? No he didn't say nothing else. I looked at him, so how you know it was me? I was standing over there by the desk there when I saw you come in. I said to myself that got to be Popeye. When did he die? He died a couple of days later. He had lost a lot of blood he was lucky we found him. So where is Eddie? He was killed by a shell a couple weeks later.

What is your name Pvt? My name is Pvt. Terry Sharpe. Well I'm glad to meet you Pvt. Sharpe as we shook hands. Oh I got to go. They just called my flight. Well I'm glad I got a chance to meet you you take it easy. He picked up his duffle bag and headed to his plane. I sat back in my seat my worse fears came true Sgt was dead. Tears started running down my face. I wish was there with him at the hospital. This one Negro soldier seen me crying and said. I know how you feel Sgt I'm glad to get the fuck out of here to he said. He just didn't know why I was crying not because I was going home I was crying, because I lost a good friend. I sat in that air station which felt like hours. Finally they called my flight number. I picked up my duffle bag and headed for my plane. I got to the line when I heard the MP's telling the Negro soldiers to dump out there stuff out of their duffle bags. These were black MP's saying this before you get on the plane we got to check your bags to see if you got any stolen items. If we find any stolen items you we be arrested and throw in the stockade. I wasn't worry about them finding anything on my way to the air station I took the diamonds out of my bag and put them down my pants. I had a feeling they were going to be checking bags and I know they ain't going to check down my pants. Dump your bag out . I did what he told me. I took his billy club and went through my stuff. You good . I put my stuff back in my bag and stood back in line. They did catch a few guys, but they just warned them and let them go. They made us stack our bags in the back of the plane. The plane was one of those planes they used during D-Day.

The seats ran along the sides of the plane the walls was paper thin.

Michael Johnson

I didn't care I just wanted it to get home safely. I sat in my seat and put my seat belt on. The plane was packed with Negro soldiers from different division all over Germany. A lot of them I didn't know was in Germany. One soldier told me the pilots flying the plane was from the Tuskegee Airmen Squadron. I heard the engines crank up. Than we started moving the plane was shaken so hard I thought it was going to shake apart, but once we got in the air it stopped. Once we got in the air everybody broke out in a loud cheer some even started crying. I wasn't going to be happy until I was home in Houston in the arms of my wife. The plane ride took 5 hours the plane itself look like it wasn't going to make it, because one of the engines went out. They told us they might have to make an emergency landing a lot of the men started to panic, but I told them to calm down. I was scared myself I was thinking I went though all that hell to die in a plane crash. Oh hell nah. When we got over London it was dark as hell They had to use torches to help us land. Hold on tight boys one pilot said it's going to be a rough landing. We hit the runway and the plane bounced once then it hit the runway hard the pilot got control and he brought it to a safe stop. My heart was pounding so hard I thought I it going to jump out of my chest. Everybody was on the edge of their seats I was so glad we landed safely, but a couple weeks earlier a plane full of white soldiers crashed on the runway when they lost both engines. I would find out that Capt. Drummond was on that plane. I felt real bad for his wife she haven't seen him for two years and on the day of their anniversary he dies in a plane crash. I'm just happy we landed safely. It was about 2200 hours when we landed in London.

This was the first I been in London since we shipped out from here. It didn't look the same.

Most of it's building was burnt or bombed out, there was no street lights. They put us in these run down barracks I didn't care we was only going to be there a couple of days. I stayed in the barracks the whole time. I only went out to to eat and to use the phone. A lot of the soldiers and sailors was acting a fool. There was a lot of fights over women somebody got shot. I heard from one soldier a few women had got raped. The black soldiers and sailors wasn't allowed to go in any of the clubs or bars. That made a lot of them mad and some even started a riot over it. The last night I was in London a big brawl broke out between the white and black soldiers. The black soldiers was trying to get on this one club called the America, but the owner told them they didn't allow Niggers in his club and he was British. When he said that the brawl broke out. All the black soldiers was arrested In stead of putting them in the stockade they put us on planes and sent us home. London left a bad taste in my mouth. If there is racist people in London I don't what to know what's in store for us when we get back home.

CHAPTER SIXTY-ONE

WE LANDED AT NORFOLK Air station in Norfolk, Va on a hot clear day. It was so hot I had to take off my uniform jacket. The diamonds in my pants was making my nuts sweat. I didn't want to take them out until I get to the barracks. I got my duffle bag and asked this Pvt where were the barracks at? I'll take you over there Sgt I'm headed that way. On my way to the barracks this black officer told us we needed to be discharged from the Army before we could go home.

So go put your things in your room and report to the administrative office to start your paperwork. They put in this barracks called Essex Hall it had two beds, a desk and two lockers to put my stuff in. I put my bag down and headed back out the door I still had those diamonds down in my pants. I wanted to take them out, but there was no locks on the barracks doors and I didn't want them to get stolen. I hurried down to the administrative office I wanted to start my paperwork, so I can get the fuck out of here. I didn't want to stay here no longer then I had to. As I got close to the administrative office I could see there was a long line. There was two lines one for whites and one for blacks the white soldiers lines had about six people helping them get their paperwork done. The black soldiers had two people trying to get all those soldiers paperwork done and the line was around the corner. I said to myself this going to take all day and to make things worse I was last in line. It was hot as hell to. Some of the guys didn't go to the barracks they took their stuff with them to the administrative office.

While I was waiting in line I got to talking with this Sgt name Boyle from Tyler, TX. He was in the 377th tank division that crossed into Germany. That was the only black tank division in Germany. He told me about all the things they did and all the promises that was made to them and they never received anything. He had a lot of bitterness in his voice when he was telling me this. I don't blame him all the shit we did for this country in this war and we ain't got nothing to show for it. I thought they didn't let black soldiers into Germany. Nah that ain't true he said. They wouldn't let us in Germany. They told us they didn't need us. Really. Yeah really.

Then I remembered the article I had in my pocket from stars and stripes about VA programs. I asked him did he know about the VA programs for veterans. No. I gave him the article so he could read it. He was shocked to learn about all these programs for veterans. We need to tell all the black soldiers about this. Come on Popeye let's go to the front of the line to tell everybody. We got to the front there was two black clerks sitting at a desk. One was a light skin medium built man with wavy hair and a thin mustache. The other was brown skin heavy man with a low cut and no facial hair. We walked up to the brown skin clerk. The back of the line is back there he said. We know where the back is I said but we got some information to put out to the black soldiers. What is it the light skin one asked. Boyle handed him the article I got from the stars and stripes. He took it from Boyle and read it. He looked at us. Yeah your right we need to tell this guys here about this. He handed it to the other clerk. What's your name Sgt? My name is Jeffery Ross and this here is Sgt Robert Boyle. Most of these guys wouldn't know nothing about these VA benefit if it wasn't for you. You guys back up and let these two Sgt get their discharge paperwork done. I thought some of the guys would get mad, but they didn't. They started passing the article around so all the soldiers can read it. It didn't take Boyle and I to get our paperwork done, but it would take another two days to get our discharge papers. The next couple of days Boyle and I hung out and

Michael Johnson

talked about home. We exchange address, so we could kept in contact with each other. I never saw Boyle again after that. We kept in contact for a while, but when I tried to get in contact with him his wife told me he died in the Korean War trying to defend some hill.

It was Friday Sept 18, 1945 I got up early that morning. I was feeling good, because this was the day I was getting the fuck out of this man's Army. I got myself together ate some breakfast and headed over to the administrative office. I got to the office

Cpl. Walls was there he helped me with my discharge was sitting at the desk. Good morning Sgt Ross. Morning Cpl. Walls. Cpl. Walls was one of them Negro's who try to talk proper and act like he white. I don't know why Negro's do that to themselves they ain't never going to be white. The white man don't want us mixing with him he outta know better then that. I guess you are here for your discharge papers right? That's right I said that with a big smile on my face. Well I got some bad news for you. What! The Col hasn't signed them yet. Why! I don't know Sgt. So when is he planning on signing them? I guess sometime today. They've been sitting on his desk the pass couple of days. Oh you in luck here he comes now. Walls stood up to saluted. Good morning Col. I turned around to saluted and guess who it was. Yep fat ass Col. Conley. Well look who's here Sgt. Ross. Morning Col. I guess you're here for your discharge papers? Yes sir I am. Well let's go to my office and see what I can do. I looked at Walls funny all he could do is shrug is shoulders. I followed the Col into his office. He unlocked the door flicked on the light and we went in. Have a seat Sgt Ross. He sat his fat ass behind this large black lacquer he stole from Germany. There also were two German style lamps that sat on two beautiful oak wood tables. The chairs and the one I was sitting in came from that house he made his headquarters back in Germany. All the furniture he had in his office he stole the from house in Germany. He took a sip of his coffee. So Sgt. Ross you are getting out of the Army? Yes sir I am. What are you going to do once you get out? I'm going to go home be with my family and then look for a job. He looked at me and said oh really. You know it's going to be hard for Negro soldiers like yourself to find a job you know they are going to hire all the white soldiers first and they will have all the good jobs. Yes I know that sir, but I have to take care of my family. I understand that Sgt. Ross, but what if you can't find a job? How are you going to take care of your family without a job? It might take you several months before you find a job. He was pissing me off about what he was saying, but he was right. What are you getting at sir?

What I'm saying Sgt. Ross is this why don't you just stay in the Army. I looked at him like he was crazy. I wanted to say have you lost your fucking mind stay in for what. Now sir why would I want to do that? For your family. My family. Look Sgt let's face the facts there ain't many opportunities for Negro soldiers and when they start closing all those factories it's really going to be limited, but a least you already have a job. You get paid every two weeks, medical, dental and housing for your family. You going to throw all that away think about Sgt.

You could come work for me at Fort Monroe. I don't about all that sir I don't want to fight in any more wars I have seen enough killing to last me a life time. Sgt Ross we are not going to fight any more wars we won this one who's going to challenge us. He had a point the world now know we have nuclear weapons ain't nobody going to fuck with us they know we will use them. Lillian did ask me in one of her letters was I going to stay in. I know if Lt. Banks were Sgt here he would get you to stay in. Yes he would sir. I haven't talk to my wife since I been back let me call her and see what she thinks. He looked at me and pulled out this gold cigarette holder. I know he got that off a German officer, because it had the Nazi symbol on it.

He took out a cigarette lit it up took a long drag and blew the smoke my way. Okay Sgt you have until 1600 hours to let me know your answer. If I don't hear from you by then I'm going to sign these discharge papers and you won't be able to serve in the Armed Forces again. You understand Sgt Ross. Yes sir I understand. Now you go call your wife. Yes sir. I got up to leave when he said to me. Oh by the way Sgt. Ross if you decide to get out you won't be getting out as a Sgt, but a Pvt. Now you think about that. I'll see you at 1600 hours Sgt or will it be Pvt. Yes sir. I saluted him and left.

CHAPTER SIXTY-TWO

I LEFT THE COL OFFICE confused about what I'm going to do I was all set to get out and he throws this shit at me. You alright Sgt. Ross? I just looked at him. You know every black soldier that comes out of his office has the same look on their faces. One soldier came out crying. Crying!

Yeah he was crying. Where is the nearest phone at? There is one across the street in the phone center. Thanks. You welcome Sgt. I left and headed over to the phone center. I felt the Col left me know choice, but to stay in I don't want to do that. I didn't want to come in any where. I got to the phone center all it was a room with four pay phones and stools. This phone center was for the Negro soldiers you could tell it wasn't kept up. It was dirty out of the four phones two of them were broken. Somebody had snatched the cord out one of them the other one was lying on the floor. The two that were working wasn't in the best shape neither. The one I was going to use the wires was hanging out of it. I pushed the wires back in, so it wouldn't cut off on me when I was talking. I started to dial, but the dial got stuck. I had to dial a couple of minutes, so it could loosen up. I dialed 0 and the operator came on. City and state please. Houston, Texas. I waited for about couple minutes then another voice came on Houston she said. Yes can you connect me to 555-6285. I called my mother in-laws house, because we didn't have a phone. I looked at my watch it was 9am. Hello a woman voice said.

The Men that Time has Forgotten

Lillian I said. No this ain't Lillian this her sister Pam. Who this? It's me. Me who? Me Popeye woman! Oh hey Jeffery I didn't recognize your voice. Where is Lillian? She just went to work.

When is she coming back? She don't get off until 4:00pm. 4pm! Yeah she works the 8am-4pm shift, but she ain't going to get home until 5pm. 5pm I thought you said she gets off at 4pm?

She does she has to go pick up Jennifer from my momma's house. Damn! Is they away you could get in contact with her? No her job ain't got know phone. Listen Pam it's important that I get in touch with her our future depends on it. Y'all future depends on it this must be very important the way you talking. Well She goes her on lunch break around 12pm. I'll go down to her job and see if she can come home for lunch. Good you do that Pam tell her I will call her back at 12pm sharp tell her to be there. Okay I will. Thank you Pam I'll talk to you later. Okay bye. Bye. I decided to stay at the phone center I didn't want somebody to use the phone and I might miss Lillian. I sat there every time somebody came I would pick up the phone like I'm using it. I looked at my watch and it was only 10am.I would have to wait until 1300 hours to call Lillian I was one hour a head of her. I still had a long time to wait ten people had already come in to use the phone. Every 5-10 minutes I would look at my watch. Damn I wish 1300pm would hurry up and get here. This one Pvt was using the other phone that worked. Sgt this one Pvt asked me are you going to use that phone. How long are you going to be? I got to make an important phone call at 1300. I'm only going to be 10-15 minutes. I looked at him and got up so he could use the phone. I stood right there just in case somebody else wanted to use the phone. The Pvt who was using the phone was laughing up a storm who ever he was talking to he kind of made the time go fast. Excuse me Sgt you inline to use the phone next? I looked at my watch it was 1130.Yeah I'm next, but you can go ahead of me. Thanks Sgt. When the one Pvt finished he got on the phone. I let 5 other Pvt go ahead of me to use the phone. When I looked at my watch it was 1215pm. When the last Pvt finished I just sat down by the phone. Another Pvt came up to me and asked could he use the phone. I told

Michael Johnson

him yeah he looked disappointed when I said that, but I didn't care. I needed to talk with my wife and him looking sad didn't bother me. A line had formed behind the two phones. Come on man hurry up. The Pvt give him the finger and kept on talking. Then he looked at me. I looked at my watch it was 1230pm. I told him he could use this phone. Thanks Sgt. You need to hurry up I got an important phone call to make. No problem Sgt. He got on the phone and started talking to who ever he called. I looked at him and at my watch to let him know his time was up. Well I got to go there are a lot of people who want to use the phone I'll talk to you later.

It's all your Sgt. I looked at my watch it was 1255pm I still had a couple of minutes left. I sat down on the stool and I picked the phone up and dialed it slow I even acted like I forgot the number. I dialed zero for the operator. City and state please. Houston, Texas. Houston the voice said. Can connect me to 555-6285 please. Hello. Lillian. Yeah is this you Jeffery. Yeah it's me baby. I'm so happy yo hear from you. Me to baby. Where you at? I'm in Norfolk, Va now. Oh so you not in England no more? No I got to Norfolk yesterday afternoon. Why you ain't call me to let me know you was back? I'm sorry baby I was trying to get my paperwork done for my discharge. Oh okay how is that going? Well that's what I want to talk with you about. Okay. My Col wants me to stay in the Army. She got real quiet. Why he want you to stay in? Well If I get out and I can't find a job what am I going to do? You no there ain't going to be any jobs for Negro soldiers. I got to take care of you and Jennifer. You right about that a lot of soldiers are coming home and nobody's hiring them. If I stay in I ain't got to worry about that. She didn't say anything. I don't know about that Jeffery it's been hard for me since you been gone I ain't seen you in almost two years. I know baby, but you will be with me we won't be apart again. So what are you saying is that I could come where you are at. Yes that's what I'm saying. Okay I can deal with that as long as I'm with you, but you gotta promise me one thing. What's that baby? You got to take me to Paris. Okay that's a promise. You ain't going to fight any more wars are you? No I ain't going to fight any more wars. How wrong was I in five years we would be in another conflict. Okay now you sure about this? Yes I'm sure baby.

Okay now I can tell that Col I'm staying. Jeffery when I come where your at? Where are we going to stay? They are going to give us a house to stay in. Our own house? Yeah baby our own home. Good I'm tried of that apartment we are going to need more room anyway.

Jennifer is getting big. How is my baby doing anyway? She's fine she's over my momma's house now I'll pick her up after work. Lillian you do you think she's going to know who I am?

Yeah she's going to know who you are Jeffery your her daddy. I know Lillian, but she ain't seen me yet. Don't worry baby I show her a picture of you all the time is that what you are worried about? Yeah I am Lillian. I don't want her to reject me. Oh baby she ain't going to reject you. So don't worry okay. Okay. I got to go back to work my lunch time is up. I'll be looking forward to seeing you soon when are you coming home? I'll be there in a couple of days. Okay I'll be looking for you. Okay baby. Well I got to go I love you. I love you to. I hung up the phone with a big smile on my face. The other soldiers wasn't to happy, because they was waiting a long time. Damn! Sgt is about time you got off that phone. It's all yours I said with a big smile on my face. Y'all boys have a nice day. As I was leaving I could hear them tell that soldier you better not be on that phone long. I was laughing as I walked out the door.

Now that I had got that over with I can go tell Col. Conley fat ass that I was staying in. I looked at my watch it was 1330pm I had enough time before I had to got back to see Col. Conley. I thought to myself am I making the right decision a lot of guys in my division are getting out. I know Sgt would have stay in and he would have encourage me to do the same. I hope the Army changes it's ways.

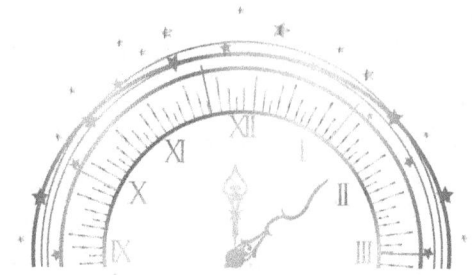

CHAPTER SIXTY-THREE

IT WAS 1400 HOURS when I got to back Col. Conley's office. I took my time getting back to him. I went to eat first, I was hungry as hell then I want to the PX to buy a gift for Lillian and my daughter. When I walked the administrative office I was met by Cpl. Walls. Good after Sgt Ross in his fake white voice. Afternoon Cpl is the Col in? Yes he is I'll tell him you are here.

He got up and went back and knocked on the door then he came back. Sgt Ross the Col will see you now. I walked back to the Col office. I knocked on the door. Come in. I walked in he was sitting behind his desk smoking his cigarette. Have a seat Sgt Ross. So have you made your decision?

Yes I did, but my wife was crying when I told her that it took me two hours to convince her that it was a good idea that I stay in. The only reason she agreed I told you said I wouldn't fight any more wars. You told her that? Yes sir and she believed me sir. Well I guess you did what you had to do. He reached over and pulled my service record from a pile he had on his desk. He opened it and put it in front of me. Now all I need you to do is sign these papers and you will be good to go. It was a lot of papers I knew I better read them first before I sign them I might be signing my life away. Sgt I'm going to grab me another cup of coffee while you read all those papers. He got his fat ass up grabbed his big ass coffee cup and walked out of the office. I started reading the papers a lot of them was simple stuff that was telling me what I was entitled to. The information in these papers were things I signed two years ago. I read the first three pages and when I got to last page I was shocked. It was a letter from the Col requesting I be admitted into the officer program. Now why would he want me to be an officer I can't stand this fat motherfucker he got a lot of good men killed in that war. I sat there for a minute thinking it wouldn't be so bad being an officer I would be in charge of my own division I would be able to get better housing, wouldn't have to wait anymore. I could help other Negro's soldiers get in the officer program. This would even give me a chance someday to go to college I always wanted to do that. I signed all the papers except the last one I could hear the Col come down the hallway. Well Sgt did you read and sign all those papers. Yes sir I did. Did you understand them? Yes I do sir. I signed them except the last page. Why what's wrong Sgt? I was wondering why you picked me to go into the officer program? Well if you must know you did a hell of a job out there the Army need Negro soldiers like yourself to lead the next generation of Negro soldiers. Things are going to change for Negros all over especially in the Army. When will I be going to school to start my officer training? I say in about a year the war just ended they are going to need time to sought everything out. There's talk going around they thinking about intergrating the Army white and black soldiers training together. Are you serious sir? Yes I am. When is this going to happen? I don't know, but it will happen. Now that is something I would like to see. I signed the last paper. He took a big sip of his coffee while I was signing it. Now since you have reenlisted I need you to rise your right hand and repeat after me. I repeated what he told me to say. It was the same oath I took two years ago. Now Sgt. Ross since you have reenlisted I'm putting you on 21 days leave, so you could move your family from Texas to Va. Before you leave you need to go see the housing officer. He will help you find a place for your family to live. Go to Cpl. Walls and he will type you up some leave papers. When you get these papers your leave will start. I will see you when you get off leave. Col sir what will I be doing? You will be in charge of the Negro soldiers at the new base

Michael Johnson

in Newport News called Fort Houston. That's way I want you back, so you can help with the move. Yes sir I said with a smile on my face. I got up to leave. Oh Sgt one more thing. The smile on my face started to fade, because I thought that he was going to tell me some bad news. I'm promoting you to 1st Sgt I already put the paperwork in you will start wearing it when you get back. Now get out of here I'll see you in three weeks. Yes sir thank you sir. I saluted and left. I got outside his office and did a little dance. I see somebody is happy. Yes Cpl. Walls I am. So you made up your mind to stay in. Yes I did and I'm here to get my leave papers. He reached in his drawer and pulled out this folder. Here sign these papers. The Col told me to type them up when he left you his office.

He knew you was staying in. He told you that? Yeah he told me to type up your promotion papers also. Let me tell you something Sgt you ain't the only one he talked into staying. Now I felt like I been had I should have known this was all a set up. It was too easy. Well it ain't nothing I can do about it now. Sgt Lt Lawson is the housing officer is waiting on you in his office. Where is his office at? Down the hallway. Lt. Lawson office was at the end of the hallway. I knocked on the door. Come in he said. He was sitting behind his desk when I walked in. Morning Lt I said I also saluted him. My name Is Sgt Jeffery Ross Col. Conley sent me down here. He said you were the Housing Officer and I needed to talk with about finding my family and I a home. He looked at my sat back in his chair took a deep breath. I don't know what the Col was thinking when he told you that we don't have any housing for Negro soldiers. What! So where is my family and I are going to stay sir. I don't know Sgt. I guess you your family going to have to find a place out in town. But sir the Col said since we moving to the new base there going to be plenty of housing. I had lied to him the Col never said that I just wanted to see what he was going to do. New base what new base? The base we are moving to in Newport News didn't you hear we was moving? No I didn't no one told me anything I wasn't told we were moving. His face turned beat red he got on the phone and called the Col. Yes sir I just heard from Sgt Ross that we're moving sir. I don't know what was being said to him on the phone, but his face went from beat red to pale white. Yes sir I will sir.

You have a good day sir. He hung the phone and looked at me. Sgt Ross I'm going to need you to fill out this package. He gave me this stack of papers to sign. You can have a seat in that room over there to read and fill out these papers. He pointed to this room next to his office. When you finish bring them back to me. I took the stack of papers from him and went into the next room. It was a small room with a couple of chairs and desk. I sat down and started filling out all that paperwork I took me about an hour and a half to fill out all that paperwork. When I finished I took the paperwork and took it back to Lt. Lawson. When I got there he was packing up to go home. Oh you finally finished. Yes sir. Well let me see if you filled all the paper out properly. He put down his briefcase and took my package from me. He looked though it real quick and throw it on his desk. I didn't like the way he did that. Sgt. Ross when you come off leave there will be a home waiting on you. Thank you sir. So when you going on leave Sgt? I'm leaving tomorrow sir. Well enjoy yourself, because when you get back we will have a lot of work to do. He made it seem like they were going to work me to death.

Well I got to get home my in-laws are here. He picked up his briefcase closed his office door and left. He left me standing there. Lt. Lawson was a tall man with brown hair and brown eyes. He had a northern accent like he was from New York or some other northern city. I would find out later he was pulled offline during the war, because he had freaked out. The office was empty everyone had gone home even Cpl. Walls. I looked at my watch it was 1700 hours. I started walking back to my barracks thinking I hope I did the right thing. I know one thing good came out of it I'm going to be a 1st Sgt. I could never guess all this would be happening to me. I got to my room I was dead tried I looked at my watch it was 1730 hours. I was hungry, but I didn't went to walk to the chow hall. I took my shirt and shoes off and flopped down on the bed.

CHAPTER SIXTY-FOUR

I STARTED TO FELL ASLEEP when I remembered the two letters Sgt had given me. He told me not to open them until I got home. Well I'm home now I got up and went over to my uniform jacket. I pulled them out of my pocket they was wrinkled up I always wanted to find out what they said. I started with the one I already started to open back in Germany. I had to be careful when I opened them, because I didn't want to tear the paper they was stuck together. It took me about 5 minutes to peel them apart. When I finally got them apart I tried to read the first page, but the ink made the letters was run together I couldn't hardly make out what it was saying. I could make out the begin Dear Popeye, but that was it. I started scanning the letter for words I could read I got down to this one part that said killed Killed! I said to myself. What the hell is Sgt talking about killed? Then it hit me he must be talking about Capt. Lewis the night we went on that fucked up mission. So Sgt did kill Capt. Lewis? Why would he do that? I started reading the next page which was better then the first page. I read to the part that said:

    I shot him Popeye, because he was gonna shoot me. When you was at that wall pinned down by that machine gun. H told me to charge that machine gun. I told him I wasn't going to do shit not by myself. He took out his 45 and said that's in order Nigger and if you don't do what I told you I will blow your Nigger brains out. I gave him the impression

The Men that Time has Forgotten

I was getting ready to charge that machine gun, but I turned around and hit him with the butt of my rifle knocking him to the ground. He said Nigger what the fuck are you doing? I'm going to make sure none of you come back alive and than he laughed. I stood there and looked at him I picked up his gun and give it back to him. He got up and pointed his gun at me. Your Nigger ass will be the first to die. He was gonna shoot me, but his gun jammed. We stood there a second looking at each other. When he tried to cock his gun again I pulled mine out and shot him in his head. I had to kill him Popeye he was gonna kill me. You know I couldn't let that happen. That's why I told you something bad happen that night. It was all a set up. They didn't think we was gonna survive, but we did. Don't stay in this man's Army Popeye. This ain't for know black man.

GET THE FUCK OUT.

I was lost for words he had killed Capt. Lewis for us knowing what those white folks would do to him if they found out he had killed a white officer. I wish I had read this letter earlier before I singed my life away. I put that letter back in it's envelope. I grabbed the other letter this one was better to read than the last one. When I opened it something fell out of it on to the floor. I got it to look for it. When I found it to my surprise it was a wedding ring. I was shocked I knew this couldn't be Sgt, because Sgt isn't married. I put it down and started reading the letter.

You must be home if you are reading this letter. That means I'm dead. I always know you was gonna make it out of here alive. You stronger then you think. All the shit you been though must men would've died in those situations. God left you alive for a reason. I want you to do me a favor. I never told you this , but I have a wife and kids back in St. Louis. We been married about ten years. I have seven kids four girls and three boys. My wife's name is Carla she one of those high yellow girls who can almost pass for white. I met her at a party my uncle was given. She one fine woman Popeye. My kids names is Rita, Brenda, Beverly, Diane, Willie the third, Larry and Charles. Brenda is the baby of the family she's six years old. Charles is the oldest he's 12 years old. I want you to go to St. Louis and tell my wife what happen to me. I wrote and told her about you already. I don't trust the Army Popeye. You know what they gonna say a bunch of bullshit. They gonna send her this letter in the mail telling her how I died for my country and all that bullshit. I want my wife and kids to know the truth.

None of that bullshit they tell all the families. Tell her the truth do this favor for me Popeye. Tell her I love her with all my heart and the kids to. Popeye I want you to know you are the best friend I have ever had. I love you like a brother. I will never forget you. I'm gonna close now, because Douglass is coming and we got to go around checking on the men guarding the road. You know how he is? I want you to take care of yourself your wife and the little one Jennifer.

Your Friend

Willie Banks the Third.

I didn't know Sgt was married and had a family back in St. Louis. He never said a word about them I wonder why. I never seen him write a letter home. He wrote this letter like he knew he was going to die. I was about to put the letter back when I seen something on the back. I turned it over to see what it said.

Popeye I almost forgot to tell you. I got some money put away in a bank in St. Louis. It's not a lot, but it some money. I made it from running moonshine with my uncle. You ain't the only one who ran moonshine. It's only $2,000.00 dollars. The account book is in a old oil can in my shed. I hid it well so nobody can find it. I didn't give you my address. It's 1309 Wilson rd, St. Louis,Mo. I ain't got know phone, so you gonna have to go over there.

Now I can go now. Here comes Douglass again.

I folded the letter and put it back in the envelope. Damn!I was planning on going home now I have to go to St. Louis. I already brought my bus ticket for Houston now I got to change it. I told Lillian I would be home in a couple of days. I got to thinking if leave for St. Louis tonight instead of tomorrow I could still get home the time I said I would there. I didn't really mind this was for a good friend who saved my life. I got dressed packed all my things and left. I turned my key to the desk. I looked at my watch it was 1917 hours it was still early. I should be able to catch a bus to St. Louis. I waved a taxi down and told him to take me to the bus station. It only took him about ten minutes to get me there. I threw him a couple of dollars and got out.

The station was packed with soldiers and sailors trying to get home. I had to use the colored entrance it was packed to. I pushed my way though the crowded bus station to the departure board. I looked on the board to see if there was any buses leaving for St. Louis. I was in luck there was one bus leaving at 2115 hours, but then the clerk put a full sign next to it. I walked over to him and asked him what did that mean. It means what it says son. No more seats on the bus. So when is the next bus leaving for St. Louis? Let me see he grabbed his clipboard. The next bus ain't leaving until 2215 hours and that one is full to. So when is the leaving?

The next one ain't leaving until 0600 tomorrow morning. 0600 tomorrow morning I need to leave tonight. I wish I could help you son, but ain't nothing I can do. Then I felt a hand on my shoulder. I turned round to see who it was. A short brown skin man wearing a sailor's uniform was standing there. Hey soldier I over heard you talking to that clerk you needed to get to St. Louis. Yeah I do. Well maybe I can help you. How? First let me introduce myself my name is George Washington Lincoln. Yeah I was named after the two Presidents before you say anything. We shook hands. My name is Jeffery Ross. So how are you going to help me George? I have a ticket to St. Louis. Okay so what do you want me from me? I need to get to Dallas,Texas I don't have a enough money to buy a ticket to get there I only have a enough to get to St. Louis. I have family there I was going to ask them to pay my way to Dallas. So what you are telling me you need to get to Dallas? Yeah. I think I can help you I got a ticket to Houston. You do. Yeah I do. So you want to trade? Sure what time does your ticket say? It's for 2115 hours. That's good let me get that ticket. We traded tickets. Thanks Jeffery. Your welcome George. Hey Jeffery you better hurry up, because that 2115 bus to St. Louis is loading up now. It's loading? I thought it wasn't going to leave until 2115. Yeah they were, but they just changed it to 2015 hours. I looked at my watch it was 2010. I picked up mu duffle bag and ran to the bus. You getting on this bus boy? This white bus driver said in a mean voice. Yes sir. Where is your ticket? I gave him my ticket. He snatched it out my hand. Now that made me mad when he did that. He looked at me you look familiar didn't you ride my bus before? No sir I don't think so. Yeah you did I remember you from about two years ago I dropped you off in Iowa. I thought about it for a minute. Then it hit me I do remember this redneck. Yeah I member you now? He looked at me in my uniform. So you were in the war?

What was your job. I brought supplies to the troops on Omaha beach during D-Day. Oh Yeah!

Yeah my division help push the Germans out of France. I also drove trucks to supplying the troops. You did all that? Yes sir I did. He had this amazed look on his face. Well I appreciate what you boys did for us and this wonder country. Thank you. He even shook my hand which shocked me. Now get on the bus son. I got my duffle bag and got on the bus. I thought he might have said get your black ass on the bus like the last time. I headed to the back of the bus where all the Negro people seat. Even though I fought this country and risk my life the rules ain't changed. There were no seats, so I had to stand the half trip. The whole trip I kept thinking how that redneck fell for that D-Day story. I wasn't even in France during D-Day. I realized that white people was suckers for stories like that. I would use these stories to get what I wanted from the Army.

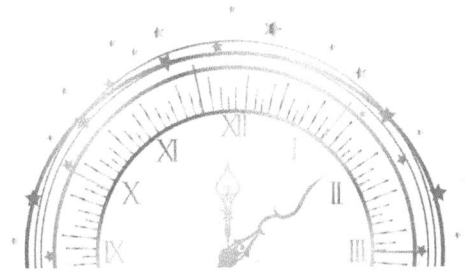

CHAPTER SIXTY-FIVE

WE FINALLY GOT TO St. Louis around 0830 hours that morning I got to sit down around 0200 hours. When I tried to get up my legs was stiff I guess it was from all that standing I had done.

I got my duffle bag and got off the bus. It was kind of cloudy and look like it was going to rain and the wind was blowing a little bit. The bus station was in downtown St. Louis it was a nice station. It was better then the one in Houston. It had painting on the wall nice chairs where you can sit, but they had what all bus stations have segregated sections. I started thinking before I did anything I better find out when the next bus to Houston was leaving. I walked over to the colored ticket counter. The clerk at the window was this short fat man with bushy eyebrows smoking a big cigar. What do you need soldier boy? Yes sir I want to know when the next bus to Houston is leaving? He looked at these papers he had on this clipboard. Well we got one leaving tonight at 9pm and two leaving tomorrow at 9am and 3pm. I'll take the one at 9am. Okay then that will be 2.00 dollars. Okay here's your ticket. I would advise you to be here early, because those seats full up quick. Alright I will. Where can I get some breakfast around here? There's Paul's diner right across the street. How's the food in there? It's good I go there everyday for breakfast he makes the best damn pancakes in St. Louis. Thanks I picked up my duffle bag and headed over to Paul's diner. When I got outside the streets was busy that morning I guess everybody was going to work. I crossed the busy intersection to Paul's diner. The outside of Paul's Diner didn't look like much it reminded me of Hattie's place back in Houston. When I opened the door and went in the inside was a different story.

    The inside of Paul's diner minded me of a white restaurant. It had booths and tables with flowers on them painting on the walls, chairs all the same color. Waiters and waitress wearing the same uniforms not like colored restaurants where what you wear to work is your uniform. I was looking around for some where to sit when a sweet voice said. My I help you? I turned around to see who it was a pretty dark brown skin young girl was standing there. She had the most beautiful brown eyes I have ever seen. Yes I would like some breakfast. You by yourself? Yes I am. She grabbed a menu a roll with a fork, spoon, knife with a napkin wrapped around them. This way. I followed her though the restaurant everybody was smiling at me as I walked passed their tables. I wasn't paying any attention to them I was watching that waitresses ass as she walked. Here you go. She gave me a booth by a window on the other side of the restaurant. She put the menu and roll on the table. My name is Donna I will be your waitress. Can I get you something to drink? Yes a cup of coffee please. Okay I'll be right back. I watched her as she walked away. Damn if I wasn't married I said to myself. I picked up the menu it was a real menu. It wasn't one of them paper ones I'm use to. This was a real menu with pictures of the food and a list of all types of dishes. They had a wide selection of pancakes, waffles, sausage, ham, bacon and even steak. Which I was shocked I ain't never had steak for breakfast. I looked over the menu to decided what I wanted to eat. Then I seen this big breakfast meal it had pancakes, sausage, eggs and grits. I decided that's what I wanted. By this time Donna had come back with my coffee. Did you decided what you wanted Yeah I want this big breakfast. The big breakfast are you sure you want that? That's a lot of food for a man your size. I looked at her what you mean by that? What I'm saying is s most truckers and construction workers eat that meal, because they do a lot of work. So I have done a lot of heavy fighting in that war. Don't let my size fool you. She smiled at me okay the big breakfast it is. She took the menu and headed to the kitchen with my order. I was sipping my coffee (which by the way was the best coffee I have ever had) I seen this tall white woman come in. She was wearing the same uniform Donna had on. That seemed odd to me a white woman walking in a place like this around all these colored folks I thought that was strange. Ten minutes later Donna brought my food to me. When I seen all that food my eyes almost popped out my head. I told you it was a lot of food you didn't believe me. It's alright I can handle it. Okay if you need anything just let me know. Alright I will. I watched her as she walked away. Damn she got a fat ass. I looked at my plate and realize this was a lot of food.

It came with 4 large pancakes, 4 sausages, 5 scrambled eggs, 2 pieces of toast and a big bowl of grits with a nice helping of butter on top. I dug in I ate the sausage, eggs and toast first. That hardly filled me up I ain't ate in a day or so. Then I started in on those pancakes and grits. I got some syrup and put it on my pancakes I cut them so I can eat them better. I was doing good until I started eating those grits. That's when I started getting full. I could see out the corner of my eye Donna and her friend looking at me. They were laughing at me trying to choke all that food down. More coffee a voice said. I looked to see who it was. It was the white woman. Yes please I said with a mouth full of pancakes. She filled my cup up with coffee. You know those two over there got a bet on you that you can't finish all that food. She said that with a smile. A bet! Yep a bet then she walked away smiling. I looked at them and smiled. This is one bet they ain't going to when. I finished the bowl of grits off. I still had two pancakes to go. I finished off one quick, but I got full after that one. My belly felt like it was about to pop, so I loosen my belt a little. I looked at the last pancake and I decided to cut it into four section. I downed the first two with no problem, but that third one I had to choke down. I looked up and I seen the white waitress looking at me smiling. I smiled back. Then I realize she wont white at all she was black. She was just a high yellow woman. Sgt told me his wife high yellow. I got to wondering is that his wife. I took a big bite of the last section. I took another bite I barely got that one down. I could see Donna and her friend looking at me.

I had this one piece left I took a deep breath and stuff it in my month. I shouldn't had done that, because when I did that it started coming back up. I got up and rushed to the bathroom. I got in the bathroom and throw all that food up. When I came out Donna and her friend was laughing at me. You alright Donna asked me. Yeah I'm fine I didn't think you can finish all that food, but you did. I couldn't let y'all win the bet. Bet who told you we had a bet? She told me I pointed at the light skin woman. Oh she did. Yeah she did. Bitch! I can't stand that high yellow bitch Donna said. She need to mine her damn business. What's her name? Her name is Carla Banks. Is she married ? Why you want to know you interested in her? No. Then why you won't to know is she married? The reason I'm asking, because I might know her husband.

What's her husband name? Willie Banks. Yep that's him Donna said. Yeah he was that fine dark skin man the other waitress said. What your name I asked the other waitress? My name is Tina Burrows. What's your name? My name is Jeffery Ross. Well glad to meet you Jeffery.

Where you from Jeffery? I'm from Houston, Texas. What you doing here in St. Louis? I came to tell her about Sgt. Where he at anyway? I just looked at her. Oh my God he's dead. Yeah he died in the war and I'm here to tell her what happen to him. You not going to tell her now are you? No I'm going to wait until she gets off work. Well you are going to be waiting a long time she don't get off until 8pm tonight and it's only 10:00am. So what are you going do for the next ten hours. She said that with a smile on her face. I don't know. Well you can go to the movie house down the street. It shows movies all day long you could go there to kill some time. I think I will do you know what's playing there? No I don't. I guess I'll find out when I get there. Can I leave my duffle bag here? Yeah I'll put it in the store room for you. Thank you Donna. Your welcome. Now where is this place at? She told me where this place was. I sat there and and chatted with them for about an hour or so than I headed to the movie house.

CHAPTER SIXTY-SIX

I LOOKED AT MY WATCH it was 1200 hours when I left Paul's Diner. I told Donna I would be back around 1930 hours to catch Carla before she got off work. I hoping Donna or Tina don't tell Carla what happen to Sgt. I wanted to do that. When I was walking to the movies I seen a phone, so I decided to call my wife to let her know I'll be home sometime tomorrow evening. I walked to the phone I made sure it was colored only. As usual the phone was broken I got mad and just headed to the movies. When I got to the movies there was nothing playing I wanted to see. The movies that were playing was Sands of Iwo Jima, The Flying Leathernecks both John Wayne movies I hate John Wayne. Some other movie with Ronald Reagan, Abbott and Costello I don't like them neither. I was looking around to find something to watch when I seen this one movie that caught my eye. The Diary of Guadalcanal. I never heard of it before, but it look like it would be good. I paid for my ticket on the colored side and went in. I didn't pay any snacks, because I was still full from that breakfast. The movie had already started when I went in. I found me a seat in the corner way in the back. The colored section of the movie theater wasn't to bad. It wasn't run down like the ones in Houston. The seats were soft there was no soda all over the floor making the floor sticky. The screen didn't have holes in it. It was really nice. I seen a young couple sitting just below me. I could see the guy trying to put his hands under her dress. She kept telling him NO, stop it until she just got tired of him and got up and left. He was left there looking stupid for a couple of minutes then he got up and went after her. I was saying to myself you better go after that I know you ain't going to let that get away from you. I sat there trying to watch the movie, but I was falling asleep. I guess I was tired from that bus ride and all that food I ate. The next thing I knew the usher was waking me up. Hey, hey he said to me. I felt him shaking me. Hey you've been sleeping for awhile. How long have I been sleeping? You slept throw five movies. What! What time is it? He looked at his watch. It's 7:30pm. What! Yeah 7:30pm. I been sleeping all that time? Yeah I guess. Damn! I need to catch Carla before she get off work. You mean Carla Banks. I looked at him. Yeah why you know her? Everybody know her she one fine woman, but she got this crazy husband name Willie. He's in the Army. I know him and I served in the same division. I hear he coming home soon. I didn't say a thing. That's why I'm here I told him. I got to go. What's your name? My name is Tony, Tony Miles. Jeffery Ross, but my friends call me Popeye. Glad to meet you Jeffery I mean Popeye. We shook hands and I left. I fixed my uniform before I left the theater. I wanted to make sure I looked good when I walked in Paul's Diner. I walking to the diner thinking how I was going to tell Carla about Sgt. This wasn't going to be easy. I got to Paul's diner around 1940 hours. I walked in I didn't see Carla.

I looked around and I seen Donna and Tina at the waitress station. Where is Carla? She left Tina said. Left! I thought she didn't get off until 8pm. She does but she left early. What time did she leave? An hour after you. An hour after me? I looked at them. Did one of y'all tell her what happen to Sgt. Tina didn't say a word. Donna started walking away. I grabbed Donna by her arm. Why did you tell her that? She just looked down. Damn! Tina you know where she lives? Yeah she lives next door to me if you wait a few minutes we can walk over there together. Okay. Where is my duffle bag? Right here. I grabbed it I looked at Donna and shook my head. I'll be outside waiting for you Tina. Okay. I was mad as hell I wanted to hurt her for telling Carla Sgt had died. I wanted to tell him that coming from me would have been better. I got outside and started thinking I can't imagine what Carla is going though right now. A few minutes later Tina came out. You ready? Yeah I'm ready. I picked up my duffle bag and we started walking towards her house. I told Donna she was wrong for telling Carla that. I told her she shouldn't have done that. Why did she do that any way? Well Donna don't like Carla.

Why? Because she's light skin. No! You see this got something to do with Willie. Sgt. Your Sgt or what ever you call him. What do you mean this got something to do with Sgt? Well Donna and Willie was engaged to get married. Really. Yeah this happen a long ways back when Willie first came to St. Louis. So what happen? Well one night Willie's uncle Charles throw this party. Yeah I know he told me about it. This is where he met Carla right? Right! Carla came to the party with her cousin Pat. Pat was messing around with Willie's uncle Charles.

Charles never liked Donna. Why? He said she thought she was to good for everybody, so introduce Carla to Willie. Carla ain't from St. Louis neither. Where is she from? She's from a small town in Missouri called Lambert. Where you from Tina? Who me I was born and raised right here in St. Louis. She said with a smile. Well anyway Willie start messing around with Carla behind Donna back. Oh yeah how did she find out. I sounded surprise, but I wasn't Sgt was a womanizer any way. Donna sister Mary Jo saw Willie and Carla kissing one day. She went back and told Donna what she saw. Donna and Carla got into this big fight. Donna beat up Carla real bad and Donna was 8 months pregnant with Willie's baby when she did that.

Donna had a baby for Sgt? Yep she had a baby girl name Wilma. He didn't tell you about that. No? Did he tell you anything about himself Jeffery? Yeah, but he never mentioned all this to me all he told me was he and Carla get seven kids together. That ain't all the kids he got.

What! He got more? Yeah your friend Sgt got kids all over he got about 20 kids. What! Yeah.

This was all a shock to me Sgt ain't never told me he had a lot of kids. We were talking so much we almost walked pass Carla's house. Well here we are that's her house right there. It don't look like anyone's home. Oh she's home. Are you sure? Yeah I'm sure. I guess this is good-bye Tina. I guess it is. I want to thank you for your help. Your welcome Jeffery. I tell you what before I leave tomorrow I'll come by and tell you good-bye. Okay that would be nice. We hugged and I watched her go in her house.

CHAPTER SIXTY-SEVEN

THE HOUSE CARLA LIVED in was small looking from outside. It was dark so I couldn't see what color it was. There were bikes and toys in the yard. I walked up to the door and knocked. At first nobody answered. Then I knocked again then a tiny voice said who is it? Jeffery Ross is your momma? Yeah wait a minute I go get her. I could hear feet running. I was waiting for Carla to come to the door when I looked over and Tina was looking out the window at me.

She waved at me and I waved back. Who is it a woman's voice asked? Yes ma'am my name is Jeffery Ross I was a friend of your husband Willie Banks. The door opened up Carla was standing there. Hello ma'am I don't mean to bother you. I put my hand out to greet her she just looked at me. What you won't Mr. Ross? I'm a friend of your husband's he might have wrote you about me. They call me Popeye. When I said that she ease up a little. Oh so your Popeye? Yeah he talked about you in some of his letters come on in. I picked up my duffle bag and went in. The hallway had no lights, but there was a table with pictures on it with a big mirror above it. I couldn't see who were in the pictures, because it was dark. Come let's sit down in the living room. We walked in the living room. She clicked on the light. The living room was pretty big. It was a long sofa against the wall with a long wooden table in front of it.

The table had a flower vase in the middle. The flowers was fake.

There was a cabinet with shelves with all types of nicknacks. Two black chairs sat at the end of the room. There was a lamp on a table next to one of the chairs. The whole living room was painted in gold. Have a seat. I sat down on the long sofa. Can I get you something to drink Mr. Ross? Yes please and you don't have to call me Mr. Ross you can call me Popeye. Okay Popeye I'll be right back. I sat there thinking she don't seem upset about Sgt death. I could hear the kids upstairs playing. Stop all that noise up there. Here you go Popeye. She brought me a cup of coffee.

Thank you. I guess she remembered what I was drinking at the diner. She sat down in one of the chairs. So Popeye what brings you to St. Louis? Well I suppose to tell you what happen to Sgt, but Donna beat me to it. How did she know he was dead? Did you tell her? No! She asked me what happen to him when I did say nothing she figured it out for herself. I want to tell you what really happen to him. She sat back, so how did he die? Before we get started Willie said you was from Houston, Texas. Yes ma'am born and raised. You come all the way from Houston to tell me this? No I was in Virginia on my way home and Sgt that's what I called him asked me to do him this favor. He did. Yes he did. Well tell me what happen? We was ordered to take this village called Norberg. I told her the whole story. When I was telling her the story she didn't seem to concerned about Sgt. Which made me mad. He gave me these two letters I pulled them out of my pocket when I opened one of them this ring fell out. I handed her the ring. She looked at it and put it on the table. I looked at her is there something wrong? You want to read the letters she just waved her hand. Then she looked at me. Let me tell you about your friend Sgt. The whole time he was over there fighting that fucking war he never sent me one red cent. What! Yeah he never sent me shit. I had to take care of everything myself. Let me tell you another thing he wasn't a very nice person to me neither.

When he got drunk you know what he would do? No! He would beat the shit out of me. You know he fucking my best friend, my sister and three of my cousins and every women he could get his fucking hands on. That woman Donna he left her for me told he loved me. I believed that black motherfucker then he turned right around and got that bitch pregnant.

Then he told me it was an accident. You know I believed him and took his sorry ass back. You know that black motherfucker got my sister pregnant. Her and I haven't spoken in six years behind that bullshit I'm glad that black motherfucker is dead. He made my life a living hell. By this time she was yelling and crying one of the kids came downstairs. It must have been the oldest boy Willie. You alright momma? Go back upstairs Willie momma alright. Momma. Didn't you hear me boy take your ass back upstairs for I beat it. He looked at me with this sad look on his face and went back upstairs. I sat there in shocked I couldn't say nothing. If you don't mind me asking how have you been taking care of you and your kids? I worked two jobs to make ends meet. They don't pay much that's why it so dark in here. I can't afford to pay my light bill. The only light that work in the whole house is this lamp. I'm about to lose this house if I don't pay my mortgage next month I'm already three months behind. He brought me this house and ever paid one day rent. He would lay around all day doing nothing while I did all the work. Do you have family around here to help you out? Yeah my sister and we ain't speaking to each other the rest of my family is back in Lambert, Missouri. I felt bad for her I wish there was a way I could help her out, but how. Then I thought about what Sgt had wrote in one of the letters about the $2,000 dollars he had in the bank. You know what Sgt told me in one of his letters that he had $2,000 dollars in a bank. She just looked at me. Willie had $2,000 dollars in a bank that's a laugh. That Nigga didn't have to nickels to rub together to make a dime where would he get $2,000 dollars from? He said he saved it up from running moonshine with his uncle. I'm serious Carla I gave her the letter to read. She looked up at me.

It says that the bank book is in the shed in a old oil can. It won't hurt to go check it out. She gets up go to the kitchen get a flashlight and goes out to the shed. I watched her she walked out the back door. Willie came back downstairs. Where my momma at. She's in the shed she will be back in a few minutes. You better go back upstairs before she sees you. So you know my daddy? Yeah he was my best friend. Where he at? He's somewhere special God is taking care of him. When he hears Carla coming back he runs back upstairs. Did you find it. Yeah. In her hand was this old beat up book. It says here he has $2,000 dollars in a bank right here in St. Louis. I'm going to go straight over there tomorrow and get this money I really do need it.

So he was thinking of you after all? I guess he was Popeye. I got something else for you to he wanted me to give to you. I got up reached in to my duffle bag and pulled out the little bag of diamonds. What is that? I opened it up took a few out and gave them to her. Sgt told me to give these to you. She took from me and looked at them. She couldn't see so she got up and walked over to the light. Her eyes lit up it like Christmas tree lights are these real diamonds?

Yep Sgt and I find them in this old house in a village we were in. You could sell them and pay off all your bills and mortgage. You could go to one those white jewelry stores and tell them your father left them to you. She looked at me with this look on her face. Now how am I going to do that? You look like your white you could pass for one of them who's going to know you a Negro. You can do that can't you? I sure can. Look Carla I know Sgt might have been a bad man and treated you bad, but he was a good friend to me and he cared a lot about you all he talked about was you and the kids. If he didn't care about you he wouldn't have asked me to come all the way to St. Louis to tell you about the money and give you a few of these diamonds. He did? Yeah he did. Is this it? I don't understand. I mean he sent you all this way to give me a few diamonds. You got a whole bag full there. I know he told you to give me more than this. I looked at her. Just a few minutes ago she didn't have a pot to piss in or a window to throw out of now she asking me for more. Sgt was already dead when I found these diamonds I was being nice by helping her out. She got some nerve. I reached in my bag and gave her a few more. She smiled thank you Popeye I'm going to buy me a new car.

Yeah you can now. Well Carla I guess I better be going. Going where you going? You got some place to stay? No? I got some money I was going to get me a hotel room. Don't be silly Popeye you could stay here tonight and leave tomorrow morning unless you trying to get over to Tina's house. Why would I want to go over there? I'm a happily married man I love my wife and I ain't trying to get over there to Tina's house. Okay then you can stay here. You could stay in the boy's room. The girls can sleep with me and the boys can sleep in the girls room.

Let me go up here and fix the room up for you. She went upstairs. I wasn't going to argue with her she was right I didn't need to be staying in hotel out in town besides I know Sgt wouldn't allow it. I could here her yelling at the kids about something they had done. I sat there thinking about my daughter and how glad I was going to be when I see her. After about 15 minutes Carla came back downstairs. Popeye the room is ready for you I know your tired?

Yes I am. Well you go get some rest. What time do you have to catch your bus tomorrow? Oh at 9am. Okay then I will wake you up around 7am, so you can eat some breakfast before you go. That would be good. I got a candle lit in the room so you could see your way around.

Okay thank you. It's the room down the hall on the left. I nodded my head and went upstairs.

The hallway was dark I had to feel my way down the hallway. I passed the master bedroom and the girl's room. I could hear them playing in the girls room. I got to the boys room and when I opened the door the smell from piss hit me. I put my duffle bag down and looked around. The room was small with one bed, a chest and a long dresser. The bed was wooden and it look like somebody made it who ever made it did a bad job. I walked around thinking I would have rather stay in a hotel in town even though the window was open the smell from the piss was still strong. It was about to drive my crazy I put my head outside the window to get some air. When I did that I could see Tina laying in bed reading a book. Popeye you alright? Yeah I'm fine. She came in the room. I know it smells bad in here Charles has a bad bladder. Oh yeah how long has he had this problem? Even since Willie left to fight. Did you take him to a doctor? No I ain't got no money, so how was I going to do that? Well you have those diamonds now you can take him to see a doctor. I will. Well I'm going to let you get some rest. I'll see you tomorrow. Okay. I really didn't want to sleep on that mattress I bet it's all pissed up. I pulled the covers back Carla had put clean sheets on the bed something told me to pull the sheets back. When I did that the whole mattress had piss spots all over it. I wanted to turn it over, but I knew the other side would be the same. I wasn't going to sleep on that nasty mattress, so I decided to sleep on the floor. I took the sheets, blanket and pillow off the bed and make me a bed on the floor just like I did in the war. I took my uniform off and hung it in the closet. Before I laid down I looked out the window to see what Tina was doing.

Her lights were out, so she must have went to bed. I laid down on that hard floor which didn't bother me when I laid my head on that pillow I was out.

CHAPTER SIXTY-EIGHT

THE NEXT MORNING CARLA woke me up at 0700 hours just like she said she would. She knocked on the door. Popeye you up. Yeah I'm up. Come on downstairs and get some breakfast before you leave. Okay I'll be down in a few minutes. I got myself together and went downstairs. She cooked me a nice breakfast of eggs, bacon and pancakes. Come on sit down. I sat down next to one of the kids. Go head Popeye help yourself. I got some eggs and bacon I didn't want any pancakes. I know why you don't went any pancakes we both started laughing. Can I have them Willie asked me. Sure. I gave him two pancakes. Popeye why did you sleep on the floor last night? I'm not use to sleeping in any beds yet the last two years I have been sleeping on the ground, so I have to get use to it again. She knew I was lying and why I slept on the floor. Charles is lucky he ain't my son I would whip his ass every time he pissed in the bed.

Do you know my daddy the youngest girl Brenda asked me? Yes I did he was my best friend.

When he coming home? I had no words for that. Carla and I just looked at each other. He'll be home soon baby. Popeye it's 7:30am you better get going you don't want to miss your bus. I looked at my watch yeah you right I want to try and get a seat. You know I had to stand for most of the bus ride here. Oh yeah, so you really better be going. I'll go get your bag for you.

Thank you Carla. Was my daddy a brave man like you? Yeah he was braver then me. Did you win any medals? No I didn't win any medals, but we saved a lot of people. Where my daddy at now? He still over there. When he coming back? How many people did he shoot? They were asking me to many questions I was saying to myself I wish Carla would hurry up. She came down with my duffle bags. Here you go Popeye. Thanks Carla. I put on my uniform jacket and cover. I'll work with you to the bus station it's on my way to work. Let me get my coat. Listen I want you all to start cleaning this house. Rita I'm leaving you in charge this place better be spotless when I get home from work. If it's not done I'm going to whip me some ass when I get back home tonight. You understand. Sir ma'am. Come on Popeye let's go. I said good-bye to the kids and we left. We started walking to the bus station. Those kids can be a handful. I know they can. Willie told me in one of his letters you have a little girl.

Yeah I do her name is Jennifer. I know the kids took you by surprise asking you all those questions about Willie. Yeah they did. So when are you going to tell them what happen to Sgt? I will tell them when the time comes. Popeye I want to think you for those diamonds I know Willie didn't tell you to give them to me I know him Popeye. You did it out of the kindness of your heart and I want to thank you for that. No problem Sgt was a good friend he saved my life if it wasn't for him I wouldn't be alive. It took us about 15 minutes to get to the bus station. Well Popeye this is where we depart. You talk care of yourself and don't be a stranger you got my address you can come visit any time you want you can bring your wife and daughter to. Okay I will. We hugged and I watched her walk into Paul's Diner. I walked across the street to the bus station. I looked at my watch it was 0745 hours I had about an hour or so to kill before they started boarding the bus. I went inside to find out where I can catch my bus at when I heard someone call my name. I looked around and didn't see anyone, so I kept on walking. I was thinking who would know my name in St. Louis, but Carla I didn't know anyone here. I was walking to my bus when I felt someone touch my shoulder. I turned around to see who it was. It was Tina. Hey didn't you hear me calling your name? Yeah I did I didn't see anyone, so I kept on walking. What are you doing here anyhow? I came to say good-bye since you didn't stop by like you said you would.

Yeah I wanted to, but Carla was walking with me. So are you going to say good-bye? She walked up to me and gave me a big kiss on my lips. Good-bye she said to bad you don't live in St. Louis we could have some fun.

You have a safe trip home. She turned and left. I stood there speechless I watched her leave.

I did know Tina was that good looking of a woman. She was a tall dark skin woman with long beautiful legs and a fat ass. I couldn't do nothing with her I was a married man. I would see her in a new magazine called Jet as a Ebony Fashion Model. She would model for ten years before marrying and settling down in L.A. I sat there for about an hour before they started boarding the bus to Houston. I gave him my ticket he clipped the ticket gave it back to me and got on the bus. Hey we are proud of your boys for what you did over there. Thank you. I got on the bus of course you know I had to sit in the back. There was plenty of seats open I put my duffle bag on the rack and took a window seat. This was going to be a long ride, so I wanted to sit back and relax. I had stand on my way to St. Louis I'll be damn if I was going to stand all the way to Houston. The bus was packed a few people had to stand up. The bus started to pull off I leaned my chair back to relax for the long ride home. I sat there thinking I ain't seen my wife in almost two years. I ain't seen my little girl at all. I wonder if she going to know who I'm. A lot of thoughts ran though my mind. One thing that did stick in my mind is the bullshit Carla was telling me about Sgt. Sgt in his own little way was a low down dirty dog.

When you get your wife's sister pregnant to can't get know lower than that. I don't care what he did before I met him he still my friend. I should have found out how many kids he had. It really doesn't matter now I'm on my way home to see my family. I wonder if they buried Sgt?

All the friends I lost over there I couldn't stop thinking about them. All these things going though my mind kept me awake. I was blessed to be alive I almost died, but the good Lord saved me for a reason. I started to get sleepy I put my cover over my face and dosed off.

We stopped in a few places, but I only got off to use the restrooms. I couldn't sleep that good, because I was to excited to be going home. We passed a sign saying Houston 200 miles. The closer we got to Houston the less people got on. We stopped in a town 60 miles outside of Houston called Clear water, Texas. This was Klan territory I heard about this town a Negro don't have a chance around here. There were a few white folks on the bus and they were scared. The bus driver didn't want to stop. This is bad country for Negros do I need to stop here? No we all said. Than the next stop will be Houston. He put the bus in gear and sped off.

That was fine with me. I'm glad nobody had to get on the bus, because they just got left. Now you know this must be a bad place when white people was scared. The bus driver did pull over to use the bathroom. We passed a sign that said 100 miles to Houston. I could feel myself getting excited. Than another sign that said 50 miles to Houston. Than 30 miles to Houston I could feel my heart beat faster. Than 20 miles. Than 10 miles I started to fix my uniform. I got my bags down off the rack. The driver said we got 5 miles before we get to Houston. We got 1 mile to Houston. When he said that my heart almost jumped out of my chest. When the driver pulled into the station I was already standing at the door. When I got off the bus he told me to take care. I will I told him. When I stepped off the bus it was there wasn't a lot of people at the bus station. As a matter of fact it was kind of empty. I looked at my watch it was 2100 hours. I guess it was empty, because the war had ended a month ago.

A few people stopped me and shook my hand telling me how they were so proud of us. They don't realize I'm glad it's over. I started walking and I realized I had forgotten where I lived. I stopped for a minute to think about. Are you lost son this man asked me? No. I was lost, but I didn't want him to know. This was embarrassing here I am so excited to be home after two years and I can't remember where I live. I started walking back toward the bus station to use the phone when I seen Fat Joe sitting his his cab across the street. He was just about to pull off when I ran over to him. Hey how you doing Fat Joe? I startle him at first, but when he saw it was me. Popeye is that you. Yeah I'm back. Damn you scared the shit out of me. How you doing boy? He tried to get out of his taxi he struggled to get out. That's alright Joe you ain't got to get out. Okay well don't stand there get in and let me take you home. I throw my duffle bag in the back and jumped in. Popeye boy we were all worried about you getting killed over there especially Mrs. Hutchinson. Yeah Lillian told me in her letters. I heard Mr. Sutton died?

Yeah that's a shame to he got run over by one of his own trucks. It was raining real bad one night. You know he was running that moonshine. Yeah I know. Well anyway it was muddy and he messed round and fell .One of those boys he had driving that truck didn't see him and ran him over. I didn't say nothing Mr. Sutton was like a father to me. I'm going to miss him not being around. I seen your wife and little yesterday she looks like you man. The only thing she ain't got is them pop eyes of yours. Oh yeah where did you see them at? They was on there way to see Mrs. Hutchinson she ain't been feeling to well lately. Well here you are. We stopped in front of my apartment building I live in. I looked out the window it looked different from what I member. I got my duffle bag got out I reached in my pocket and gave Joe a couple of dollars. Don't worry about that Popeye this rides on me. Welcome home. Thanks Joe. We shook hands and he drove off. I stood there for a minute looking at the building than I started walking towards the door.

CHAPTER SIXTY-NINE

I TURNED TO WALK GO inside and Mr. Hopkins was standing on the porch. Welcome home soldier boy I see you came home in one piece. I walked up to the porch and we shook hands. We didn't think you was going to make it back alive. Well I did by the grace of God. I stood there for a minute thinking about what I was going to do or say. What are you waiting for boy you better go in there and see your wife and baby. Is she home? Yeah she home. I picked up my duffle bag and started walking down the long hallway. Popeye just in case you forgot the apartment number it's apt A. Thanks Mr. Hopkins I'm glad he told me I had forgotten that to. I slowly walked down the hallway to my apartment. My heart was beating fast I even started to sweat a little. I stopped in front of the door I was going to knock, but I stopped. I looked down the hallway and Mr. Hopkins was looking at me. He nodded his head to tell me to go head and knock then he went in his apartment. I put my ear to the door to see if I could hear anything I heard a little girl's voice. I knocked softly the first time. The little girl's voice stopped.

I knocked a little harder this time. Who is it? I didn't say anything. Who is it she asked again.

It's me Lillian. She opened the door when she seen me standing there she screamed so loud people came out their apartments to see what was going on. It's alright folks you can go back into your apartment she just glad to see her husband he just go home from the war. Lillian was hugging me so tight she almost choked me to death. Baby, baby you choking me. I'm sorry baby come in. She pulled me so fast in the house I didn't have time to grabbed my duffle bag. Wait a minute baby let me get my duffle bag I got my duffle bag and went in the house.

The apartment liked different from what I remember. We kissed a long passionate kiss. I started getting hard, but I knew I would come later. I'm so happy your home. She took by my hand and walked me around the apartment. You like what I did to the apartment? Yeah It's real nice you did a nice job fixing it up. I looked around the house to see toys on the floor.

Where is she Lillian? She's in the room. Can I see her? Sure silly you can she's your daughter. Come on she grabbed me by my hand. I hesitated a little. What are you doing come on baby. I took a deep breath then we walked in the room. When we walked in the room Jennifer was sitting on the bed. Lillian walked over to Jennifer. Jennifer looks who here. I couldn't move I just stood there. When I saw that beautiful baby sitting on the bed a tear dropped from my eye. Come here baby. Jennifer crawled into Lillian's arms. she brought her over to me. Jennifer you know who this is? Jennifer looked at me to say No. That's daddy Lillian told her. She's beautiful. She didn't look like me like Joe said she looked more like Lillian. I glad she looks like Lillian, because I didn't what her looking like me with pop eyes I don't want her getting teased like I did when I was a kid. Here hold her. I don't know Lillian I might dropped her she so small. She handed Jennifer to me. You ain't going to dropped her.

You need to learn how to hold her you going to be doing it a lot. I took her from Lillian I held that tiny bundle in my arms. We looked at each other if she could talk. She probably say who the hell is this? I walked around the apartment with her. I couldn't believe this was my child, but I tell you what I going to make sure she get's the best. When did you get back? I got back around 20 minutes ago. Why didn't you call me I would've come down to the station to meet you. I wanted to surprise you and Jennifer. I got all your letters and your Sgt Willie

Banks wrote me to. He said you were in the hospital, because you had caught the flu. Yeah I did and I had it real bad I was in the hospital for about three days. Sgt had lied to Lillian he knew I got shot, but I guess he didn't want to worry her. I'm glad he didn't tell her the truth she would've had a heart attack if she find out I got shot. He also said he was going to come see us when the war was over. Did you and him come back together? No we didn't. Why? I looked at her Oh my God he died in the war? Yeah he died saving my life and a few others so we could get away, but he didn't make it. Did the Army tell his wife? No I did. What did you do write her? No I went to St. Louis to tell her in person. She looked at me. Sgt wrote me this letter asking me if he died would I go to St. Louis and tell his wife. He would've done the same for me if I asked him to. Well how did she take it? She took it pretty well better then I thought she would. I didn't want to tell her all the things Carla said about Sgt. What's his wife's name? Carla. Did they have any kids? Yeah they got seven kids three boys and four girls. Did she tell the kids?

No she didn't she said she will tell them when the time comes. I hope she going to be alright.

Oh yeah she'll be fine. Talking about Sgt and his wife got me to think about those diamonds in my duffle bag. Here hold her I brought you something back from Germany. I went back into the living room opened up my bag and I pulled the little bag of diamonds. I notice it felt a little light. I opened it and seen that some of the diamonds was gone. I looked at Lillian. What?

That bitch took some more of my diamonds. That's why she was taking her so long to bring my duffle bag down to me. Well a least she didn't take them all. If she had done that I would have gone back to St. Louis and killed her. What you got there Jeffery? I pulled one of the diamonds out of the bag and gave it to her. She looked at it. Jeffery this is beautiful where did you get this from? I found them in a empty house in Germany. In Germany them white folks know anything about this? No I had to stink them out of the country. You know if they had caught you you would've gone to jail. Yeah I know and for a long time the one I gave her was a small one. This is beautiful Jeffery what you going to do with them? I'm going to go to Mr. Bernstein and ask him how much can I get for he knows a lot about diamonds. How much you think he going to give you for them? I don't know, but I'm going to go over there tomorrow and find out. How many do you got in that bag? I poured the rest out on the bed. it was a lot more than I thought. I shook the bag to see if I got them all. Than this big red one fell out I didn't know it was in the bag. I picked it up it was about the size of a quarter. Wow like at the size of this one Lillian. Yeah this one is beautiful. I wonder how many carrots it has. Carrots! Yeah carrots. What's a carrot? It's what a diamond is made of. I didn't know what a carrot was myself I just said something to keep her from asking me questions. This would look nice as a ring. She took it from me and put it on her finger. Yeah that would be nice. Then we heard a knock at the door. You expecting somebody? No! Well go see who it is while I put these diamonds back in the bag. Lillian left the room to go see who was knocking on the door. Who is it? It's me Lillian your brother William. Lillian let him in. Where he at William Lillian? I heard William coming walking towards the room. I put the bag of diamonds under the pillow. Hey Popeye welcome home he gave me a big hug. Thanks William. I see you made it back in one piece. Yeah I did. Man a lot of us didn't think you was going to make it back. Well I'm here.

Yeah you are. Come on out here and see the rest of the family. We walked out to the living room and Lillian's whole family was there. Who told y'all I was home? Fat Joe told me you was home William said. Welcome home Lillian's momma said while giving me a kiss I'm glad you made it home safe. Thank God you made it home safe Mrs. Hutchinson said while giving me a hug. I'm sorry about what happen to Mr. Sutton I told her. A sad look came over her face. Thank you baby. I never mentioned I know that she was married to Mr. Sutton. I'm glad you made it home safe Jeffery. Thank you Pam. Somebody put their hands over my eyes.

This is got to be Patrice. She gave me a kiss on my cheek. Glad you made it home safe.

Where the guy you was going to marry? Oh him he went back to his wife. His wife! Yeah his wife she caught us together one night. I told her that man was married she didn't believe me.

Mrs. Hutchinson said. I'm sorry Patrice. I'm not I'm glad he's gone he was know good anyway.

You have really grown up since I been gone. Let me take a look at you. How old are you now?

I'm 18 years old now. She whispered in my ear to bad you married my sister it could be you and me. I just smiled, but I knew she was right. If I wasn't married to Lillian I would've jumped all over here. That will never happen Lillian is the best thing that ever happen to me. Now we got Jennifer I got a family now. Once again welcome home. She brushed up against me when she walked passed me. Come on baby we going over to my momma's for dinner. Where your daddy at? He home waiting on you to come by. Well let's go I'm hungry. Y'all get the baby and let's go. Give me my baby I'll carry her. We were about to leave when Lillian said wait a minute let me get my cigarettes. Your cigarettes! When you start smoking? When Willie wrote me and said you got shot. So you knew I got shot? Yep I needed something to calm my nerves. It was either smoking or drinking and you know I don't drink. Well I'm back now, so it ain't know reason to smoke now especially since we got Jennifer it ain't gonna be good for her. She looked at the cigarette pack and through it in the trash. Okay I'll stop smoking if you promise to spend a lot of time with Jennifer. I promise. She kissed me on the lips and we walked out the door.

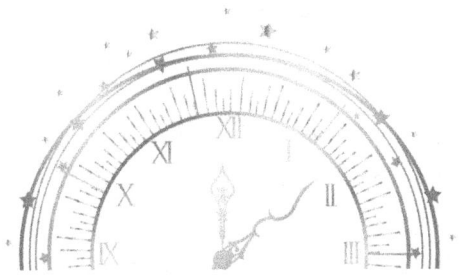

CHAPTER SEVENTY

IT WAS A WARM sunny day on June 6, 1994 in Normandy, France. I didn't expect to be here again, but Maj. Gen Conley talked me into coming to the 50th Anniversary of the D-Day invasion. The bad memories that I had left here over 50 years ago I didn't want to relive. I had lost my wife Lillian a few months earlier to lung cancer. We were married 53 years. She didn't stop smoking when I asked her to. She would sneak around smoking behind my back. When I caught her I was very angry with her. I couldn't stop her, so I told her she could smoke and she don't have to hide it anymore. Now I wish I had been hard on her more to get her stop.

She find out she had cancer in 1991 during a routine physical. They had taken some x-rays and find she had cancer of the lungs. It didn't seem to bother her, but it tore me apart. I watched her for three years die slowly before my eyes. I would go off by myself and just cry.

She would tell me why you so sad I'm the one that got cancer. I need you to be strong for the kids she would tell me. She finally passed away in April of 1994 I'm still getting over her death When Conley asked me to come and celebrate this Anniversary I told him no at first. Than after he called me several time he convinced to go. I retired from the Army in 1982 as a Lt. Gen after 40 years of service I worked my way up the ladder it wasn't easy, but I did it. I used the G.I. Bill to go to college and I earned two bachelor's degree in English and Mathematics.

Michael Johnson

I decided to major in English when I was a kid I spoke some bad English I didn't want my kids talking like me I wanted them to speak proper English. I didn't want white people thinking they were stupid. I even taught English and Math for 12 years before I retired from that. I was commissioned a 2nd Lt in 1948 when I finished officer school. That's the year President Truman desegregated the military. Gen. Conley made sure I went to school he told me if I went to school I would never have to fight another war. He was wrong I did go to war as a matter of fact I fought in two more wars. The Korean War and I did two tours of the Vietnam War. I got promoted to Col after my second tour in Vietnam 1968. I didn't do any fighting in Vietnam, but Korea was a different story. I worked for Conley for a while he turned out to be a decent man not the redneck I thought he was. After I got promoted to Col after Vietnam I didn't work for him any more. In 1972 I was promoted to Brigadier General that's when I got my first command and in 1975 I was promoted to Major General. We kept in touch though out the years he and his wife June came to Lillian's funeral. I was blessed to have my first command in Texas at Fort Bliss. We lived a good life. We brought a beautiful home in the suburbs of our hometown of Houston. We had five more children three boys and two girls five of them graduated from college our oldest child Jennifer became a school teacher and she married a preacher they have four children. Our second oldest Jeffery Jr became a doctor. He has his own patience in Atlanta. His oldest son Jeffery the third is also a doctor he's in the Army. He served in Desert Shield and Desert Storm. He lives in Hampton, Va with his family.

Our third child Willie (I named him after Sgt) is a commercial pilot for Delta airlines. He followed my footsteps and went into the military. He flew fighter jets for the Navy he retired as a Commander he lives in L.A. now. He's not married, but he his a daughter name Monica. Our fourth and fifth children Patrice (which we named after her aunt Patrice) and Daniel were a big part of the civil rights movement in Houston. Daniel was died in an automobile accident in 1967 he and some friends were going to Dallas to register voters and some car ran them off the road. He was the only one killed he was only 17 years old.

I don't think it was an accident I believe he was killed, because of what he was doing for civil rights movement. That hurt my wife and me to our hearts. I was very angry about it to it reminded me of how my father was killed. I knew who killed my father, but they never found out who killed my son. Patrice became a congresswoman in Washington D.C. She went there to fight for civil rights and just stayed. Now she's running for the Senate seat for Maryland. I'm proud of all my children they did well for themselves. I can't say that for my wife's sister and brothers. Let me start with William. He went from running moonshine to running drugs. He became the biggest drug dealer/ gangster in Houston he ran all the wards. He was killed when a drug deal went bad some people say he was set up by his ex-girlfriend. She was the niece of Bobby Joe who he killed in that moonshine run we did back in 1942. He was only 32 years old. Lillian momma called her and told her. We were living in Virginia when that happen. Mrs. Hutchinson she died in 1978 she was 75 years old. I buried her next to Mr. Sutton she left everything to me which was the house which I sold to a buyer. The one thing that really got me was the safe deposit box full of money saving bonds, stocks and jewelry. I knew Mrs. Hutchinson had money, but not this much. The box had over $300,000 dollars in cash. The jewelry was worth $25,000 itself. We took take money and cashed in the saving bonds and stocks and put it in the bank. The jewelry I gave to Lillian. Pam did good for a while. She did marry Reggie and they had a couple of children they moved to L.A. They opened a store in Watts section of town and lost it during the Watts riots of 1965. A couple years later they got a divorce and everything for her went downhill from there. She started drinking a lot. One day she went to the hospital complaining of stomach pains, but they could find anything wrong so they sent her home. One of her friends went to check on her, because they haven't heard from her.

When she went over to Pam's apartment that's when she found her dead. Her body was shipped back to Houston. She's buried in the same cemetery where Mrs. Hutchinson and Mr. Sutton are buried. Now as for Patrice she did well for herself she went to collage graduated at the top of her class in nursing. Than she a job working at a Hospital in

Houston she worked there until she met her husband Larry Fulton. He was a Sgt in the Army. They married and they moved to North Carolina where they live today. They have two children name Valerie and Larry Jr. She told me she married him, because he reminded him of me. Lillian's daddy Roscoe died of a heart attack in 1985. Her momma died in 1991 of complications from diabetes the same year Lillian found out she had cancer. That was a real hard time for all of us. I looked back on all the things that has happen I think God for what he has done for me.

Carla Sgt's wife did good for herself to. Those diamonds I gave her some jeweler brought them from her she took the money and brought her a home, a new car then she put all her kids though college. One thing that bothered me is she never talked about Sgt again. One of her son's Charles became a big time football player he played several years in the NFL I can't remember what team he played for. I was sitting on the bed thinking about how blessed I was 4:45pm when phone rang broke my thoughts. I walked over and answered it. Jeffery a voice said. Yes Gen. Are you coming to the ceremony with us? Yes sir I am. Well it's going to start in an hour I've been waiting on you in the lobby for 15 minutes. It's going to take us at least 30 minutes to get there. I want to get some good seats before it starts. Okay Jack I'll be down in a few minutes. Okay Jeffery hurry up. I was wearing this brown suit I had brought just for this occasion it was sharp to. It was double breasted and I had brown shoes to go with it. I walked downstairs to the lobby where Gen (Jack) was waiting with his wife and son. This was the first time I had seen him in since Lillian died. He looked like he lost a little weight, but he still had that big belly of his. Hey Jeffery his wife said. She gave me a hug. I'm sorry to hear about Lillian's death. She was a wonderful woman. Yes she was. Lillian used to always tease me saying June liked me. I would laugh it off, but I think she was right she was always stirring at me which made me very nerves. Hey Jeffery. Hey Jack how you doing? I'm fine you ready to go? Yeah let's go. Hey Vincent How you doing? I'm doing good. Where's your wife at. She decided not to come she home with the kids. Vincent was an officer in the Air Force he flew F- 18 fighters for the Air Force he also was part of Desert

Shield/ Desert Storm. He was 8 years younger than my son Jeffery Jr. Well you tell her I said hello when you get back home. I will.

We left the hotel and jumped in the car that was waiting on us. I sat in the front while they sat in the back. We headed toward the Normandy beach cemetery. I don't know why I'm even going there. We (black soldiers) didn't enter the war until Aug of 1944 at least that what I thought. I find out reading some records that there were about 2,000 black soldiers who took part in the D-Day invasion. I know what happen on those beaches, but all my friends are buried in unmarked graves all over Europe. They are not here to celebrate what they did in this war. When is someone going to thank them for what they did. Everything is always about what the white man did and all their heroes. There are no mention of the Black soldiers who fought racism, discrimination, hate and the lack of good leadership we were given. I guess that's way I'm here to represent those men who were forgotten. Those were my brothers who died out there and I'll be damn if they are going to be forgotten. All these thoughts ran though my mind as we arrived at the ceremony.

CHAPTER SEVENTY-ONE

WE GOT OUT IN front of the ceremonial grounds. Pay the cabbie Vincent. He gave the driver a few Francs. Lets try and find us some good seats. We walked passed the thousands of graves to our seats. There was thousands of people out there looking for loves ones who died in the war. I wondered to myself is Sgt name on one of those graves. I stood there looking around to see if I knew or saw any of the guys I saved with. There were a few black veterans, but I didn't see any one I served with. Come on Jeffery June said the ceremony is about to start. We had seats in the front row. I could see the looks on those white men faces saying what is he doing here I didn't care I earned this place. They can kiss my black ass. There were top officials from all over the world there including President Clinton. His wife Hilary and their daughter was there also. The media from all over the world were there to cover this big event. We stood up for the national anthem for the U.S., England, France and Canada. It seemed like we was standing forever. After all that we sat down for about five hours listening to all these countries telling what there country did in the war. They talked about all the different people, companies and divisions who gave their lives to defeat the Nazis. Not once did they mention the contributions the black soldiers did. That made me mad that's why I told my kids what happen for real over here and not to listen to all that bullshit they always telling hem about us. President Clinton got back up there and said a few words to the crowd and with that the ceremony ended.

Well that was nice June said. Yeah it was. Jeffery you coming with us we are going to walk down to the beach? No y'all go ahead I'm going to walk to the cemetery. The cemetery? Yeah I'm going to give thanks to the soldiers who gave their lives for us. Okay if we don't meet up we will see you back at the hotel. Okay. They started walking towards the beach and I started walking towards the cemetery. I got to the entrance to the cemetery all the graves had flags on them for what country the soldier was from. There was a lot American flags then any other country. I started walking looking at the headstones. The headstones were all white with the soldier's name, rate and the day he died. The Jewish headstone were different they had the star of David on them I didn't know why, but there must be a reason. Even in the graveyard where people are suppose to be at rest there is still racism. I walked up and down the isles on the cemetery and I notice this one American flag had came out the ground. I walked over to this headstone to put it back in it's place when did that I couldn't believe my eyes. The name on the headstone couldn't be who I think it was. I took my glasses out of my pocket, so I could read the name. The name read 1st Sgt. Willie D. Banks. I wonder to myself could this be Sgt or was this another person with the same name. I looked at the headstone what convince me it was him was the day he died. That was the same day we were in the village of Norberg.

That was the last time I saw him alive I fell down on one knee and started to cry. The memory of that day started coming back I regret that I left Sgt there to die. I'm sorry Sgt I said I didn't mean to leave you like that you were the best friend I ever had. I pulled my handkerchief out to wipe my eyes when a bird flew over and sat on Sgt grave. It looked at me and smiled at me I smiled back then it flew away I knew it was Sgt saying goodbye. I stood up as it flew away and disappear into the sky. I finally got the chance to say goodbye. I said my last goodby to Sgt and started walking out the cemetery when I saw this white woman kneeling down by this grave saying a prayer. I wanted to walk around her, because I didn't want to disturb her. I tried to but she was right in the isle. I tired to squeeze pass her, but her feet were in the way. I just stepped over her and started walking out the cemetery. I looked back to she did I disturb her.

She was still praying when I started thinking she looks like someone I knew. I stood there for a minute until she finished when she finished she stood up. She was a tall woman with black hair with gray streaks in it. She was wearing a white dress with blue flowers on it. She turned to walk away when I realize it was Ingrid the young girl we found hiding in that basement in that store in Germany. She looked at me. I said Ingrid. Jeffery is that you. Yes it's me.

What are you doing here? I came here to pay my last respects to my friends who die in the war. What are you doing here? I'm putting flowers on my husband's grave. Your husband! Yes he was a soldier in the English Army he died six years ago of lung cancer. I'm sorry to here that.

My wife died a couple of months ago of lung cancer to we were married 53 years. Oh I'm sorry 53 years is a long time to be married. How long were you and your husband married?

We were married for 39 years. I met him in 1947 after the war he helped me escape to West Germany before the Russians took over East Germany. I went to England to studying to be a doctor we got married in 1949. So your a doctor? Yes I've been practicing for over 40 years now. So what do you do? I'm retired now I retired from the military after 40 years of service.

Then I became a school teacher for awhile then I retired from that. What did you teach? I taught English. English that's good. You look good Ingrid. Thank you Jeffery. That's a nice suit you got on. Thank you I brought this suit just for this occasion. I thought I would never see you again Jeffery the night you left I was very sad I was falling in love with you. I was shocked when she said that I barely knew this woman and she was falling in love with me. She also was young at that time. My grand parents didn't like that I was falling for a black man. Are your grandparents still alive? No they died a few years after the war. That war took a lot out of them. What was your husband's name? His name was Patrick Hayes. He was a officer in the British Army he was part of

D-Day. I met him while he was stationed in Germany he helped me escape to West Germany we got married a couple years later. Did you have any children?

Yes we did we had two boys and two girls. Did you and your wife have children? Yes we have three boys and two girls. That's wonderful. Yes it is I'm proud of all of them. They did well for themselves. So who grave was you paying respects to? Oh that was my best friend who died saving my life. Who was he? His name was Willie Banks, but I called him Sgt. I'm surprised he's buried here. Why? We weren't part of D-Day we came over a couple of months later.

Most of the black soldiers are buried out there somewhere. I stopped and looked out over the beautiful hills all I have is the memories of them. They were all good men and they weren't even mentioned in that ceremony. He was probably buried by the German civilians who found dead American soldiers all over Germany. She put her hand on my shoulder to comfort me.

I'm sorry Jeffery. Thanks Ingrid I better be getting back to the hotel I got a long flight tomorrow. So your leaving tomorrow? Yes I am why you asking? I was just wondering if you would stay a couple more days, so we can catch up on each other. I thought about for a minute. I really ain't got nothing to do. Yes I'll stay a couple more days, but I got to call my son and tell him. He going to pick me up from the airport I don't want him waiting for me and I don't show up. Okay you do that she said with a smile on her face. I could show you around and we could even go to that village where you found me in that basement. I would like that.

Come on would you like a cup of tea? Yes I would. I know a nice small place in town where we can talk. She grabbed my by my arm and we started walking into town.

This book is dedicated to all the black men who fought and died in World War II for a country who didn't even consider them equals, but stood tall in the face of racism, discrimination, segregation and still did their job. My you rest in peace where ever you lay and my God bless you for your sacrifices.

www.ingramcontent.com/pod-product-compliance
Lightning Source LLC
Chambersburg PA
CBHW071426070526
44578CB00001B/20